I0282809

The Biggest Thing in Show Business

THE BIGGEST THING IN SHOW BUSINESS

Living It Up with Martin & Lewis

MURRAY SOLOMON
MATTHEW POMERANCE

SUNY
PRESS

COVER: Portrait of Martin & Lewis. Courtesy PhotoFest, New York.
Published by State University of New York Press, Albany
© 2024 State University of New York
All rights reserved
Printed in the United States of America

No part of this book may be used or reproduced in any manner whatsoever without written permission. No part of this book may be stored in a retrieval system or transmitted in any form or by any means including electronic, electrostatic, magnetic tape, mechanical, photocopying, recording, or otherwise without the prior permission in writing of the publisher.

For information, contact State University of New York Press, Albany, NY
www.sunypress.edu

Library of Congress Cataloging-in-Publication Data

Names: Pomerance, Murray, 1946- author. | Solomon, Matthew, author.
Title: The biggest thing in show business : living it up with Martin & Lewis / Murray Pomerance and Matthew Solomon.
Description: Albany : State University of New York Press, 2024. | Includes bibliographical references and index.
Identifiers: LCCN 2023022980 | ISBN 9781438496528 (hardcover) | ISBN 9781438496542 (ebook) | ISBN 9781438496535 (paperback)
Subjects: LCSH: Martin and Lewis (Comedy team) | Martin, Dean, 1917-1995. | Lewis, Jerry, 1926-2017. | Entertainers—United States—Biography.
Classification: LCC PN2285 .P64 2024 | DDC 791.092 [B]—dc23/eng/20230810
LC record available at https://lccn.loc.gov/2023022980

10 9 8 7 6 5 4 3 2 1

for the sidewalks of old New York

You could get a parrot. You could be talking to it, and it could be talking to you. You probably wouldn't be talking to each other. But it would be talk.

JUDY HOLLIDAY, IN *IT SHOULD HAPPEN TO YOU*

This is not an essay. And, good lord, not a treatise. First of all, it is a batch of reflections. Reflections—in the form of a brush. Sticking in all directions.

SERGEI M. EISENSTEIN, 1928

· Acknowledgments ·

Matthew & Murray are sincerely grateful to Olivier Bahizi (Ann Arbor), the late Peter Bogdanovich (Los Angeles), Tifenn Brisset (Bali), Jeffrey Alan Brodrick (Grand Rapids), John Bruns (Charleston), Michael Campochiaro (Albany), Jennifer Chapman (Ann Arbor), Brandon Cronenberg (Toronto), Derek Davidson (New York), Erich Dietrich (Abu Dhabi), Julia Dudley (Syracuse), the late Leslie A. Fiedler (Buffalo), Sandy Grabman (Albany, GA), Philip Hallman (Ann Arbor), Aimee Harrison (Durham), Burke Hilsabeck (Greeley, CO), Charles Hsuen (Halifax), Todd Ifft (New York), Tim Jones (Pittsburgh), Ann Kaplan (New York), Vincent Longo (Ann Arbor), Douglas Messerli (Los Angeles), Ryan Morris (Albany), James Peltz (Albany), Nellie Perret (Toronto), Ariel Pomerance (Toronto), Stephanie Rosen (Ann Arbor), Bill Rothman (Miami), Dan Sacco (Toronto), Eric Schramm (Dallas), Scott Smith (Ann Arbor), Neil Verma (Chicago), and Matt Yockey (Toledo).

· In These Pages ·

II

III

AN AMERICAN UTOPIA

[1]

In his *Painting and Experience in Fifteenth-Century Italy*, a book first published in 1972 and with which Dean Martin and Jerry Lewis were no doubt both entirely unfamiliar, art historian Michael Baxandall proposed the existence of a "period eye," a way of seeing that was specific to the culture and the period of fifteenth-century Italy that informed the ways painters represented objects and the ways viewers perceived them. In one of the book's most virtuosic sections, Baxandall sizes up Niccolò da Tolentino's hat (we will return to hats, given both Martin and Lewis's manifest delight in haberdashery) in one of the three panels in Paolo Uccello's triptych *The Battle of San Romano*, which now hangs in the National Gallery in London and is dated between 1438 and 1440. In the painting, which depicts an equestrian battle between knights and other combatants, one figure stands out from the others, military commander Tolentino, mounted upon a white steed in the middle foreground. Although Tolentino wields a lance, it is not his weapon that draws the viewer's attention but rather the huge red and gold cylindrical fabric headpiece atop his head.

Baxandall connects the unusual size and shape of Tolentino's ballooning, oversized, turban-like hat (which may or may not have been a decorative cover for a functionally protective helmet) to the fifteenth-century learned perceptual skill of *gauging*, which was important for the primary audience for Uccello's painting during the fifteenth century, the merchant class. Baxandall explains,

> It is an important fact of art history that commodities have come regularly in standard-sized containers only since the nineteenth century: previously a container—the barrel, sack or bale—was unique, and calculating its volume quickly and accurately was a condition of business. . . . An obvious way for the painter to invoke the gauger's response was to make pointed use of the repertory of stock objects used in the gauging exercises, the familiar things the beholder would have been made to learn his geometry on—cisterns, brick towers, paved floors and the rest. (86–87)

What is especially useful about Baxandall's analysis is his meticulous attention to the ways commercial factors can help determine the ways artists represent things as well as how viewers of artworks perceive those representations. Although Italian art and classic Hollywood cinema are grounded in Renaissance perspective, the ways relatively objective optical qualities are perceived and understood varied culturally and historically. (Walter Benjamin reached similar conclusions about visual perception in modernity.)

Five hundred years after Uccello and the painters of the Renaissance, Martin & Lewis worked with their own repertory of stock objects—automobiles, cigarettes, glasses, golf clubs, hats—and they relied just as much on a "period eye"—their own, as well as those of the millions who enjoyed them. If, following from Baxandall, one imagined a *period eye and ear* that were very specific to the United States from 1946 to 1956, one could begin to understand the incomparable multimedia oeuvre of Martin & Lewis. In the decade after World War II, the duo keenly developed a sensitivity to cultural vibrations, ubiquitous but bordering on the imperceptible, while practicing a kind of cultural mimicry that remediated the culture in audiovisual form.

In doing this they were of course playing to—and with—a prevailing myth of American culture at the time: harmonic prosperity.

[2]

While in England the aftermath of World War II was a bitter and extended adversity, America, especially middle-class America, prospered as never before. By 1946, the American myth involved contentment, consumption, congratulation, and confidence. If women were leaving the work force to some degree, and redomesticating the home, their familial efforts, coupled with new housing construction and, in the mid-1950s, the birth of the Interstate Highway System, led to a new regime of household glamour that involved furnishing, decoration, leisure fashion, and the automobile, not to mention, in numbers exponentially growing after the war, television sets for importing knowledge, awareness, and pleasure. Advertising burgeoned. Harmony, both fabricated and apparently natural, ruled.

It was a time in which innocence was naturalized—a state of mind and experience so widespread and pervasive in affairs both official and casual that it went without being spoken of, even without being noticed. There was certainly a peculiar innocence to the typical Martin & Lewis routine, an absence of cynicism. Here is but one telling example. There is a *Colgate Comedy Hour* skit (performed, like all *Comedy Hour* shows, before a live audience) about a problematic waiter (who will surely be Jerry): we open with Dean behind a cash register with a bucket of soup in front of him. On a blackboard behind, it says that soup is 15 cents. A crowd of customers leaves and he sighs with relief, then treats himself to a sip of the soup from a ladle. Exaggerated facial expression of disgust. (Audience chuckles.) He says, to no one in particular, that he's going to change the sign so it reads ten cents. Major, major, major explosion of laughter in the extraordinarily receptive studio audience—the best joke they've ever heard!!! In society broadly, people and things were taken to be what they claimed to be (Watergate was decades away and an advertised bowl of soup was a *good* bowl of soup). Daydream mixed with everyday perception, while people desired, while they secretly confessed, while they sipped their Manhattans and Vodka Gibsons and Whiskey Sours, while they told and cackled at jokes ribald, caustic, stereotyped, even profane. *A rabbi, a priest, and a minister walked into a bar, and the rabbi said. . . .* There was as yet no buried subculture of sharp-edged critical discourse (Lenny Bruce and Mort Sahl had comparatively tiny audiences), no carping jealousy and distaste, no broad resentment to kindle incendiary thoughts. Here is part of Sandra Gilbert's (b. 1936) 1984 sonnet, "The Ladies' Home Journal," looking back to the 1950s:

The brilliant stills of food, the cozy
Glossy, bygone life—mashed potatoes
Posing as whipped cream, a neat mom
Conjuring shapes from chaos, trimming the flame—
How we ached for all that . . .

The *ache* was extensive, yawning, as though everlasting. If we always wanted more we were satisfied with what we were given. It was funny enough when cigar-chomping George Burns looked askance at his beloved wife, Gracie Allen, and confided to the camera how goofy she was—we knew already. It was newsworthy enough for Dwight Eisenhower to be quoted on the noontime news (yes, news at noontime) speaking (for young TV watchers of course unintelligibly) of détentes and plans and forthright futures. It was lavish and luscious enough to sit in a restaurant with a linen tablecloth and slowly devour half a grapefruit with a maraschino cherry on top.

If postwar America was densely populated, at least in the cities, the myth alleged that there was never a crowd, certainly not the "lonely crowd" David Riesman pointed to, since every happy adventurer had a place to stand, room to move, and an ultra-couth etiquette that forbade barging in, elbowing, presumption, obnoxiousness, or eating your ten-inch-high chocolate cake with a spoon. Duncan Hines and Betty Crocker, the ultimate couple,[1] along with Aunt Jemima,[2] dictated affairs of the home; Ann Landers[3] dictated affairs of the heart; motion pictures dictated melodies, singing patterns, legitimate hopes, proper love, and the colors of life. As to those colors, they dripped into curtain fabric, dresses, bathing suits, kitchen appliances, toilet seats, hand towels, soap, building exteriors, and with an astonishing panache, cars. Saturated robin's-egg turquoise . . . apple pink . . . picnic-grass green . . . sunset

1 Betty Crocker was not a person but a publicity construct from General Mills (see Marling). Hines (1880–1959) was the author, three times a week, of the syndicated column, "Adventures in Good Eating at Home."

2 Under the label "Aunt Jemima," the Aunt Jemima Milling Company produced a quick pancake mix from 1889 through 2021, at which point the current ownership changed the name. The figure of the African American cook iconizing the packaging was brought to life at the Chicago Exposition of 1893 by Nancy Green.

3 The nickname "Ann Landers" was created by advice columnist Ruth Crowley in 1948 at the *Chicago Sun-Times*.

gold. (We will return to colors below.) The world of black or gray wartime automobiles was behind us, as was the technology behind the war, insofar as it could be recognized as such; much of that technology was redesigned and repackaged as gleaming, "new" consumer products. Behind us, too, at least in popular awareness, was the Great Machine—the Moloch of Lang's *Metropolis* (1927)—because the economic queen's chapped lips were hidden behind advertising's lipstick. Now, according to the myth, we were inhabiting the Elysian Fields of popular culture, basking in suntan oil, waving our hair, culturing proper relationships with our neighbors who were good because we had a good white picket fence between us.

Around Dean & Jerry as they jived and jittered, crooned and cackled, cooed and kibbitzed, a sense of peace and progressive tranquility was everywhere. The forces of market capitalism were content to grind ahead methodically without infringing on the sacred territories of selfhood, family unity, and fun by pressing for urgency, speed, and untold-of profit. All that would come later, but even the thought of capital expansion was covered by comparatively small-scale development, such as the fabulous domestic architectures of Frank Lloyd Wright and Richard Neutra. It was adventure enough to take the family for a Sunday afternoon drive into the country to see the orange groves or peach trees in blossom. There was sufficient festival in the official holidays, added to which were intensive commercializations of Mother's and Father's Days for good measure. Spring Break from college was not yet; easy air travel was not yet; standby fares were not yet; and you could still wander into The Automat and for one single nickel get what was indisputably a "good cup of coffee."

Not that there was no luxury. Luxury was for the movie stars. Designer of, among many, many films, *Gaslight* (1944), *The Postman Always Rings Twice* (1946), *Easter Parade* (1948), and Doris Day's gowns in *Midnight Lace* (1960), Irene Lentz Gibbons (who went professionally as Irene) was implored by Bullock's Wilshire to open a salon there, and she was given a palatial space with doric columns and enough carpeted emptiness between the thickly upholstered lounge chairs for a Broadway chorus to dance out her new fashions. In Hitchcock's *Rear Window* (1954), Grace Kelly's Lisa could, with perfect aplomb and no more excitement than in checking a new shade of lipstick, have lunch for two delivered from "21," uniformed waiter included. Movies consistently showed brave people undertaking big-time exploits, or lovers falling in love as lovers do, or marriages in which a husband and wife, occupying some vast thickly carpeted and sleekly upholstered zone, and splayed, of course, upon matching twin beds (the Motion Picture Production Code was in effect until 1966), squabbled over something that would very shortly turn out to be nothing. Horror films were small in number if preposterous, science-fiction films generally projected a sterile future (some of the best based on sleek artistic renderings by Chesley Bonestell), and most westerns showed the triumph of horseback-riding white cowboys.

The age was an image of itself, an image that by now has become (only) a caricature.[4] What might seem astonishing today, in our age of photorealism, is that most graphic expression in the public domain was handled by skilled artists using their hands to make drawings or paintings. Advertising images in magazines were still very largely hand-drawn; posters were printed from hand-made paintings; greeting cards showed the telltale hand of the artist, the one who knew without a thought how to draw snow-laden pines settled in gentle snow-covered nooks nearby a gentle white country church. One saw photographic images in the front vitrines of movie theaters, ballyhooing the film currently on show (and usually with stills specially prepared for the purpose, sometimes hand-colored). Here, and with all styles of animation and abbreviation far and wide, the presumption was that the viewer would be able to fill in the gaps from a generally shared storehold of knowledge about the world as defined in the culture. One group of viewers, one vast audience, pitching together into one deep well of knowledge, doubt, understanding, and questioning. The bubbles on cartoons could be abbreviated; the drawings themselves could be abbreviated; everybody knew how to leap to the unstated meaning, which artists and advertisers considered too verbose or too complex or too frenetic to fully include in the presentation. The "meaning" of pop culture certainly did not promise to be some dark and troubling secret.

For life taken generally, then, the myth affirmed that everything was good and everybody was happy, more or less—everybody was at least content or without the fervor to scream for change (with the McCarthy hearings this fundamental tenet came into the spotlight). Everybody presumably had their own safe place, however modest or palatial, their own room to move, and the universally affirmed etiquette in the West was that you didn't barge into other

4 Some readers may need to be reassured that contemporary takeoffs on the 1950s today are generally devoid of actual cultural reference: they are made by people, and they star people, far too young to have tasted the time.

people's space, you didn't race to grab before they could the goodies they had set their hearts upon: there were goodies enough for all. (Hitler grabbed and pushed; the U.S.S.R. grabbed and pushed; we did not, on both sides of the 49th Parallel.) Courtesy was everywhere, in place of angst, tension, conflict, loathing, bloodshed (so that, just as in the days of early Hollywood chronicled inimitably by Kenneth Anger, bloody crimes were rare and spectacular enough to gain notoriety, not the meat of everyday entertainment). Somewhere, somehow, there existed a wise ruling body that organized things for the benefit of all, for what Robert K. Merton and other structural-functional sociologists of the time regarded as a coherent and stable society, not very unlike the domain of which Voltaire's Pangloss touted, "All's for the best in this best of all possible worlds."[5]

[3]

Such a beautiful world!, where the sun is always shining! Were there also fears, horrors, anxieties, pains, and troubles, not so shiny and not so much fun? The answer is, that if these darknesses existed they were kept inside, locked away. In short, utopia required that dystopia be repressed. Repressed, repressed, and thoroughly repressed . . .

And two young performers stumbled onto a stage together and pointed to it. Opened the gateway so that the repressed could return . . .

What, we must ask, happens when the repressed returns? *The repressed:* not an armory for destruction and the infliction of agony, not an eraser, not a discomfiting probe, but instead a kind of energy source, a creative irritation, that blurred the boundaries between things, rubbed off the labels, stood people on their heads, warped language, blurred expression anywhere and everywhere regardless of propriety and good form.

And what if the repressed showed up as a kind of marriage, between movement and cacophony on one side and harmonic poise on the other, between the need never to be interrupted and the urgent need to just get a word in edgewise . . .

5 Leonard Bernstein's *Candide* was first performed in 1956.

All of this very much in the light, available for all to catch, on a stage, on a movie screen, on the pages of a vastly circulated magazine, in posters, in comic books, on the radio. A repressed that returned to take over show business.

But when we call Martin & Lewis the *biggest* thing in show business, what can we possibly mean? Show business: not just movies, not radio, not television, not magazines, not newspapers, not posters, not record albums . . . BUT ALL OF IT! However commonplace or dilute a referent the 1950s may have become, however much decades taken in themselves might be thought a historiographically suspect grouping that posits some kind of internal coherence on the basis of sheer decimal coincidence, here we propose to examine the idea that something meaningful in the atmosphere of our culture occurred between one July night in 1946 and another in 1956. At the same time, there is nothing approximate in designating a decade of Martin & Lewis as a timespan of perfect, mathematically bounded precision.

In looking at Dean & Jerry we face backward with a very keen attention to a warning proposed by Stephen Jay Gould, who felt it urgent to avoid what he called "Whiggish history,"

> the idea of history as a tale of progress, permitting us to judge past figures by their role in fostering enlightenment *as we now understand it.* (*Time's Arrow* 4; emphasis added)

Gould goes on to quote Herbert Butterfield's proscription against imagining that history "can give us judgments of value—against assuming that this ideal or that person can be proved to have been wrong by the mere lapse of time" (105–6; qtd. in Gould *Time's Arrow* 5).

[4]

Considering their development as individual performers before 1946 and their solo work after the 1956 break-up, one finds in the collaborative work a strange tension between a relentless, sometimes explosive spontaneity and a dominating (sometimes condescending) calm, a jerky, surprising, breathtaking unpredictability and an easygoing, even lazy swagger. On television, their on-camera takes were, daringly, often only marginally rehearsed, and dependent to a large degree on their sensibilities at the working moment. On film sets, where considerable forethought and arrangement are necessary, for financial reasons and on account of film's intensively collaborative nature, they still performed with some degree of spontaneity and improvisation.

Since Dean & Jerry stopped working together, there has never, to this day, appeared anyone in front of an audience to match them. Not by way of any medium. Not only are Martin & Lewis gone, but the culture that yearned for them and fed upon them is gone, too. A culture that is the progenitor of our own, though more generous, forgiving, eager, and unspoiled, and hungry to eat them up.

The Beatles were right: what you get depends entirely on what you give. What we take from Martin & Lewis, together or singly, depends a lot on how we *read* them, as indicators, as symbols, as figureheads, and as human beings; depends on our frame of mind before the performance commences and all through the internal agonies as it bumps, falls, glides, careens, or races along. What, indeed, does it mean to *read*—or gauge—in a case like this (not that there are any other cases in this category)? For considering a performative duo like Dean Martin & Jerry Lewis, what sensibility, consciousness, dream-state, relaxation, and spontaneity might be both useful and required? If we were to think about Dean & Jerry, would our thinking imagine them constituting a solid object, with sides and boundaries? A single organism with limbs jutting in several different directions? A legal document with a beginning, middle, and end? Or something more akin to an apparently boundless ocean of performative power, which can be considered only one wave at a time? Given that by now Dean & Jerry have been dropped from daily currency and are rendered, if at all, as ghosts of what they once were, how can we reasonably think about them otherwise than in an apparently discontinuous and respectfully wacky way? Further, are we to think of *DeanandJerry* or *Martin&Lewis* as a single, fused being, as a pair of individual pieces bound together by contract, love, or what have you, or as only a superficial figuration in the public's mind?

[5]

No performers had ever been so conscious of marketing, of what we would today call cross-platforming, of merchandising the self, of licensing rights to the self, and of hitting audiences across all conceivable entertainment markets more or less at one time: stand-up stage acts, recordings both solo and together, radio broadcasting, television, motion pictures, comic books, coloring books, coffee mugs, cuff links, decals, glue, playing cards, puppets (including a two-faced model with Dean's face on one side and Jerry's on the other), salt-and-pepper shakers, sheet music, tape dispensers, and more.[6] Frank Krutnik testifies to the astoundingly swift rise of the duo, and the extensive width of their popularity:

> The speed with which Martin and Lewis attained such prominence was quite remarkable. So, too, was the range of audiences they persuaded to embrace their wild, bewitching liveness—from the sophisticated urbanites who applauded them in the clubs, to the families who watched them on TV, to their ardent and occasionally hysterical young fans. Norman Taurog, director of five of the team's films, testifies to the excessive emotions they could inspire among their young enthusiasts. During their record-breaking two-week engagement at New York's Paramount Theater in July 1951, the streets were jammed with teenagers. ("Sex" 111)

It hardly mattered, from the time of the American entry to World War II onward, what you wanted to do in your spare time, Dean & Jerry would be there doing it with you. And one paid for them to do it. They were money, big money, big big big big money.

If our culture has developed an obsession with box office figures, comparing weekend grosses as if they were sports scores and using them as some sort of a measure of a film's success, we prefer not to play that game. Not only are historical box-office figures notoriously inaccurate, even if reliably accurate numbers were available we are not entirely confident those numbers would provide any measurable account of the magnitude of space that Martin & Lewis occupied in American culture and the American popular imagination. Let us say, when the fireworks go off in front of you, you're way beyond counting the sparkles: Dean's sparkles, Jerry's sparkles, Dean & Jerry's twin sparkles!

One tiny indicator of how popular and recognizable Dean & Jerry were is in the opening skit from the June 24, 1951, *Comedy Hour*: a group has gathered at the airport to welcome "Martin & Lewis," but when the eagerly awaited stars get off the airplane, they're *Tony* Martin and *Joe* Louis—the extremely

6 Jeffrey Alan Brodrick, "Jerry Lewis Collectibles," http://jerrylewisunauthorized.com/jlcollect.html; Brodrick, telephone conversation with Solomon, February 5, 2023.

popular nightclub singer (married to Cyd Charisse) and the world heavyweight boxing champ.[7] When Martin & Lewis arrive soon after, it's utterly anticlimactic, the joke being that Dean Martin and Jerry Lewis are not such a big deal. Audiences quickly grasp that while Dean might have been able to go fifteen rounds with Tony verse by verse, Jerry against Joe would have lasted about ten seconds. Indeed, when Joe barely tickles Jerry with his glove, "the wimp" immediately drops to the stage in a messy heap.

(The beauty of that: [i] that Jerry transitions from standing straight up to being a bundle on the floor in a quarter of a second; [ii] that what happens is precisely what one would expect to happen, *but bigger*, Joe barely tickling instead of punching, Jerry not just reeling but entirely disappearing from view.)

A similar riff characterizes the December 30, 1951, *Colgate Comedy Hour* broadcast in which an assembled roomful of children at the "Birdwheel Public School" are totally uninterested in the two celebrities to whom their teacher introduces them so excitedly. Dean & Jerry tell a few jokes, but the children do not laugh—Jerry asks if this is a "midget Nuremberg trial." "What's-all-the-big-deal-about?" moments like these serve well to reinforce that Dean & Jerry are absolutely a big deal; the biggest deal imaginable at that time, in fact exactly a deal big enough to make self-deprecating jokes about itself. Only a very big deal can look in the mirror and say, "So?" An audience of around 29 million viewers watched them on television at this time (Hayde 130). In America there were some 152 million souls. Thus, roughly one in five living Americans were watching Dean & Jerry on the *Colgate Comedy Hour.*

A market share to be envied, no doubt. But there are curious and provocative ways in which everything about Martin & Lewis spurred envy. Envy, frenzy, confusion, delirium. In order to touch their madness it helps to have a little madness in your own fingertips.

7 A version of a gag they had performed on their October 21, 1949, radio broadcast with guest George Jessel.

USER'S MANUAL

Dean Martin and Jerry Lewis performed together for ten years exactly, from "July 25, 1946 to July 25, 1956, to the day, which was Martin & Lewis's beginning and demise, same day" (Lewis interview). More than the same day, the same hour, 10:00 p.m.—*exactly* one decade. Like a Roman candle, the duo flared spectacularly and vanished from sight. We felt compelled to think about it.

After almost a decade of moving toward, away from, toward, and away from the subject of this book, we finally got together in mutual home isolation during the early first summer of the COVID-19 pandemic, each unable to leave not only the country but also the house, each more or less tethered to a computer (like so many others around the world).

To catch, even a little, Dean & Jerry's spirit of presence, of sudden incarnation, of improvisation, of unpredictable emergence and joy, we made the decision to sidestep a conventional research and writing process for this work.[1] What we sensed the need for was a book in which both of the co-authors were intensely co-present moment by moment as themselves, just as, with a marvelous and immeasurable electricity, Dean & Jerry always were. Inspired by our subjects themselves, we also wanted to get off to a fast start—no tedious introductions. This meant beginning not in the library but inside the Martin & Lewis world, if we could get there.

Our path took us online, and more specifically to a shared Google document to which we both continually and simultaneously contributed. We began "meeting" using FaceTime, and later Zoom, more or less daily, but irregularly, and often on a whim if both happened to be available and one initiated a continuation of the conversation. Our typical working method was synchronous, both writing, revising, and rewriting in the shared document while remaining connected both visually and aurally through a call open in another window. Sometimes we read aloud as we typed or asked the other, "Does that seem right?" or "Are you OK with that?" or even "What did you mean by that?" Often, we revised each other's prose almost as soon as it appeared onscreen, shifting the color of the text to highlight those changes and seek the approval of the other, who would turn the text black to indicate agreement on phrasing and word choices. We also each frequently looked up references and details online using keyword searches while also performing close readings on various documents, articles, books, radio shows, television programs, and films that entered the discussion using multiple windows on our respective computers, while relying on countless online searches to establish both generalities and specific details quickly.

While co-writing synchronously, one was sometimes a few sentences ahead of the other, but we would typically both circle back or ahead to converge on single sentences to hammer out our differences in real time, reconciling our

1 One precedent for the fragmentary composition of this book (although not its dialogism) in the scholarly literature of cinema and media studies is Charney, *Empty Moments* 49–53. Although Charney's book contains neither introduction nor explicit reflection on method, effectively setting readers adrift—one of the key terms for the book—in a series of fragmented, loosely connected, sections, Charney reveals a debt to the literary and intellectual montage of Walter Benjamin and Sergei Eisenstein, as we do, and does not designate its seven sections as "chapters."

respective viewpoints—not to mention the idiosyncrasies of our respective writing styles. Neither of us wanted to linger too long on any one sentence, paragraph, or section since, like our subjects, we both placed a premium on speed, spontaneity, flexibility, and pinpoint attentiveness. Also like Dean & Jerry, we found ourselves constantly jumping on one another, both verbally and compositionally, and rather than acting to reduce this action we allowed it to triumph over commonplace rationalities. This, after all, was the most intimate way to understand the Martin & Lewis phenomenon, the leaping, the nonsequiturs, the bizarre transitions, the unmatched textures, the *in-your-face*ness of it all. We often found it useful to insert images or frame-grabs directly into the text, although only a small portion of these images was retained for publication. To keep moving, we often flagged passages that we knew needed revision in a brilliant color, returning to them later individually, or together at our next working session. We wanted the manuscript to move briskly: you had to race when you watched and listened to Martin & Lewis.

But, like what our subjects did on live television, we were pushing the limits of the available technology. Video calls perpetually froze, text searches for things we each remembered writing somehow eluded us in the shared document. Internet connectivity was compromised because the continually updating Google document was competing for bandwidth with our ongoing FaceTime or Zoom connection. Interrupting onscreen messages appeared frequently: "Poor Connection: The video will resume automatically when the connection improves" or even worse, "Page Unresponsive: You can wait for it to become responsive or exit the page." Is this what it was like to work live onstage and on radio and live television? Like trying to make love to a marble statue?

Readers should not be surprised or disoriented to find here verbal and theoretical leaps into staccato bursts, frequent interruptions and asides, and unapologetic non sequiturs. Having watched and listened to scores of hours of film, television, and radio, we have come to recognize that this mode, this discontinuous, heterogeneous aesthetic—postmodern *avant le lettre*—is the most appropriate form for this prose to take. And we recognize, too, that now is the time for appreciative minds to take such an approach. Our method has been deliberately nonlinear, deliberately spontaneous, deliberately interruptive, deliberately disregardful of convention. To grapple with Martin & Lewis as a cultural phenomenon in all of their complexities and connections, a systematic approach governed by chronology or by a single central argument would not suffice: whatever desire we might have had for comprehensiveness was overwhelmed by the impulse for spontaneity as driving force. This is not a history book, although we recognize that our subject is historically bounded and accessible to historical methods (among others), as well as being neatly encapsulated by the exact decade spanning the tenure of the partnership.

Capturing the essence of Dean & Jerry—and yes, there was an essence, however quicksilver its appearance—presents challenges that will melt away if you are willing to hop into our metaphorical 1956 cherry-red (extremely gigantic) Chrysler New Yorker—never mind Mr. Bascomb, the massive Great Dane taking up most of the back seat! The journey begins. Here we go. To Dean & Jerry's Hollywood. Or Bust!

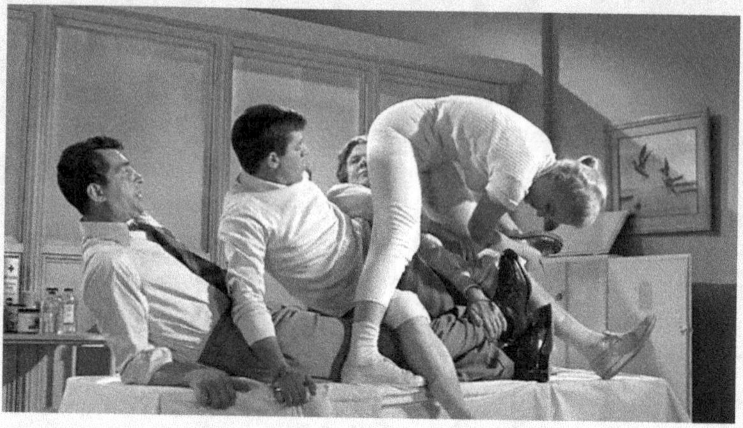

CAN YOU RELAX?

We generally think of modern life—"modern" life—as beginning with World War I (with development in Weimar Germany); continuing through World War II and the Korean War as well; and suffusing all of cultural experience through at least the whole decade of the 1950s. The scurry, thrust, and control of modern life, the multi-directionality, the hyper-spontaneity, the fragmentation, obvious still today, underpin all of Martin & Lewis's work, and are openly signaled there. Therefore, the viewer who needs the calm security of traditional forms, the bucolic meditativeness of the nineteenth century in its most classical style—let us say, the neo-Victorian viewer—finds Martin & Lewis comedy threatening, if not altogether ugly. It can be fascinating, in fact, to observe the lengths to which some audiences, scholarly and lay, will go to disavow their own squeamishness as Dean & Jerry live it up. Ugly was their shtick, in a particular and fascinating way—not in the way that the comedy of later performers such as Eddie

Murphy, Sam Kinison, Andrew Dice Clay, Joey Diaz, Bill Burr, and Bert Kraisher might be thought "ugly," but in a way entirely idiosyncratic, special, unheralded, musical, blithe, uncertain, and specific to their period. One needs to recognize how the typical Martin & Lewis routine is a play on *improbable emergence seen retrospectively as logical.*

Consider a number of discrete events that are enchained . . . each one arrived at (with apparent logic, as one looks back) from the one before . . . yet every arrival unpredictable as it happens. Every A becomes an utterly improbable B. Yet when we rest for a second at B and look back to A, we understand how B is a perfect, even inevitable follow-up. Improbability is seen *retrospectively* as logical, but seen that way *only* retrospectively, since there is no way one can use some established logical system for guessing what will come next. One can never see the future, but the past always looks like the "perfect preparation."

Martin & Lewis turn the classic flow chart, with its clean lines, clearly marked directional vectors, carefully delimited hierarchies, and typically binary outcomes into a Rube Goldberg device, all the parts obviously connected but in mysterious ways seen, if at all, only in retrospect. During the action itself, every movement comes as a surprise, yet one that directly connects with what came previously. What we get are displacements and substitutions and wholly unpredictable consequences. Yet, there is no individual phase that is not, in its individuality, clearly articulated and wholly logical, predictable, conforming to the expected laws of the universe. Martin & Lewis's work leaps into situations, almost always without an introduction, even when those situations mock up an implicit "introduction" as part of a scene.

To illustrate their method, here is consideration of the opening of *Living It Up* (Norman Taurog, 1954), a key film in the Martin & Lewis oeuvre while at the same time a beautiful send-up of the history of comedy as we know it. Jerry is stationmaster of the railroad depot at Desert Hole, New Mexico (elev. 1 ft., Fairyland of Enchantment), an arid nowhere in the Southwest, but he is going to be sent on a journey that will bring him to midtown Manhattan and the heights of a penthouse. How will he begin to get from one condition (Desert Hole) to the other (Manhattan)? A fragmented opening, to be sure:

Credits have rolled over a montage of Manhattan locations, uptown, downtown, East Side, West Side, with an invisible chorus enthusiastically chanting "Every street's a boulevard in old New York." We arrive at Grand Central Station as the credits end, and a swift wipe brings a brilliant, saturated, fire-engine red Superchief into view, flying screen-left to -right toward us down the track; we pan rightward, eager to catch all of it.

[1]

DESERT HOLE: Isaiah Jackson (Walter Baldwin), retiring stationmaster, is in high spirits, because in *exactly 28 seconds* he will be climbing aboard the eastbound Skyrocket. A new life! Dejected Homer (Jerry Lewis) is reassured that he will now step into the stationmaster's shoes, and in *exactly fifty-two years* he will be getting a pension, too. Climbing aboard, Jackson hands Homer a titillating New York City tourist brochure. "Sleep with this under your pillow. . . . I'll mail ya' a card from the Copacabana!"[1] The train pulls out.

[2]

But Homer makes a move! With a suit he's had hanging in wait, he leaps onto a boxcar in motion.

1 10 East 60th Street, ironically the site of Martin & Lewis's final stage appearance together, July 25, 1956. See Podell-Raber 69–72.

[3]

Homer changes into the formal wear, ready for the Big City, but suddenly the train comes to a halt. "Wow, that was a short trip!" His car is uncoupled; the rest of the train pulls off. "Hey, come back, I'm here!!!!" But a military transport train rushing up (on the same track) collides with his boxcar, throwing Homer into the hay. Confused by the jolt, he has no view. Now another engine couples at the front and the train moves on. Climbing up to the boxcar roof to see what's up, he finds military types who chase him along the length of the train.

Now the promised journey to New York is scotched.

[4]

As Homer races along the tops of the train cars, we can note that all around as far as the eye can see is desert, and he is somehow going to have to get off this moving train. He runs with syncopated, jerky, graceless (Jerry Lewis style) desperation, and, leaping from a car, lands on first one and then a second massive rubber boat resting on a flatcar. These act like trampolines, and the second one bounces him up, up, up, and off into the dirt beside the rails. Standing up and looking around, Homer sees some ancient abandoned jalopies. He gets into one and drives off.

[5]

Magically, the beat-up old car is full of gas. But as he drives we are given to see what Homer cannot, that this particular car has a warning sign tacked to the front bumper. He is jovial. We see trouble coming.

[6]

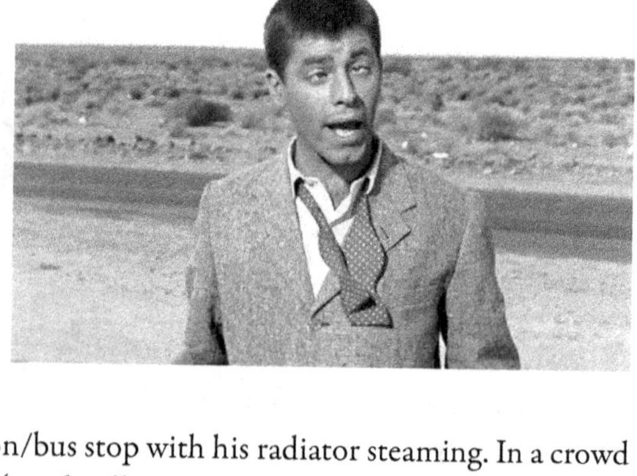

He arrives at a filling station/bus stop with his radiator steaming. In a crowd waiting nearby, one man (vaudeville performer Franklyn Farnum) points frantically, "Radioactive car! Run for yer life!" "Can I get some water?" Homer sweetly asks an old attendant, "What's all the commotion, everybody running away?"

"I'll be dad-burned if I know!" The old coot is eager to know what kind of car it is.

Wiping off the radiator hood Homer reads "Radioactive." "What—you never heard of a radio active?" with delight . . . until the penny drops. A huge double-take. Homer collapses to the ground.

*

All the progressions in this sequence—1>2, 2>3, 3>4, 4>5, and 5>6—with their repetitive up-down, down-up movements, are improbable in themselves as they happen; yet entirely logical when seen in retrospect. We continually don't know where we are going, but once we get there the move seems uncontestable. Just regard the chain:

[1] Dejected Homer, with an eternity before him before he can go to the Big City . . . BUT 2, Taking the leap he hops on the train anyway.
[2] Taking the leap he hops on the train, BUT 3, is he going anywhere?, the train has halted.
[3] The train has halted, BUT 4, now it is bumped unceremoniously. . .
[4] The train is bumped unceremoniously, BUT 5, he climbs up to the roof, sees desert all around, gets in a chase with the military, and bounces off into the desert.
[5] He's in the desert, BUT 6, he finds a car and drives it away.
[6] He's driving a car BUT he discovers it's radioactive.

Each ensuing moment is one among a great number of hypothetical possibilities—there is no way to predict with surety which will ensue. Yet when we have moved forward and look back, we see the perfect logic of the continuity.

Here are two faces of modernity, one unstoppable and transcontinental, the other blocking and ineffective:

> The Plan for New York ||| The halted train. Running away from the military ||| Bouncing off the train. Driving a car ||| Finding out it's radioactive.

And both faces motor forward movement: the flow chart vs. the Rube Goldberg device. What seems especially important is that Jerry is the human at the switch, (mis)managing the transitions. *Dean, as we are about to see, often appears to be managing Jerry's mismanagement.*

The central question for those who would understand or appreciate Dean & Jerry, their push & pull, their poise & their bounce, and for those who would read this book, is, "Can you relax?"

CAN YOU LISTEN?

[1]

It is revealing that in the 1960s, Dean Martin should have been a central member of The Rat Pack, a "band of brothers" formed a decade earlier by Humphrey Bogart and Lauren Bacall but by this time (Bogart died in 1957) including principally five Las Vegas performers (and associated hangers-on, like Jerry Lewis): Joey Bishop, Peter Lawford, Sammy Davis Jr., Frank Sinatra, and Martin. Frank, Sammy, and Dean were generally considered the center of the group, and all three, paragons of casualness, were the highest paid and—Tony Bennett aside—most highly regarded male vocalists in America. Three men, three voices. Sinatra had impeccable diction and a soaring style of breathing that made for long, dramatic phrasings and punchy rhythmical play. He gave the impression, when singing, of being meticulously rehearsed, indeed of having worked out every syllable of harmony and every breath. The Man in Charge. Davis's method was born of jazz, and syncopation riddled his personality and delivery. Of the three, he had the most operatic voice, simply in terms of its size and range, and when he performed in company with, or in the vicinity of, his Rat Pack chums one sensed him restraining himself, not quite letting the cat out of the bag. More than losing himself in a song, Davis would lose himself in his sound, and watching him sing at the top of his form was like watching a wondrous child exposed for the first time to echoes. With his witty elocutionary style, Sinatra turned melody into a riposte. With his playful dynamism, Davis turned melody into a prayer.

But Dean Martin:

To watch Dean Martin sing was to see him stand and smile, while music flowed out of him without any effort at all. He sang without breathing. He sang without thinking about it, beforehand or during. He sang without caring about the song; it was only a pretext for the voice. His métier was singing, not the delivery of compositions, and so, in a way, every song he sang was like every other, the inimitable Dean Martin style flowing through the superficial façade of the text. As to melody—he was, somehow, outside of it, flying above.

People would say, *singing came naturally to Dean,* and that was the response he inspired. A cloud = a cloud; Dean Martin = a singer. He stood in calmness while time beat its way out of him. An unhurried man, untroubled, even unconcerned. Superior. A later legend that he was a supreme alcoholic (the flaw!) gave the impression that he was on another plane while performing, one might think *not even really there.* If he drank heavily, however, so did all his friends and associates; so did most of show business; and so did a major portion of the North American bourgeoisie from the early 1950s onward. The consumer utopia was flowering but over the half-buried bodies of the middle class, and citizens lived their lives in what Thoreau called "quiet desperation," slaving all day in office prisons and dragging home at night exhausted, worried, fearing the future, uncertain of the stability of their jobs, desperate for a release.

[2]

What was the popular amusement derived by audiences from Dean's singing-that-wasn't-singing? A young man stands in place (without twitching, while his partner twitches without standing), song oozing out of him instead of breath. Heavens, he doesn't need to breathe! The song breathes for him. Dino is a *troubador* come to life, courtly singer-poet-composer of the eleventh through the early fourteenth century (the true *troubadour* tradition died with the Black Plague). The beckoning, assuaging, placating, soothing, desirous, more desirous, always desirous, yearning, always yearning male at the foot of the tower, singing to his Princess, defending her glory with his life if need be and surely defending his honor, and proclaiming in rhythmic repetition the truth of passions. Think of Romeo under the balcony, or a meowling tomcat under his favorite's window. But soused. Floating on an inner stream under inner moonlight.

Trademark *troubador* material, some of the bouquet Dean breathed:

- "You're Nobody Till Somebody Loves You" (Russ Morgan, Larry Stock, James Cavanaugh, 1944):
  You're nobody until somebody loves you
  You're nobody 'til somebody cares . . .

- "Everybody Loves Somebody" (Sam Coslow, Irving Taylor, Ken Lane, 1947):
  Everybody loves somebody sometime
  Everybody falls in love somehow
  Something in your kiss just told me
  My sometime is now.

- "That's Amore" (Harry Warren, Jack Brooks, 1953):
  When the moon hits your eye like a big pizza pie
  That's amore
  When the world seems to shine like you've had too much wine
  That's amore
  Bells will ring ting-a-ling-a-ling, ting a-ling a-ling
  And you'll sing "Vita bella"
  Hearts will play tippy-tippy-tay, tippy-tippy-tay
  Like a gay tarantella . . .

- "Memories Are Made of This" (Terry Gilkyson, Richard Dehr, Frank Miller, 1955):
  Take one tender kiss,
  Add one stolen night of bliss,
  One girl; one boy; some grief; some joy:
  Memories are made of this.
- "Volare" ["Nel blu, dipinto di blu"] (Franco Migliacci, Domenico Modugno, 1958):
  Let's fly way up to the clouds
  Away from the madd'ning crowds
  We can sing in the glow of a star that I know of
  Where lovers enjoy peace of mind . . .
- "Ain't That a Kick in the Head" (Jimmy Van Heusen, Sammy Cahn, 1960):
  How lucky can one guy be
  I kissed her and she kissed me . . .

Courtly love was the basis of American pop songs as the jazz age diminished after the War and until the British invasion of the 1960s. Implied, inevitably, was the hungry and exhilarated male fallen into the swoon of his lover's embrace, or wishing to fall, or fearing not to fall, or regretting having avoided falling, or falling and falling again, or hoping to fall, or praying to fall. This was the case no matter who was singing, and many of Dean's big successes were covered as well by some of his friends and numerous other singers of lesser reputation. But when these words of love's yearning emerged from his glowing self, they became not only universalized in a peculiar way but also eternal. Eternal because, as he did not seem to take breath, time did not seem to pass. What he said was true, had always been true and would continue to be true forever. Alternatives to the courtly love arrangement for men (such as same-sex bonding) did not emerge into the popular limelight for decades, frequently hiding at the time under the umbrella of "confirmed bachelorhood"; for women, before Betty Friedan's *The Feminine Mystique* in 1963, the popular myth dictated that sex was not to be initiated; or desired. Martin was reinvoking the verities of love that had stood for centuries, as far as anybody could tell. Certainly as far as pop culture bothered to proclaim.

Note that courtly love's yearning was not then, nor ever had been, sexual hunger; its devotions were not pathways carved toward the bedroom; its passions were suitable, restrained; its nobility and its subservience to form were a long way from the "love" we would mean if we hunted for it in film performances then or today. Not sex, not heat, not coy allure, not flirtation—none of this, bluntly, on the airwaves. If one could at least in part embody this elixir, one could reach an audience of all ages and all attitudes.

And if one was crooning beside a Jerry Lewis, one could be interrupted as though by a series of hand grenades.

PART I

IN THE PLAYROOM

Play and art are born of a surplus of vital energy, not needed by the adult or child for the satisfaction of his immediate needs, and therefore available for the free and pleasant transformation into dancing.

—ROGER CAILLOIS (163)

Expanded, the statement "This is play" looks something like this: "These actions in which we now engage do not denote what those actions *for which they stand* would denote."

—GREGORY BATESON (180)

[1]

In his best-selling *Book of Baby and Child Care*, first published in 1946, Dr. Benjamin Spock[1] had insisted, "Play is serious business" (235), claiming of children, "They are training themselves for useful work later.... He [the child] is striving every hour of every day to graduate to more difficult achievements, and to do what the older kids and grownups do" (236).[2] However, unlike Spock's widely accepted and highly functionalist schema (which was strongly endorsed as orthodoxy within American culture), Dean & Jerry's play is developmentally regressive and persistently nonconstructive. They are *actually* adults at the same time as being children for whom adulthood is out of the question.

Spock was a big believer in the "play pen," a phrase that acknowledges the primary function of this portable piece of furniture as a container for limiting the animalistic energies of infants and toddlers. "Set up in the living room or the kitchen where the mother is working, it gives him the company that he can't have in his own room, and a chance to see everything that is going on.... *In good weather he can sit safely in his play pen on the porch and watch the world go by*" (145; emphasis ours).[3] But just *seeing* "everything that is going on" or just *watching* "the world go by" is never ever enough for Dean & Jerry, who also insist, in two idiosyncratic ways, on disrupting the passive spectatorship of others both within and beyond the diegesis of the enacted fictions in which they appear.

1 Benjamin McLane Spock, M.D. (1903–1998), the major guru and icon of the postwar baby boom years, offering to prospective mothers and current parents what were taken as infallible recipes for healthy child-rearing.

2 We have maintained Spock's use of the masculine pronoun not only because it is textually faithful to the original source, but also because it is apposite to the subjects at hand.

3 See also Spock 196–200.

[2]

A crib that effectively functions as a playpen was central to a Dean & Jerry sketch on the November 12, 1950, broadcast of the *Colgate Comedy Hour*:[4]

Begin in a living room set—a drastically simplified version of this iconic American postwar domestic environment that couldn't be real—taken up by an oversized crib that is covered at the side by a blanket. "Father" and "Mother" are going out for the evening as the baby-sitter, an attractive young woman in a tight sweater with ribbons in her hair, arrives. "Daddy's little boy" is in her care (Father [Jerry] remarks, yucking it up, "It's a shame you're not taking care of Daddy . . . Wooowwwww!"). Instead of staying home to get cozy with the babysitter, he has donned his hat and coat to go out with his wife for the evening. Call this a critique of middle-class sentimentality, certainly a fingering of the staleness many Americans at the time believed took over marriage's excitement once a child was in the picture. As soon as she is alone with the kid, the babysitter's boyfriend (Dean) comes in through the window, picks her up in an embrace, and leaps onto the couch with her (all with slightly elevated zest from Martin). And then, with hardly a tick of surprise for the audience, and quite as though cued by the sexual passion a few feet away, baby starts wailing in the crib. Wailing, screeching, bawling, tossing stuffed animals—*but still invisible.* Who could this baby be but . . . Jerry.

And soon enough, yes, baby pops up and leaps out. Jerry in a full-length flannel zip-up pajama. Screaming, demanding, screaming, demanding, screaming, and not getting the attention he wants. The sitter goes to the kitchen to get the baby some milk and the boyfriend tries unsuccessfully to quiet him, then goes to join the babysitter in the kitchen, *leaving the baby to amuse himself.* (Spock advocated not "spoiling" a baby by giving it "extra attention when he's uncomfortable" [98]). Baby says, to us as much as to himself, "What shall I do? I'll watch television!"—a reflection on widespread

4 For five years, 1950–1955, the structure of *The Colgate Comedy Hour* juxtaposed Dean & Jerry with other singers and comedians through an alternating hosting arrangement—Milton Berle, Bob Hope, Abbott and Costello, for example; a frequent critical and fan refrain involved comparisons with other stars. The show originated from the stage of the El Capitan Theater in Los Angeles (still on Hollywood Blvd. across the road from Grauman's Chinese) and New York's International Theater (on Columbus Circle).

child-rearing practices whereby children would be left unattended in front of a television set. (An early case of television itself being used recursively on television.)[5]

The television here is what would be for contemporary audiences today a Lilliputian article, fondled by Jerry almost as though it were a pet or a jewel. Whatever Baby is watching now, seated at first on the end of the couch and soon falling over in "hysterics," we cannot see, but he is going into paroxysms of withdrawal, gaping, groaning, squealing, twisting, stretching, and freezing. A lovely, layered moment for the critical eye:

[a] We will not be bothered noticing that the creature self-defining as a "baby" is actually not one, because a signal convention of physical comedy is that whatever a character calls himself, we take him to be.

[b] This Lewisian baby is watching television, *quite as viewers of 1950 were watching television at that very moment.* Note, then, how as early as then Martin & Lewis were arranging for viewers a recursive experience of watching on the little screen somebody who is watching somebody on the little screen.

[c] The baby reacts to television *physically*, as though the program works for him like an exercise routine. If watching Lewis/Baby gesticulate we do not react in so vivid a way, we do feel ourselves reacting through our bodies. "If the onlookers laugh when the clown suddenly finds himself falling like a stone," writes Erving Goffman, "it is because they had all along been projecting their musculature and sensibilities sympathetically into his walk" (381). Thus, in his Baby guise Lewis is projecting his own audience's present response, but at the same time infantilizing them.

Not long later, after an animated game of charades with the precociously verbal child, the boyfriend manages to wrangle the "baby" back into the crib. But coming our way waits an astonishing punchline. Baby, invisible to the camera again, is whining offscreen in Jerry's unmistakable voice. Mother and Father have returned. Jerry/Father shouts at the baby to quiet down as Baby argues and tosses things out of the crib.

But suddenly up pops Baby, glaring, while Papa stands beside him, glaring, too. *Both Papa and Baby appear to be Jerry Lewis.*

5 Caldwell 22–24.

Dean shouts and puts his hands to his ears in utter disbelief at the sight of two Jerrys (as though one is trouble enough)! Two identical prognathic jaws jutting, two fixed gazes of irritation. We must recollect that in the early 1950s, a program like this one was being broadcast *live* to East Coast audiences, so that split-screening (very well developed in cinema since 1945) was out of the question and in any event the use of special effects for television was immature. Clearly the "Baby" here can only be a double (Sammy Petrillo, sixteen years old [Levy 144ff; Hayde 77–80]), but Lewis has been meticulous in rehearsing the finale pose with a camera, so that the perfect angle (in this case a complete profile—unavailable as such to the cackling studio audience) can be found for making the shot successfully.[6] The skit is finished before we can swallow the wonder.

[3]

Martin & Lewis did not name playrooms "playrooms." One of their talents was to convert any and all spaces they traversed into places specialized for play. Playrooms are an unmistakably ersatz rendering of the real world, in which scale and dimension are made malleable, where the typical parameters for verisimilitude do not apply (that is, things will get "broken" without really being broken), and where there is space enough for rough-housing and physicality, if not much more than that. They are not practical spaces. Child's play can be schematic, it does not require objects from the world of actuality and can proceed entirely without three-dimensional volume. Hence most Martin & Lewis characters are completely flat—cardboard cutouts—with little more substance than that of a doll, reducible to a few attributes that can be taken in at a glimpse (as in early melodrama), easily and swiftly legible for the viewer prone to channel changing[7] or those just glancing up at the television set.

6 The "Jerry" vocalizations featured in the finale, as well as the young performer's striking resemblance to Lewis when Baby stands up, gave Petrillo some on-camera exposure as a courtesy.

7 In the early 1950s, there were only a small number of channels available on anyone's television set, typically major networks. Remote-control devices like Flash-Matic Tuning, the Lazy Bones Remote Control Channel Selector, Magic Brain Remote TV Control, and Remot-O-Matic were soon offered as expensive extras on upscale television sets. See "TV Remote Controls," *Consumer Reports*

And as in a children's theatrical, there may be a script upon which the play is premised but it is quickly abandoned for less predictable ad-libbing and novel turns that may never have been anticipated or discussed in rehearsals.[8] Scott Bukatman has paid specific attention to Dean's characteristic way of performing with Jerry, noting that the films they made together miss the strengths of Martin's performance style, based as it is on an easy informality. In the *Colgate Comedy Hour* episodes, on the other hand, Martin reveals an ability to follow and respond to Lewis, providing a measure of control while sharing in the delights of comic anarchy. The warmth of the partnership and the evident affection of the two for each other are in evidence here to a much greater degree than in any of their films as a team.

Further, for Bukatman, "The value of Dean Martin to the team has been broadly misunderstood or even lost entirely" ("Paralysis" 190). We would hasten to modify the romanticization of their personal relationship while attending to the nuances of how Martin's stolidity worked in tandem with a performed personality so very different. What looks like "easy informality" was hard work.

Martin had a tendency to hover with "ease" on the edge of a routine, inserting himself strategically while frequently following Lewis's lead by embellishing the proceedings, feigning mock surprise or outrage, and occasionally finding ways to oppose or obstruct him. It was as though Martin was at the other end of a telephone, in a wild and unmappable "conversation." Lewis would push against the limits of perfunctory stage settings, circumventing walls between adjacent onstage "rooms" rather than bothering with the pretense of flimsy fake "doors" while making a joke of ordinary barriers like "walls" and "windows." In Dean & Jerry's playrooms no mirrors were allowed—they would reflect the cameras and the audience, and break with whatever minimal verisimilitude was involved. There were no real windows

(March 1956): 109–12. These remote controls also had a mute control for those who had "the urge to silence an announcer or erase a commercial, but lacked the energy to do it" (109). Remote muting devices like the Blab-off were also available at a much lower cost: "A flick of the switch will then turn the TV pitchman into a pantomimist." See "Remote Control Devices for Radio and Television," *Consumer Reports* (November 1955): 523.

8 There is a real similarity here to the lazzi of the commedia dell'arte. See Gordon. Martin & Lewis are using the "ad-lib," which has very early roots in the Commedia.

through which the outside world could be whiffed: there is apparently no outside world. Around this time, André Bazin was extolling cinema's ability to give viewers a window on the world, but Bazin ain't in this playroom. Nor, with television, is there a fourth wall. These playrooms are glass houses into which everyone can see and millions upon millions of fans refrained from throwing anything that would resemble a stone.

In Norman Taurog's *You're Never Too Young* (1955), Dean plays Bob Miles, athletics instructor at Mrs. Brendan's School for Girls. His fiancée, Nancy Collins (Diana Lynn), also teaches there. Jerry plays Wilbur Hoolick, an aspiring master barber pursued on a train by Noonan, a violent jewel thief (Raymond Burr).[9] Unable to pay full fare, Wilbur masquerades (ridiculously) as an eleven-year-old boy and ends up being comforted by Nancy in her compartment. But a rival for Bob's affection, badly situated to see Wilbur correctly, reports Nancy to the schoolmistress as having been alone with a strange man. A meeting of the board will decide whether or not she is to be dismissed from her job. Wilbur and Bob turn the board meeting into a playroom, pulling mounted swords and pistols off the walls and putting them to violent use, running up and down a table top, swinging from a chandelier, and throwing two school mugs into a fireplace. Even the most august of formal hearings is turned into a playful free-for-all. Bob is drawn into the high-jinks even as he attempts to manage the misbehaving "child" whose juvenile antics demonstrate the baselessness of the charges against Nancy. She is exonerated, of course, but the headmistress's office is reduced to chaos.

[4]

Any movie set can seem a private universe, a playroom, cut off from the entirely separate everyday world in which viewers sit watching. How do the sets used by Martin & Lewis have a special quality? Where typically a set or location is a fictional zone in which characters live and play—characters directly shown or characters implied—in Dean & Jerry's work the set or

9 It was not irregular in major studios like Paramount in the 1950s for players who had established a strong character role in one picture to be used again not long later in a role not so very different. For Burr, this film came out when his performance as Lars Thorwald in Hitchcock's *Rear Window* (1954) was still fresh for audiences.

location is a meta-fictional zone in which performers live and play (only and very obviously dressing up as characters). Note how their dressing rooms are often shown as part of a skit or film. A meta-fictional zone: a place that only and self-avowedly "plays at" being what we take it for, just as the actors do. A giveaway example can be found in one of Jerry's solo films from 1964, Frank Tashlin's *The Disorderly Orderly.* In "Hollywood" as envisioned in the finale chase—one of the supremely great chase scenes ever filmed—the "city" (composed, actually, of views in many different areas) exists only as a zone for Jerry to zoom, zigzag, slalom, and speed through in a purloined ambulance.[10] In the same fashion, in *Living It Up* the streets of Manhattan exist only for Dean & Jerry to sing and dance in, as though urban life generally doesn't exist there.[11]

After "making it" during the late 1940s, Lewis's version of "living it up" was, in 1958, a new house (not his first)—a mansion on Bel Air's St. Cloud Road formerly owned by Louis B. Mayer—and a fleet of no fewer than fourteen automobiles. And why not? His seven-year deal with Paramount was for fourteen films for a grand total of ten million dollars. That same year, Dean was in two of the top ten biggest grossing films of the year, *Some Came Running* and *The Young Lions*, getting paid $200,000 per film (Tosches 309, 315).[12]

Lewis looked for larger and more lavish playrooms, expansive but inherently bounded settings—whether constructed in the studio, like the massive dormitory constructed for *The Ladies Man* (1961),[13] or situated in real-world

10 He is like a prototype for what would come to be known as the skate-boarder, and this sequence showed the way for Noel Black's *Skaterdater* (1966), where young boarders take advantage of every urban nuance they can find for hair-raising feats, especially a skateboard "duel" down a hilly street.

11 A trope of urban transformation that would be paid homage by the Egyptian filmmaker Youssef Chahine in his *Alexandria Now and Forever* (1989).

12 The era of movie star mega-salaries more or less commenced with Sylvester Stallone and *Rambo* in 1985, by which point studio control of filmmaking was defunct and stars were representing themselves on one-shot deals, not resting with seven-year studio contracts. Making *North by Northwest* at MGM in 1958–59, the mega-star Cary Grant earned $300,000. Jerry and Dean were making huge money.

13 For sheer size, Jerry's dormitory set, built by Ross Bellah on Paramount's Stage 18, outstripped *Rear Window* (1954), whose set by Joseph MacMillan Johnson was photographed on the same stage.

settings like Miami Beach's Fontainebleau Hotel in *The Bellboy* (1960)[14] or the San Diego Hilton and Sea World in *The Big Mouth* (1967). In films like these, actual locations became playgrounds of sorts for a series of loosely connected gags involving a relatively circumscribed space confining various denizens (such as Milton Berle, Slapsie Maxie Rosenbloom, and Walter Winchell). On one hand, the elaborate setting is a clear throwback to what Tom Gunning and André Gaudreault called the "cinema of attractions," cast in a distinctively spatial—rather than temporal—framework. The closest analogs are perhaps silent film comedies set in amusement parks, from *Rube and Mandy at Coney Island* (Edwin S. Porter, 1903) to the Coney Island sequences in *Speedy* (Ted Wilde, 1928). *Some Came Running* (1958) ends on a fairground midway among carnival games and rides, with Bama (Dean) in a Stetson hat racing through the crowds to try to prevent a murder. Three months after its release, Dean could again be seen onscreen in a cowboy hat as Chance in *Rio Bravo* (1959), which takes place in a backlot Western town a few miles outside Tucson, that feels a bit like an amusement park version of the Old West in which the characters move between a set of stock locations (saloon, hotel, main street, stables) and never venture beyond the edge of town. In *The Bellboy,* Lewis cavorts around the Fontainebleau, never uttering a word.

[5]

Play spaces for Dean & Jerry could be invented spontaneously. *The unlikely playroom.* There is a billboard at the beginning of *Artists and Models* (1955) that functions like a treehouse with an orifice entryway located within a gigantic pair of ruby-red lips. Eugene Fullstack (Jerry) hides in there, completely hidden by the facade of the sign, addictively absorbed in reading comic books aloud while Rick Todd (Dean) paints the exterior and hums, a bit like a suburban father working on maintaining his son's playhouse while the youngster acts out the violent doings of The Bat Lady, undisturbed in his

14 Shawn Levy recounts how Lewis, committed to Paramount for a film, was on a stand-up gig at the Fontainebleau in January 1960 during which he "had an epiphany. He would make the movie there, a movie about a bellboy, done all in pantomime. If he could convince owner Ben Novak to let him use the hotel as a set, he'd save a fortune in production costs" (246).

secret hideaway that is ironically just out of view of Manhattan passersby.[15] A supreme irony of the billboard playroom is that, then as now, audiences were wholly familiar with billboard advertising, especially its ability to magnify effects (as here, with the inviting lips selling cigarettes [and presaging *Attack of the 50-foot Woman* (1958)]). Looking at any billboard, no one was misled into thinking that its advertisement was offering up "the real"; they thought it was *playing* on offering the real, and that they could "play along" by running out and making a purchase—even this being a kind of play act. To see Dean & Jerry playing with this playing is both to elevate their activity and to highlight it as philosophical. Everyday gawkers probably never thought about what lay behind the screen of their neighborhood movie theaters any more than street walkers pacing to work thought about what might be behind a billboard. As typically perceived and treated by viewers, then, the billboard was as flat, as "paper thin" as the walls of an avowedly artificial set, the joke here being that while this "set" looks paper thin in fact it covers a three-dimensional world.

Going "behind the screen" was, for almost everyone, only a metaphorical journey.

Behind the formal facade of Dean & Jerry's world is a whole lot of play-acting: irreverent, casual if not absolutely spontaneous, preposterous from the point of view of rational, well-socialized thought. With elegant, strategic timing, Dean would insinuate himself into a situation where he had no place, intruding casually but bluntly on the peace of a silent moment and instigating some kind of chaos. Be very cautious about underestimating Dean's power to input, challenge, and disrupt. He only appears to be doing very little, to be couth, calm, and collected, but his role in fingering the trigger is crucial.

Jerry's body is preternaturally malleable. After his back seizes up while posing for a drawing, Dean takes him to a massage parlor in *Artists and Models.* Gawky uncoordinated Jerry ends up plastered on the table under the hands of a battleship Scandinavian Viking woman (Patti Ross), who kneads him like a clump of dough. But if this were to be taken as a serious massage, it might well commence and end this way, only. Instead, before we can count

15 The Bat Lady alludes to 1940s comic book heroines like Black Cat and Miss Fury. See Hope Nicholson, *The Spectacular Sisterhood of Superwomen: Awesome Female Characters from Comic Book History* (Philadelphia: Quirk Books, 2017), 28–30, 37–39. On the historical context for 1950s comic book regulation, see also Amy Kiste Nyberg, *Seal of Approval: The History of the Comics Code* (Jackson: University Press of Mississippi, 1998) and Frederic Wertham.

to ten, Jerry has been wrapped up into nothing less than a pretzel. He is only playing as a normal body, then, and the masseuse is only playing at giving him a normal rubdown—thus the joke. Not in response to this 1955 film, but surely existing in the same atmosphere and perhaps even for the same reasons, Joe McVicker's Play-Doh[16] was invented a year later and soon furnished with a Technicolor palette when marketed to the American public in 1956. A skilled amateur sculptor at play could even "play-doh" a "Jerry" having a "massage."

In *Artists and Models,* with Dean & Jerry's help, Frank Tashlin was making an image that could challenge not only the process of optical reception—seeing *isn't* believing—and not only the mechanism of dramatic presentation—the facade is nothing but a facade—but also the prevailing political economy of an era in which acquisition was a primary piety. The billboard face touted product, allure, and the application of skilled labor, but here all of that was merely the cover-up for what the film could claim was actually going on: self-indulgence, slacking off, neurosis. So what you see *isn't* what you get. Play to the very depth is the keynote for Dean & Jerry, and with his innate sense of its variability Tashlin was one of their great supports.

The deepest kind of play twists survival itself. In *Artists and Models,* Rick is quite literally a "starving artist" and Eugene is jobless. They have no food to eat and no money to buy it with. Eugene makes an elaborate show of preparing a single solitary Navy bean for their evening meal—perhaps a take on Chaplin's dining on a boot with Big Jim in *The Gold Rush*.[17] They have dressed for a nice supper in expensive shirts and nice clean trousers, but their plates are empty. Jerry pantomimes popping the cork of a bottle of champagne, heard as diegetic sound. But Dean is puzzled:

16 Play-Doh began as a wallpaper cleaning compound formulated to remove wall soot created by coal-burning furnaces. But when cleaner-burning furnaces came into use, by the mid-1950s, it was colored, reformulated for odor, and remarketed as a toy (see Walsh 115–20). Use of the Play-Doh form and idea in *Artists and Models* was exceptionally contemporary. A similar product, "Miracle Play Clay," was the centerpiece of a skit on the January 10, 1954, episode of the *Comedy Hour*. In the 1940s and 1950s, wallpapering was a widespread interior decorating choice, and many furnaces were coal-burning.

17 Just a few years before Dean & Jerry teamed up, in 1942, Chaplin rereleased a reedited version of *The Gold Rush* with a new score and Chaplin's voiceover narration. See Solomon, *The Gold Rush* 73–77, 91–92.

JERRY: See, I'm just makin' believe that we're both very rich wealthy millionaires, with money... and I'm makin' believe. [*Pours "champagne" into imaginary glass*]

DEAN: I hope the bubbles didn't tickle your nosey. [*Smile*]

JERRY (*in medium shot, scrunching his nose up as if to pull it back into his head. He's focused at f8. Screen left at f4 the candle nearest him is a monster, with a flame longer than his head*) Just a little tickle.

They get up and Jerry glides over to the right rear of the shot, where his artist's table sits empty. He twice slaps both hands down on it, *palms up!,* and then drops one finger to make a piano note sound. Then again. Dean is curious. He walks over and tries to play a note but jams his finger into the table. Jerry starts up the romantic melody, "When You Pretend," picked up by Dean:

The happiness you find is all a state of mind
That's true my friend
And life is filled with happy endings
When you pretend
(Harry Warren and Jack Brooks)

What is being invoked here by "pretend"??? In a *deus ex machina* in this scene, a steak drops down from the upstairs apartment the unseen denizens of which are heard only in offscreen sound and resemble Ralph and Alice Kramden arguing in *The Honeymooners* [1955–1956]). We are in The Land of Plenty, all things Can Happen, with gritty working-class TV realism-minimalism just beyond the frame, out of sight, heard but not seen. Not that we are to believe in magic happening in the everyday if we can have the relief of magic happening onscreen. Happening, too, by virtue of artifice. Karal Ann Marling comments on the "complex sensual dialectic" of 1950s women's "New" fashions as their artifice affected those who bought and wore them:

> They did experience actual physical changes—a corporeal transformation—within their own persons when they put on New Look clothes. They felt a constant pressure at the waistline, a fluttery of drapery around the legs, the friction of flesh and close-fitting fabric across the breasts.... The autoerotic aspects of the Dior ensemble are clear enough to women who wore New Look styles.... The frivolous externals of fashion may themselves trigger deeply internalized consequences. (16)

Dean & Jerry hardly look poor, their clothing is immaculate, their apartment is richly furnished, they have colorful pictures on the walls. So the "poverty" is also a pretend game, helping consumers "imagine" how it would be if they couldn't consume and feel especially wonderful if they could. David Halberstam notes how by 1955, while "a new young generation of Americans was breaking away from the habits of its parents," a new middle class was emerging and creating as a byproduct a brand-new consuming class: the young. *Scholastic* magazine's Institute of Student Opinion showed that by early 1956 there were 13 million teenagers in the country, with a total income of $7 billion a year,[18] which was 26 percent more than only three years earlier. The average teenager, the magazine said, had an income of $10.55 a week. That figure seemed remarkable at the time; it was close to what the average American family had had in disposable income, after all essential bills were paid, fifteen years earlier (473).

[6]

The walls of Dean & Jerry's play space are literally paper thin. Consider Homer's enormous hotel-room "hospice" in *Living It Up*: there is room here for a small army to congregate, and the walls are spread far apart, but outside the picture windows the City of New York hovers like a painted poster, even when Homer goes out on the balcony. No one here is trying to establish that the hospital room is far off the ground, because we have been directed by the script to consider it that way.

Or the *Comedy Hour* for May 20, 1951. Here we see a mailbox and doorbell marked "Dean Martin." Dissolving "inside," we are in a large (mansion-like) space with a huge dining table, double doors, immensely high walls ornamentally plastered, a plush sofa, and so on. Dean is there in a trenchcoat, just arrived, and chatting with his maid. Jerry will momentarily make an entrance as the newly hired valet, in tails, and scat singing loudly, "Abba dabba dabba dabba!" Go no further. As we come in, we have the startled (yet, being fans of the show, not so startled) realization of how much flatness lies before us. Some of the furniture near the wall, the plasterwork, a chiffonier with a vase of flowers on top—all this is painted on a flat backdrop, totally ersatz, totally

18 In 2023 dollars, more than $76 billion.

suggestive and only that. We are watching the interaction between Dean and the maid, that between Dean and Jerry, and so on, but never for an instant taking any of this as happening in a real place. When Jerry starts bustling around, wiping the top of a little table, an instant reaction is: fear that he is going to rub up against the scenery, since at first—and logically for him—he seems unaware of the place he inhabits. This "home" is only for Dean & Jerry to toot around in, and the same can be said for the theater in which the *Comedy Hour* was shot, to the precincts of which one or the other of the team would feel quite easy in migrating on the least inspiration. The "studio-theater" as playroom. The "mansion" as playroom. The playroom anywhere and everywhere.

[7]

If anything and anywhere can be a playroom, then play itself can be anywhere and everywhere. Relationships, business, professions can be play. Crime may not pay, as the old adage goes, but it can be play, just as law can be play, school can be play, and even religion can be play. The effect of this stretch was to offer the idea of degravitizing the serious side of economic life: the devotion to acquisition, for instance, the postwar "rat race," the obsession with the "business of America being business" (as President Calvin Coolidge famously asserted) or even the sanctity of the middle-class home—ironic, since Dean and Jerry acquired such homes, and massively; and both of them lived in perfectly routine middle-class luxury. Middle-class luxury, note, not aristocratic luxury (which was reserved for a very very very small slice of the population). The biggest fortunes in America weren't stashed in Hollywood or nearby in the Holmby Hills, the Palisades, Bel Air, Brentwood—all these, albeit ultra-lavish, were middle-class neighborhoods. What dominated the culture were middle-class values no matter how extraordinary was the opulence. Most Hollywood portrayals of aristocracy, American and European, were framed from a middle-class point of view and worked from the "movie-star home" as model. Look at "Big Jack's" middle-class domain—and values—in *That's My Boy* (1951) as a lower end of the scale, and the house in the northwest in *You're Never Too Young* for its opposite.

[8]

With their trademark thrilling hyper-flatness, and their deft transcendence of social-class gravity, comic books are a frequent prop in the world of Dean & Jerry, nowhere more than in *Artists and Models*. They are colored garishly with inked hues not borrowed from the everyday world, they are as depth-free as the paper they are printed on, filled to overflowing with wild, entirely irrational movement. Martin & Lewis even spun their own comic series, *The Adventures of Dean Martin and Jerry Lewis*, published by DC Comics from 1952 to 1957. In these "paratexts," as literary theorist Gérard Genette might call them, the respective personae were drawn into individual panels, Jerry with a jutting jaw, chiseled chin dimple, and angular—read, neurotic—posture, Dean erect and stalwart and with his wavy hair nicely Brylcreemed.[19] Jerry's screeching and Dean's warbling would both have to sit in the waiting room.

Jerry defaces a drawn "Dean" during the final broadcast of the 1950–1951 *Comedy Hour* season. He inserts a huge mustache on Dean's "face," announcing: "I been wantin' to do dat for five months!" as the audience howls with delight. In the eponymous ball in *Artists and Models*, special effects cinematography[20] allows Dean and Jerry, decked out in artists' smocks, wielding palettes and brushes, to apply paint not only to the bodies of their models, but also to thin air! Pure bold flying swatches of coloration! Again with the defacement and the thin-air painting, we are seeing playroom antics, the development of flat, cut-out figurines and their arbitrary application to diegetic space. One might have argued that artists' renderings (even the renderings of performance artists) were as important as—or more important than—the people being rendered. Triumph of illusion *as* illusion; flatness *as* flatness.

19 Brylcreem (created in Birmingham England in 1928) came in tubes, like toothpaste, and young men very often slathered their hair with it to make the waves stand solid and the hairmop glow in the light. "A Little Dab'll Do Ya!"

20 By the acknowledged "king" of Hollywood special-effects photography, Paramount's Farciot Edouart, assisted by John P. Fulton. The artist responsible for the paintings themselves is uncredited.

[9]

In theirs as in many other playrooms around America, the distinction between humans and animals became inconsequential. Another kind of flattening, this time between what we like to think of as different, if compatible, biological forms, and in some ways an echo of Johan Huizinga: "Since the reality of play extends beyond the sphere of human life it cannot have its foundations in any rational nexus, because this would limit it to mankind" (3). In film theorizing and filmmaking, Huizinga's principle is carried fluidly to new extremes (see, for one example, Lippit).

This "primitive anthropomorphism," as Huizinga named it, is what Sergei Eisenstein was musing upon in his unfinished masterpiece translated into English as *Eisenstein on Disney* (of which the form is an intellectual montage of media analysis, autobiography, quotations, and images that is one of the guiding inspirations for this book). There, "Eisenstein pays particular attention to the 'unity of man and animal' on which [Walt] Disney's entire oeuvre is founded" (Solomon, "Sergei Eisenstein" 83, quoting Eisenstein 133). But, in a child's playroom—*Peter Pan* begins with Peter wanting to return there again and again—animals (live, stuffed, or otherwise) and toys have as much or more status than humans. These include the many dogs Virgil Yokum (Jerry) cares for as an apprentice veterinarian in *Money From Home* (1953, 3D); the "pedigreed basset hound, a gift from the governor of Kentucky" for the supposedly terminally ill Homer (Jerry) perched on the nightstand in the bedroom of their hotel suite in *Living It Up;* Mr. Bascomb the great Dane lounging around the convertible in *Hollywood or Bust* (1956); the six pups Stanley (Jerry) is duty-bound to walk in a pack in *The Bellboy*; the numerous dogs Norman Pfeiffer walks for wealthy clients in *Who's Minding the Store* (1963), where he is also joined on a sofa by an enormous, fluffy-faced English Sheepdog. In *The Nutty Professor* (1963) Julius Kelp is nursed by a somewhat-too-intelligent raven—a raven maven. *The Geisha Boy* (1958) has Gerald with Harry the Rabbit (the magic rabbit, although for Jerry's characters, who seem magical in their own right, any animal they touch becomes magical, too). In the sequences involving all of these animals, human comedians momentarily take a "back seat."

As to the animals, Dean barely tolerates them.

[10]

Play invokes contortion. Frequently in diatribes with Dean, Jerry would contort both his body and his face so that the simian/human resemblance was emphasized (the received idea being that some round-headed, round-faced people look more like chimps than other people do). In *The Expression of the Emotions in Man and Animals* (1872), Charles Darwin emphasized that many of the most elemental expressions of human emotions find striking analogs in the animal kingdom, and enlisted photographer Oscar Rejlander to illustrate. These expressions of extreme emotion—baring of the teeth, contraction of the *orbicularis oris*, raising of eyebrows, tautening of the cheeks—are the nodal points of Lewis's performance style, quite as though he stayed up late studying these photographs as aids. Martin & Lewis's comedy suggests that we could spend more time with animals; or more, that, given the omnipresence of the animal side of ourselves, we are already spending more time with animals than we typically like to admit. Certainly civilized society—at least society civilized through the mega-agency of capitalism—forces structures that are profoundly at odds with nature. This "enforcement" is also a theme, not so salient, in Frank Tashlin's 1946 "children's book" *The Bear That Wasn't*—the ultimate anti-corporate, anti-human parable: "You're not a Bear. You're a silly man who needs a shave and wears a fur coat" (n.p.). Interestingly, by the time he came to direct movies with Martin & Lewis, Tashlin was showing us characters who might not have been "bears" but they also weren't just "silly men" wearing costumes: Jerry became a kind of interstitial being.

The easy coexistence, apparent fellowship, and frequent close contact between humans and animals we see in the Martin & Lewis multiverse also suggests that the behavior of humans and animals is not so different. A repeated bit on the *Comedy Hour* had Dean & Jerry licking each other's faces and kissing one another—and occasionally others—full on the mouth. The licking was so frequent that "Don't lick it!" became a catchphrase during the 1950–1951 season. Was Jerry struggling onscreen to become Dean's pet? Were the two of them applying to become ours?

A tacit requirement of middle-class life in America was a kind of hermetic sealing away of the "civilized" from the "raw," the childlike, the animal, the bodily, the ludic, the erotic—the maintenance of order: hierarchical order, taxonomic order, spatial and temporal order, normative order above all. To what extent, Dean & Jerry openly wondered, do we constrain, imprison, restrict, or else liberate ourselves and our families? Cultural historian Clifford E. Clark Jr. reflected upon American family life in the 1950s:

> Given the more permissive attitude toward child rearing encouraged by Dr. Spock and others, families felt that they needed a room where the children could play without disturbing the adults or *threatening the furniture.* In . . . a model home built outside New York City in 1951 to exhibit the very latest in comfort, children were given a very large space, *divided by a partition,* in which to play. . . . Another reason for having a . . . playroom . . . was to separate the *world of the television* from that of the adults who might want to read or have some peace and quiet to themselves. . . . A separate . . . playroom allowed the children to play their music or to engage in more active games with their friends without disturbing the other member of the house. (215; emphasis added)

In October 1950, Jerry and his wife, Patti,[21] "paid sixty-five thousand dollars for their first real home, a twelve-room, five-and-a-half-bath, ranch-style house . . . in Pacific Palisades":

> It was handsomely appointed within, with pine-paneled dens and plenty of storage rooms for Jerry's troves of goodies. The backyard was expansive, a large garden where Jerry and Patti would build an outbuilding for entertaining. There was a vacant lot next door, which Jerry later bought and converted into a baseball field for his sons and their friends. For two rootless children grown up, it was like living in a dream. (Levy 131–32)

In the Palisades house, at 1119 Amalfi Drive, Jerry made a private playroom for himself, his family, and invited guests and instituted, in his backyard, a virtual playhouse/theater. This was for him a supreme way of playing house.

[II]

Shawn Levy describes the Lewis Playhouse in some detail, a part of Jerry's homelife he wholly neglects to mention in his 2005 memoir:

> He upgraded his equipment and outfitted the summer house in his backyard into a full-scale theater—the Gar-Ron Playhouse. He paid prime

21 Patti Palmer, Jerry's first wife from 1944 to 1980.

> rates to have a laboratory process his film overnight. He even coerced Dean into joining in. . . . Gar-Ron films were premiered in catered, black-tie parties at the Lewis house, for which, oddly, Hollywood turned out: The Wallises,[22] Darryl Zanuck,[23] columnist Sidney Skolsky,[24] Ronald Reagan and new wife, Nancy Davis.[25] Jerry hired klieg lights, doormen, a red carpet. He commissioned a film crew to record the event newsreel-style. He designed an Oscar-inspired statuette,[26] "The Jerry Lewis Award," to present to his stars. (151–52)

"The things I did while in the company of my buddies were artfully planned so as to win over their loyalty and affection" (qtd. in Levy 153). Thus, Lewis's compulsions to develop expertise in filmmaking and dramatization were at play early on. "What," Levy asks, "were the Gar-Ron weekends, in fact, other than an effort to convert his house into a Catskills hotel, complete with a pool, a softball diamond, a garden playhouse, and a *tummler* prodding the guests into becoming part of the show?" (153).[27]

Dean, more or less at the same time, and living at 1317 Londonderry Place, West L.A., was in slapstick of another kind. Only months before, he had ended an eight-year marriage (his first) and gained custody of four children, the oldest aged seven and the youngest only around one. His new wife, Jeanne Biegger (an Orange-Bowl Queen) would give birth to Dean Paul Martin not long later. Family life was his life (his marriage to Jeanne lasted twenty-seven years), and the playroom space he supervised belonged to his children. If

22 Major producer Hal Wallis (1898–1986) and his partner Louise Fazenda (1895–1962). By the time of the Playhouse he had produced *My Friend Irma* (1949) and *My Friend Irma Goes West* (1950) and was at work on *That's My Boy*, with many films to follow.

23 Darryl F. Zanuck (1902–1979), writer and later head of Twentieth Century Fox.

24 Sidney Skolsky (1905–1983), Hollywood gossip columnist.

25 Ronald Wilson Reagan (1911–2004), 40th president of the United States, 1981–1989), and his wife Nancy Davis (1921–2016), both former film stars.

26 Skolsky was fabled to have coined the nickname "Oscar" for the Academy Award.

27 See also Hayde 185–86. A *tummler* is a quasi-busker who preps audiences for the comedian's laughs.

Jerry liked to offer his family play in the backyard, Dean preferred to keep his within the walls of his ultra-modern house.

There is of course another, very different, angle from which to view Jerry's Gar-Ron escapades. While he and family were occupying their dream residence in Pacific Palisades, still for him, itching and pressing from some obscure "within," there prodded a driving need to break out of domestic confinement, create some kind of play space that the home could not predictably enough offer and in which one could be transformed. Let us say that if Dean was taking the "playroom" idea with perfect conventionality, Jerry wanted to go crazy with it.

[12]

Although Dr. Spock wasn't calling for actual confinement of babies and young children, it turned out there was no way to avoid at least the look of a corral in many middle-class homes, given the smart new pieces of furniture for babying that commercial interests started flogging. So, in thinking about the Spock era, about the Martin & Lewis aesthetic commitment to behavioral transgression onstage and before the camera, and more generally about the sense of order established or violated by them, one cannot avoid coming quickly to the issue of containment. Containment in genre, containment in propriety, containment in theatrical space. Containment as confinement; social form as imprisonment. Stand here, not there. Stay put. Sit down and be quiet.

Dean & Jerry were fluent and fluid about breaking through genre boundaries (out of one playpen, into another) through both mixing and blunt destruction. They migrated out of and back into theatrical frame-space apparently at will. In fact, they made a career not only of "frame-breaking" in a Brechtian sense but also, and more generally, of wandering not just far but "way too far." As Orson Welles put it to Peter Bogdanovich, "You're too young to have seen him in the Copacabana with Dean and of course in those days he just went too far—everywhere. Way too far and it just made you sick" (Welles and Bogdanovich).[28] Fractured social and behavioral norms—through vocal loudness, gestural hyper-extension, blatantly performed "incomprehension"; not

28 Welles added, "Because when he goes too far, he's heaven. Just when he doesn't go too far, he's unendurable."

to say Dean's almost unmentionable irritation, frustration, and exasperation at being chained to this Thing—extended into the audience's expectations about performance and so-called normative boundaries between performers and themselves, between sacred stage space and public space.

However conventional it was for comedy generally, the Martin & Lewis frame breaking, that Dean & Jerry brought to new levels of disruption and direct address, was fostered in its early days by the liveness of live television and as it grew was matured in front of the movie camera. Frame breaking, sentence breaking, relationship breaking, scenery breaking, attention breaking, peace breaking, rhythm breaking . . . breaking as an art form. Breaking as truth. Breaking as life.

To have a smash hit, make a smash.

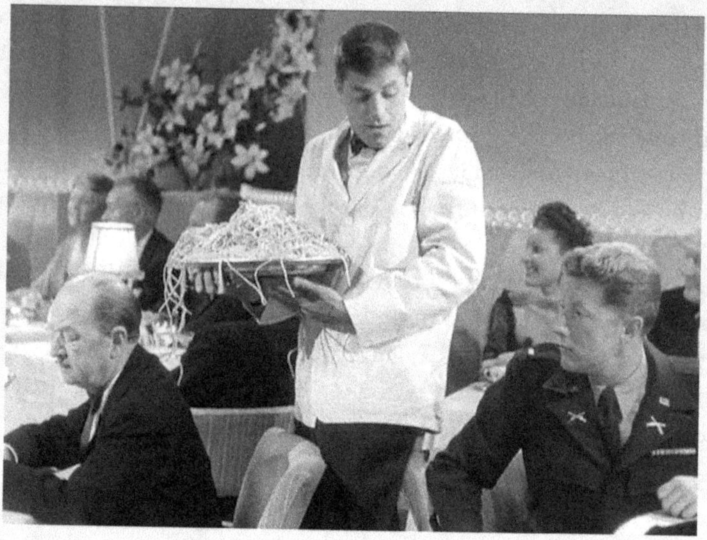

SMASH AND CRASH

[1]

Dean and Jerry organized an early attack upon three of the central pillars of the built environment of American family life, as outlined by Clifford E. Clark Jr.:

- the sanctity of furniture,
- the use of a partition to divide the (children's) play space away from (adult) family space, and
- separation of the adult world, a putative island of tranquility, from the palpable distractions of "the world of the television."

In the typical Martin & Lewis routine we find them:

- forever compromising the furniture; and
- knocking down or circumventing artificial partitions, often compromising the physical space of the studio itself; and
- collapsing the boundary between adult space—in the viewer's real experience—and "the world of the television."

Most viewers fixed upon Martin & Lewis on television saw them in a world not at all like the world where the television was.

In a sketch on the June 24, 1951, episode of the *Colgate Comedy Hour*, Dean is the rough-and-tough "gang" leader who has hurled a baseball through the first-floor window of a nearby Brownstone apartment. But Dean has no real baseball. He's just working this move through pantomime, winding up and hurling in an elegant imitation of a major league pitcher. And the timing of the studio "broken-glass" sound effect is way off, so that the crash of the window happens first (a visual effect would be produced with breakaway "glass"; for a sound effect a technician would have hammered through a pane of glass set in a containing frame) and Dean's gestural follow-through comes second. He ad-libs to cover, laughing good-naturedly, but the secret is given away: the television world is a package of meaningless nonsense compared with the sober "real" world.

[2]

Martin & Lewis are about transgression, not socialization. Perhaps one never comes closer than in the January 10, 1954, *Comedy Hour* episode in which Jerry is missing from the opening number but turns up in the orchestra blowing on a trumpet. Dean pronounces Jerry "incorrigible."

JERRY (in an exaggerated double-take, stammering with seeming incomprehension): What? What? What?

DEAN (repeating himself): Incorrigible!

JERRY (still stammering): What, what does that mean? What does that mean?

DEAN (struggling to come up with a definition, then snapping back): What's the difference? A dummy like you wouldn't understand anyhow.

But instantly, a visibly different person, Jerry stands up: "Oh, is that so?" And pausing, arms behind his back, the well-behaved student in the schoolroom, he intones straight out of the dictionary,

> JERRY: Incorrigible means not corrigible, incapable of being corrected or amended, not reformable, unmanageable, unruly, delinquent, one who lacks purpose or attachment with an incapacity for fixity or steadiness.

Dean is dumbfounded and so are we, and the studio audience applauds as Jerry smiles and takes a bow.

> JERRY: I'll take my trumpet and go and you may sing, you peasant!

Expectations smashed. Recognitions smashed. Language twisted. Language made both precise and meaningless at the same time.

In a discussion of automatism and some of Jerry's characterizations, Scott Bukatman works to catch the spirit by referring to the "jerking and the twitching" and the falling and the spilling and the stuttering and the spluttering and the "Laaaadyyyy!" and the "Whoa, Dean!" and the dangling and the spinning, and the breaking and the whole thing with the lack of bodily control ("Idiocy" 186).[1]

But these artful impressionistic descriptions tend to miss the importance of social structure and interaction on the formation of not only language but speech capacity. Jerry's characters can be examined productively as suffering from experiential and social deficits, not mental debility or loss of control or neurotic quirks or ego collapse. The character's situated condition makes it impossible or unlikely that he will do what others manage quite easily; makes it likely that he will "get things wrong."

[3]

Few violations of dramatic form work by actually compromising the physical nature of the "stage." If Jerry walks up to eat the camera's lens, he must not

1 Nor was Bukatman commenting here about "stuttering" and "spluttering" for the first time. In a 1991 discussion of Lewis's filmmaking that points to his creation of his screen character, we have reference to "articulation delayed and denied," and to "a stutter that structures the phenomenon of the filmmaker as a discursive metaphor" ("Paralysis" 188).

actually try to bite into it. But getting wet in a dry shooting situation is a tricky play, a compromise to the electrical grid for one thing and a palpable ruination of the star image for another. Either Dean or Jerry was always "all wet." Consider their "Singin' in the Rain" bit from the November 12, 1950 broadcast of the *Comedy Hour*.[2] A long preamble has Jerry more or less settled around a drum set in front of the band—the Union band!—with Dean clutching the microphone stand as his dearest friend, and Jerry clutching wire brushes. They are spatting, spitting, arguing, denying, vituperating, exculpating, Dean generally berating Jerry for horsing around too much. Finally some sort of peace settles and Dean makes to sing.

Jerry comes up very close and warns him that he's going to "get him," and leaves the stage.

Dean is doing a very rhythmic, and, one might say, minimally melodic rendition of Nacio Herb Brown and Arthur Freed's "Singin' in the Rain," when Jerry creeps on from the side and pours a pitcher of water over his head.

Audience explosion into laughter.

Exit Jerry.

Reenter Jerry with an even larger container of water.

More laughter.

Exit Jerry.

Reenter Jerry with a still larger container of water.

Audience hysterics.

Exit Jerry.

Reenter Jerry with a whole bucket of water that he throws in Dean's face.

On and on this way, all through the "song"—"I'm siiiiingin' in the rain, just siiingin' in the rain . . ."—with Dean finally finding his wits. He tells Jerry to "stand there," meaning, right at center stage at the microphone. Jerry looks around helplessly as Dean walks off, but does as he is commanded to do. Now, with Jerry at the mic, Dean returns with his own supply of water.

And again.

2 Episodes from *The Colgate Comedy Hour,* to whatever extent they may be available to fans and scholars today, can be seen only because of the kinescope process, which was the spot recording of a show, from a television screen, onto film (often 16 mm). Because Colgate needed their show—a key example of early live television—to air both in New York and Los Angeles, and because of the time lag between, the L.A. version was aired through the agency of the kinescope, while the East Coast version went out live.

And again.

And shampoo, too.

Water on both of them, their clothing drenched, the floor a lake into which Jerry plummets head-first and tries doing a crawl. Finally they stand up, sopping, side by side, friends again, for an extended good-night to the television audience.

Pure Commedia dell'arte.

Note, too, the strange and useful etiquette: that before "getting" Dean, Jerry warns him. More: when Jerry is ordered to stand at the microphone he instantly obeys, looking around *helplessly* as though some force is keeping him in position. Dean's command has, for all intents and purposes, "imprisoned" him in place, and he looks to the audience for "help." Powerful Dean, weak and helpless Jerry.

[4]

Three angles on Dean & Jerry are worth noting, because with them the fabric that was unendingly being teased and pulled, the fabric that came close to the precipice of being torn asunder, was that of their bond, call it friendship, affiliation, unity:

[A] Their antagonism is only "antagonism," always turned into mutual acceptance. They bark, they don't bite. Theirs is free play, in which everything is only what one prefers at the moment to imagine it is. And free play is neither an imitation of nor a window upon the real world, nor a suggestion that it should properly be replicated there. The comedy comes in our willing acceptance of the "guidelines" of such play, our "playing along," which is to say, wandering and wondering in our imagination; in this way we are liberated from the cuffs of what bourgeois ambitions allow.

[B] The "Singin' in the Rain" reciprocal drenching number might make us wonder how it could have happened that such uncontrolled zaniness and shapeless chaos were not only permitted on television but produced intentionally there. A pithier question: how has that carnival ceased to exist? How has all that unfettered play been evacuated from our scene? Has Western culture been subjected, now for seven decades, to a gradual, systematic, premeditated, meticulous straightening, cleansing, purifying, and elevation in the name of a limited "good"?[3] Time does not erode the delirious thought of letting go—but letting go only so far (although very often it might have been difficult to see that). Jerry Lewis and Dean Martin didn't do profanity, nor sexually explicit material of any kind: "Dean and I never worked blue" (Lewis interview).

[C] Look again at that moment when Dean is swamped after "Singin'," and perfunctorily tells Jerry to wait there: *and Jerry obeys.* A comedian stands trembling at a microphone, apparently with clear insight as to a torture to which he is presently to be subjected since Dean is, if anything, not mysterious and—can we believe this?—a torturer.

And how is it that Jerry obeys?

Jerry knows that he *is* the act—*he*, not what it is that he does—and to run or walk away is to abandon not only the geographical spot where Dean will drop his water but also the performance altogether. Come what may, don't give up the show. *Presence is the show.* Or: the show must go on—"go on" not as in "take place" but as in "continue to its natural end." So Jerry is trapped by the show, and in his role there. "Wait there" means "*I* am leaving the stage *but we are not.*"

However—

"The show" is always *the camera.* And thus, what we have in this little instant is the performer imprisoned by the camera that is showing him, caught and pinioned in his own display. Dumbstruck in the business of being a display, being visible, being seen. To translate this into values: for Jerry, being thrown into the Amazon and attacked by piranha is less horrible, far less horrible, than not being seen. *Not being seen* is the END. In this respect, our "Jerrele" epitomizes not only his own limitlessly effervescent self but every performer who stands before the camera.

In short, smash anything and everything, BUT DO NOT SMASH the comic's being there to be smashed, and DO NOT BREAK THE CAMERA, the magical talisman that makes the show shown.

3 In *Easy Living* (1937) we find Jean Arthur and Ray Milland in the middle of exactly the kind of comic chaos Dean & Jerry produced and lived in routinely, as they attempt to survive a cataclysm at The Automat.

[5]

About radio, movies, and comic books Dr. Spock had very definite prescriptions (304–7), with discussion of television appropriately added in his second edition, published in 1957. For Spock, in categorical if unstated opposition to the frenzied warnings of Fredric Wertham,[4] comic books, like play, were "serious business" and had "a positive, constructive value" (304). Reading them was a developmental phase through which children had to pass. Wertham, who published multiple scathing attacks on popular culture, including most notably *Seduction of the Innocent* (1954), is almost directly satirized in *Artists and Models* when Jerry's Eugene appears on a television program:

Audience applause for Eugene, just introduced as a guest on WTEV Channel 2's "The Better America Forum," a panel show hosted by Dr. Baker (Art Baker). We are seeing this on a color television set displayed inside a store window. The subject of the program today is "the ever-growing threat and menace of the cheap pulps, found on all newsstands, masquerading under the titles of comic books." Eugene, an avid if not frenzied reader of comic books for the past fifteen years, represents an example of "what can happen to the human brain on a steady diet of comic books," according to the program's host.

Rick, standing on the sidewalk (with us), is surprised to see his roommate on television, but even more amazed to hear that he has somehow become a spokesperson for anti-comics crusaders, since he himself has just secured a job as a comic-book illustrator that will allow them to pay their rent (so Jerry is "undoing" Dean yet again, and on television). Horrified, he attempts to dissuade Eugene from expressing his new views—speaking right through the television set in a store display behind the store's huge vitrine. Dean seems to be speaking directly to Jerry—as though plate glass, the store, the television aren't there. Eugene, in a different world altogether, is babbling:

> EUGENE: I am here to talk to the children and to the parents of the children, because if there weren't parents, there wouldn't be children, and

4 Who claimed publicly and also to Democratic senator Estes Kefauver's United States Senate Special Committee to Investigate Crime in Interstate Commerce that comic books incited delinquency in children.

vice versa. What I mean is that parents are necessary if you want children and children are necessary if parents want them, if you know what I mean.

Eugene proceeds speaking with words that are perfectly timed to work doubly, both in the ongoing conversation taking place on the televised talk show and in a separate conversation with Rick directly:

RICK: Eugene, what are you doing in there? ("In there": [a] inside this box; [b] inside the frame of that TV show)

EUGENE: I'm here to tell you how bad comic books are—for you. I never thought they were bad myself until my friend Rick Todd told me how bad they were—

Rick, who spends his time chasing girls, has apparently lectured Eugene about what a waste of time comic books are.

RICK (with his new job illustrating comic books): I was wrong. Boy was I wrong!

EUGENE: —And how right he was.

RICK: No, I was wrong, you dope.

EUGENE: And I almost became a dope reading comic books, and I realize that is why I am now a little retarded.

(That is: other people tend to think I'm retarded.)

Eugene's blather about adults being necessary if you want children bears its own strange interest, not least because he seems like a total incompetent thrust onto a stage, with no clue as to how to fill time. "Children are necessary if parents want them," he says, "if you know what I mean." We very much *do* know what he means, to such a degree that in truth it's totally unnecessary for him to have made the comment except that *Eugene (Jerry) desperately needs to utter something.* Not to show that he knows it, not to offer the content of the speech as content, but *to say the magic words.* He's not telling us something about the world, then; he's *telling us that he's telling us.* All of a sudden, words start pouring out of Jerry like lava out of an erupting volcano. Then, after a syllable or two, he becomes aware that words are pouring out and he keeps making words to account for, to half-apologize for, the outpouring, but now: he has to account for the half-apologetic words accounting for the outpouring, and so on. And so on and so on and on and on. Vibrant recursion. Talk as echo chamber.

To twist the screw a little further, in scatter speeches like this Jerry tends to look around helplessly as though he's (a) totally aware words are pouring out of his mouth, (b) totally aware that they don't make sense, and (c) completely helpless to stop this from happening—as though we all know such things happen because they happen to anyone and everyone all the time. (In short, this is how we all speak!) The tacit command to FILL TIME takes precedence over the idea of having something to say.

Eugene is trying to mimic the (for him, alien) discourse used by proponents of comic book censorship on the panel (including a professor, a child psychologist, and [Rick's love interest] Abigail [Dorothy Malone], herself a reformed comic book author). In this way he is attempting to say what he thinks his fellow panelists and their audience want to hear, essentially to make *their* statement as though it were his own, a clear case of what Mikhail Bakhtin refers to as "another's speech in another's language" (324). His babble is aimed at both the television audience within the film and the audience of the film—but with a split meaning: to the diegetic audience, the censorial view will seem sensible; to us pleasurably watching these folk watching (these animated folk), such censorship is nonsense.

For Spock, "The child must go through a period of blood-and-thunder adventure, where superhuman might and right always win at the last minute." Parents should set healthy limits: "If, on the other hand, a child lives entirely in his imagination, in stories, radio, and movies, he needs help, both from school and from parents, in finding the joy of friendships and games" (305). As to "developmental phases," Eugene lives entirely, unapologetically, and unselfconsciously in his own imagination, an imagination generated through and circumscribed by his addictive and exclusive consumption of comic books. His real-world friendship with Rick is a source of joy to himself, perhaps less so to Rick. What games they play—the "bean banquet"—are entirely Eugene's, and Rick is a reluctant—if not unwilling—participant. Dean & Jerry's comic-book allusions, imitations, replications, and references were not contrary to Spock's ideas, and were also a very long way from—if, indeed, in the same universe as—the thrilled attention to their favorite comic-book CGI movies one finds now in the twenty-first century from very largely (chronologically) adult audiences.

[6]

Eugene Fullstack's almost unbelievable immersion in the comic-book imagination is a wonder to behold: his *residence* in the billboard, his inability to take the comic book away from his face, his, in Dr. Spock's terms, entire failure to progress away from a childish way of being. But when we find him babbling on television and Rick "conversing" with him magically through the boundaries of the medium, we are also facing a truly extraordinary mini-essay, on Dean & Jerry's part, about filmic continuity in conversational moments, about the way when we watch shot/reverse shot back-and-forths between speakers we never for a moment have the sense of a tissue or boundary breaking (although there is nothing in view *but* breakage, à la editing). In *Artists and Models,* the breaking-through is openly avowed and demonstrated by virtue of Rick standing outside the shop and away from the television, yet speaking directly in what he thinks is a grammatical way to someone who's *on* television. Tashlin's care in sound editing has made *us* find the grammar, too. During the period when this film came out, and for years afterward, in certain theaters (such as the Waverly in New York's Greenwich Village and the Culver in Culver City, we each recall) audiences routinely spoke to characters on the screen as though they were inhabiting the same space. And in 1956 people were listening to this:

> Two different worlds
> We live in two different worlds
> But we will show them
> As we walk together in the sun
> That our two different worlds are one.
> (Al Frisch and Sid Wayne)

[7]

Dean & Jerry made a habit of breaking frame, interacting with camera operators on the *Comedy Hour*—conversing with the method through which they were being shown conversing. A particularly frenzied example can be seen in the February 10, 1952, broadcast when Jerry turns the simple act of introducing one of Dean's songs into a furious game of hide-and-seek with the three camera operators and the director of the show. As Jerry begins his introduction, one of the cameras approaches to a fairly tight close-up. But Jerry reacts when the director switches to another camera—performers see an "on" light atop the camera that signals it's in use—which is now shooting him in right profile. "Excuse me, I was talking," he says with irritation, but quickly the camera switches again, now shooting his *left* profile. He turns and makes a face at the camera, only to find that the camera has been switched yet again, now to a frontal close-up. He pauses for a beat and continues his introduction, only to find that the camera has again been switched, now to the right profile again. Losing patience, he speaks directly to the cameraman: "Here, you're very rude," only to find that the camera has switched back to the left profile. "I was talking to *him*," he continues, then whirls to face the camera, crossing his eyes. "Here, I'll have to ask you not to be so impertinent." He turns back and the camera switches to a frontal close-up. He turns right, then turns back quickly, then starts turning back and forth. The camera switches back to the right profile. "Now here—well, well, if you want to fool around, try and follow me!" Jerry yells, ducking his head and bowing up and down as the cameras attempt to go along, with only a blur visible for a few seconds. Recovering "composure," the director switches to a medium shot that shows Jerry cavorting onstage while the two other cameras are both bobbing in unison, attempting to follow his wildly unpredictable movements. "I got everybody crazy!" Jerry yells triumphantly with the camera switching to the left profile before settling on a frontal close-up as he bares his teeth and raises his hands like claws. "You know the television director Kingman Moore sitting in the booth and all you people are seeing me do these crazy things," bending down and disappearing momentarily, "you think he's going crazy? This man gets up in the morning, 7 o'clock on Sunday, he looks out the window and he says, 'It's Martin & Lewis day,'" Jerry raises his eyebrows, "and he runs down to the theater and he gives all the cues, he says 2-camera, 3-camera, 1-camera, 4-camera, and then it's one minute to five, and he says, 'cue music' and we're on the air. And Dean and I walk through the curtains. The TV director looks at us, he takes a sigh, and says 'Ugh!'"

Conceptually and philosophically, the issues raised here are fascinating:

[a] That by virtue of opening his mouth and uttering words in a certain (clearly visible) direction, the performer is invoking the means whereby he is being shown to the world, thus both performing *on* TV and pointing *to* TV at once.

[b] That through switching points of view we not only gain a wider appreciation for the production space (the studio/theater where the *Comedy Hour* is being shot) but also find ourselves with the feeling we can achieve no possible orientation, as seemingly confirmed by moments in the broadcast of this brief interrupted monologue when only a blur is visible or when successive images of Jerry's face are fleetingly superimposed. Every angle shows (the same) "Jerry" and with equal fidelity, but as a different form and with a different background. Or:

[c] Is the viewer both being prepared for, and assumedly already activating, a fully Cubist point of view?

[d] That Jerry seems to be making friends with *the cameras themselves,* personified. But also,

[e] Even when we do not see the camera(s), every move Jerry makes causes us to imagine that we do—since he is playing to one of the three cameras employed in a live television broadcast, to some particular camera every time he changes orientation. As he plays, however, we now begin to see not Jerry playing but the camera he is playing to, see through presuming and imagining. Thus, the cameras take over the shot, even from outside it. This set-up reveals itself as a 3-camera set-up, and Jerry is merely the elusive subject the cameras are trying to train upon. *For us,* the spirit of personality seems to migrate from Jerry and jump to the (desperate) cameras, which are obliged to join his game whether they want to or not! Soon enough at least two of the three cameras become "Jerries," our frenetic subjects. Therefore,

[f] We have a clear demonstration of comedy reaching out of the performer's body and into the contiguous space, say, the throbs of humorous play infecting the devices as though they are flesh.

This is all more than frame-breaking; it is breaking the machines and the system that make the frame.

[8]

The on-camera "game" reached a crescendo in the December 30, 1951, *Comedy Hour* broadcast in which, looking glum, with head bowed, Jerry made a seemingly earnest entreaty to the television audience around the country—"fifty million listeners," as he says—to help him find his Uncle Louie, who has been missing some thirty years, and about whom his Aunt Jean in Brooklyn continues to worry.[5] Explaining what he's doing, Jerry says, quite gravely, "Now, this is no joke. And we miss him very much, especially the older folks in the family," and he implores anyone "if they ever saw my Uncle Louie they should call me on the phone and tell me, or maybe send a wire or write a letter." He unrolls a photograph of the man for the camera, hoping that someone somewhere will recognize his uncle.

No sooner does he do this than he receives a telephone call. The telephone is brought onstage, cord trailing behind it, and Jerry agrees to pay $20,000 in exchange for the location of his long-lost uncle. "Tell me where's my Uncle Louie? Where? . . . Where!?! . . . Where!?!"

"All right, thank you very much! I'm so happy I found him, I'll call my Aunt Jean and tell her!" beams Jerry. "Thank you very much, I found my Uncle Louie, thank you!!" He is running off the stage for the long-awaited reunion but stops short when he comes to the first of the KNBH-NBC cameras, behind which stands . . . Uncle Louie, looking exactly like the photograph we just saw! Jerry tackles him to the floor and showers him with kisses. Has he been behind the camera since the start of the *Comedy Hour* with Jerry never even noticing?[6] Has he been following Jerry around the world?

[9]

While to the undiscerning eye Dean & Jerry may have seemed like overactive flippers in a pinball machine, their work was constantly—and with sober aim—commenting upon, even critiquing conventionalized behaviors,

5 Something of an homage to 1930s screwball comedies, in which aunts, uncles, cousins, and grandparents are relentlessly if inconsequentially invoked loudly by central characters.

6 Uncle Louie is Harry Hines (1889–1967), who, six months earlier, to the day, was seen by audiences as the man who crawls under the carousel in Hitchcock's *Strangers on a Train* (1951). Hitchcock was filled with guilt shooting this scene, because Hines's life was in fact in danger. Later, Hines also appeared uncredited in *Friendly Persuasion* (1956), *Jailhouse Rock* (1957), *Party Girl* (1958), *Lonely Are the Brave* (1962), *All Fall Down* (1962), and *The Cincinnati Kid* (1965), among many other films.

expectations, routine activities, value systems, and hopes in the society around. They weren't just twitching—they were pointing. (Pointing to an audience that would never allow itself to be pointed at, but that could enjoy laughing at strangers twitching.)

Consider Lewis's screaming baby in the "I'll Watch TV" skit. We have a comment here on the postwar baby boom and the kind of problem people very generally thought it might produce: Dr. Spock's boom, as it later came to be thought—"Oh, are you a Spock baby?"—which was immense in North America. Babies here, babies there, babies everywhere, and all of them crying and whining and screaming and mewling, demanding and demanding, without end, so that Jerry's exaggeration of these vocal effects is merely an attempt to replicate the overall volume of this social phenomenon. The postulate to feed the baby on demand was a key feature of Spock's philosophy. Jerry and his wife Patti had a youngster of their own, Gary (born 1945), who was a charter member of this boom. The much-touted myth of joyful parenthood was complex. Young parents were widely expected to be entirely unaccustomed to and unprepared for this rearing of young children to which they were now dedicated, and therefore they were understandably taken aback by the problems of child care. They craved the solitude and silence of the golden years before conception, the newcomer's interrupting noises a constant cue of their discomfort.[7]

But parodists are always taking aim. The November 30, 1952, broadcast of the *Comedy Hour* took direct aim at the ubiquity of Spock and his recommendations for middle-class parenting. The skit was prefaced by a short introduction by an announcer in coat, tie, and eyeglasses standing in front of the curtain, who noted "two distinctively different schools of child psychology: the old and the new." The old school, he explained, embraced the principle of "spare the rod and spoil the child" and involved punishing and scolding disobedient children. "The new school, however, insists that a child should be allowed to follow his natural instincts. These people have read books on how to raise their children. They've learned never to spank their child for fear of frustrating him." After a brief cutaway shot showing "parents of the old school"—a medium two-shot of a man slapping his hand with a belt, eyes wide with fury, as a woman looks on sternly, arms akimbo—the announcer segues to "the parents of the new school": Dean with arms crossed,

7 Thirty years later, Dr. Richard Ferber advocated for parents to let them "cry it out." This method came to be known as "Ferberization."

unexpectedly paternal with eyeglasses and sweater, leaning on a couch next to a woman who has a book open to examine its pages intently. "They have allowed their child to follow his natural instincts. He has been brought up by the book," the announcer says, as a dissolve takes us into a set dressed to look like a family living room, for the skit proper.

> FATHER: What are we going to do about Rodney?
>
> MOTHER: Will you stop worrying, Paul?[8] Dr. Marvin says he's going to grow out of this stage.
>
> FATHER (visibly irritated): Will you stop with this book!
>
> MOTHER (continuing to refer to *the book*): Dr. Marvin says he has to have freedom of expression. (*She clutches the open book in one hand.*) It's right here in the book—just, just pretend like nothing happened. . . . It says right here on page forty-seven . . .

Their child, Rodney (Jerry), seems to have also read *the book* (or at least has come to understand its contents by osmosis). Indeed, he demonstrates to both of his parents exactly what "old school" parents were still actually doing to their children, smacking both "daddy dear" and "mummy darling" on the face before breaking a vase of flowers over her head and knocking her off the couch onto the floor. Still holding on to the open book, she stands up:

> MOTHER: Well, thank heavens he's so uninhibited! (*She exits.*)

Left alone with the child, "daddy darling" threatens violence, but Rodney responds, high-pitched and squeaky, by picking up the book:

> RODNEY (cautioning): Daddy, remember Dr. Marvin's book . . . (There are copies of "Dr. Marvin's book" stashed everywhere in this house.)

Dr. Spock's wisdom notwithstanding, a child's imaginative faculties enriched through radio, books, movies, and other cultural forms would not always necessarily prove educational. In *Pardners* (Norman Taurog, 1956) the "development"—both narrative and character—of the fully adult Wade Kingsley Jr. (Jerry) appears to have been set back by the murder of his father Wade Kingsley Sr. (Jerry again!) on the day he was born. We find Wade is fascinated by

8 Dean's middle name that Jerry called him familiarly.

a mechanical horse he is riding. This is a much more elaborate version of the small coin-operated rides that proliferated during the 1950s outside grocery markets, as a means of keeping young children entertained while a parent—read, mother—shopped for the food to feed them. Dressed to the nines in a blue cowboy suit, cowboy hat, red boots, and furry chaps, Wade bounces in the saddle (in VistaVision!). But his pointless and decidedly unconstructive fun—the mechanical horse does not transport him anywhere, it just goes up and down, unlike the many real horses we see in the film after Kingsley Jr. and Slim Mosely Jr. (Dean) return from 1910 New York to the West. Dr. Spock might be chagrined at Wade's definite inability to learn real horseback riding from this toy device. But why on earth would Wade ever need to know how to ride a real horse!

[10]

Smashing expectations and conventions is one thing. Smashing the unstated "rules" by which we regulate activity in the physical world is another, especially when those "rules" involve material goods and ownership, that is, capital production and financial control. All of Dean & Jerry's early visual work came under the aegis of sponsorship, and when they "went nuts" on camera they were operating in the context of what were presumably to be taken as objects produced for serious profit and most reverently cherished by those who acquired them—the products in the sponsor's commercials. These often became the object of Dean and Jerry's play.

The radiant object is central in the Martin & Lewis routine, the material thread that connects us in the viewing present to Martin & Lewis in the past, that energizes our contemporary scrutiny to the historical Martin & Lewis: a cherry-red 1956 Chrysler New Yorker, for instance, whether or not it was the very car used in making *Hollywood or Bust*; a shoe once worn by Lewis, whether or not it was the one that popped off during an especially physical routine (and just as quickly became a prop telephone) during the October 15, 1950, *Comedy Hour;* a microphone and microphone stand like the ones used by NBC during the early 1950s, whether or not it was one into which Martin himself sang any one of his many mellifluous melodies: consumable as all such things were originally they are definitely consumer products now, Dean-and-Jerry souvenirs.

Play involves toys and tends to fetishize objects. These objects are the slender threads that connect the world of play and of play-acting scenarios to the real world and real-world situations mediated within the playroom. (Without such an objective anchor, play would morph into mime.) Play and "reality" must not bleed into one another. Gregory Bateson: "Play is a phenomenon in which the actions of 'play' are related to, or denote, *other* actions of 'not play'" (181; emphasis added). Indeed, one cluster of signals that helps us see "play" differentiated from "actuality" is exactly the arbitrary, often warped, and always transformational use of objects: an object used as though it were something else (a shoe used as a telephone), an object used as itself but not at all in the way people would use it in everyday life (sneakers looking like sneakers but being worn on the wrong feet).

[11]

An interesting kerfuffle took place during the September 17, 1950, *Comedy Hour* broadcast that included a skit in which Martin was manager of a completely empty movie theater, drastically discounting admission prices at the box office and accosting passersby to try to stimulate business. This, all while insisting "movies are better than ever"—a phrase that both he and the usher dutifully intone (it is also printed on a sign under the marquee). Lewis played Melvin, a youngster dribbling a basketball on the sidewalk, who is far more interested in going home to watch television than in paying even a discounted admission price to watch a movie in a theater (he also balks at the obligatory box of popcorn that is pushed on him).[9] Interestingly, with this skit Dean & Jerry "aroused the anger of the Council of Motion Picture Organizations because they poked fun at exhibitors; [Hal] Wallis had no other choice but to issue an apology" (Dick 153) on behalf of the duo, presumably because it was his responsibility as producer of their motion pictures to have the boys better controlled.[10]

9 Between the late 1940s and the late 1950s there was an astronomical upsurge in American household television ownership, to such a degree that the movie industry felt threatened at the prospect of losing its audience to the small screen.

10 (1898–1986). Also producer of *The Stooge* (1951), *Sailor Beware* (1952), *Jumping Jacks* (1952), *Scared Stiff* (1953), *Money from Home*, *3 Ring Circus* (1953), *Artists and Models*, and *Hollywood or Bust*.

Impromptu snatched moments (like Melvin's diatribe) never vanished from the Martin & Lewis playing field. If they were not lambasting commercial products, or breaking the fourth wall by conversing with audiences and cameramen, they could pilfer a sponsor's stage to hype their own movies, and did so frequently, sometimes one of them standing patiently aside as the partner did the work, sometimes trying to speak in choral unison, sometimes just doing the old "interrupt" routine that audiences already anticipated with a thrill of joy. Watching any of these self-promotional plugs now, riffs of the highest order, it is easy to shudder with embarrassment at the thought that the prizes of one's gaze might be in such awkward straits as to require their movie hype to come out of their own mouths (remember, this was before backstage interviews where a star could casually drop reference to a current project; such interviews are omnipresent, even much abbreviated now—as on Instagram). Were Dean & Jerry's films so insignificant the studio didn't even bother to notice let alone promote them . . . ? But no, when Martin & Lewis had a new film, hype about it was everywhere. Doing their own plugs was a way for them to implore prospective audiences *personally* to see the film. The commercial became friendship.

[12]

It is too easy to neglect the fact that Dean & Jerry were children of the Thirties, a time when, as Alfred Kazin recollected, the "deliverance of mankind from material hardship [was] very far from the realities of . . . life," when successful Americans "spent their days thinking up slogans to make you buy toothpaste, soap and deodorants" (6, 8–9). In 1932, Dean was a fifteen-year-old adolescent (the term "teenager" wasn't invented until the mid-1950s) and Jerry, just like his "Kid" character (as he often claimed), was six (old enough to see what was going on).

The Thirties: one experienced the decade of the Great Depression and a roiling uncertainty between two world wars. America fronted by Herbert Hoover (Rep., who had seen the country plunge into the Depression) and then Franklin D. Roosevelt (Dem., who offered a "New Deal"). *Trouble in Paradise, It Happened One Night, Top Hat, My Man Godfrey,* and *The Awful Truth* were all notable films of the time. And in the banner year of 1939, *The Wizard of Oz* and *Gone with the Wind* and *Stagecoach* came out. Dean was then a callow and still insecure twenty-two, shiningly handsome to look at yet typically naive as to the power of looks, graceful movement, and a nifty singing voice. Jerry was a wired thirteen. Dean's formative teen years had spanned the decade, as had Jerry's even more formative childhood. One didn't need to be drafted into the Army to understand the catastrophe war produced on civilian life in the early years of the 1940s, just as one didn't need to have been a farmer to experience the effects of the Dust Bowl (1934 onward) or of the massive urbanization of American life on the food supply. One doesn't need to have millions invested on Wall Street in order to understand how (as shown so powerfully in *Splendor in the Grass* [1962]) an economy can collapse like a house of cards.

Today, it is virtually impossible to acquire a ticket for voyaging to that time. Restagings of history don't do the trick, not even the marvelous *Bonnie and Clyde* (1967). Critics, scholars, and artists who were alive and who endured the times could feel hunger in their bones, and could make gestures or statements of keen reflection, but their audiences would fail to grasp the taste and the truth, unless they came from the same generation; a very rare exception is the brilliant Morris Dickstein (1940–2021; childhood on the Lower East Side):

> The Depression seemed to have no visible end.... To many who believed that the United States was essentially a middle-class nation, a land of progress and opportunity in which everyone could *become* middle class, the Depression not only challenged America's economy and its political system, but also undermined the central myths and beliefs on which the system was founded. (217)

Some look from a contemporary point of view today at L. Frank Baum's *The Wonderful Wizard of Oz* (1900), for example, as a political comment about the Gold Standard coded as a festive children's play. But MGM's film, coming as it did at a moment when the Depression leached into the War—the news from Europe was darkening the horizon, just like that twister—had a far more tangible meaning for viewers of all ages. *Stagecoach* can easily be taken, too lightly, as warm-hearted, sentimental reflection of a bucolic pastoral agrarian time, now that isolationism was mounting, farms were being foreclosed, and bread lines continuing—the explicit setting of Ford's *The Grapes of Wrath* one year later—but it was a keen-edged portrait of the rich and easy in contest with those who had to fight for existence. When in the twenty-first century, more than fifteen years after his death, we read Leslie

Fiedler's description of the spirit of the 1930s, it can seem, though written elegantly, as incomprehensible to our experience as the pharaohs' hieroglyphs:

> Here in the poet's sense of the word, is the true "myth" of the '30s: the sense of sterility, the despair, the outrage before the senseless waste of the human turned crazy laughter and at last art; but for most people this is too strong, too "morbid," too real a vision to be endured. And so we do not have finally any shared myth of the age. ("Search" 169)

The despair. The outrage. Crazy laughter. Fiedler was born the same year as Dean Martin, and in the same city as Jerry Lewis. He was both of them, but neither of them (like all of us, but far more articulately).

SONG OF THE SOUTH

[1]

"Don't hit me!" we hear from Jerry, like a refrain.

Or: "Don't hit me again!"

Or: "No Dean, I didn't mean—!"

Not that Dean does repeatedly hit Jerry; but that Jerry repeatedly cries out a fear of being hit—the fear of punishment from above. Dean & Jerry wrestle with a power imbalance. We sense it, we see it, we feel it.

These fleeting panic moments, rarely sustained beyond a few words or a posture, are a kind of "tell" that reveal an underlying dynamic that has many of the hallmarks of an abusive fraternal relationship. Dean is often quick to raise his fist, threatening to strike Jerry if he makes a mistake. Jerry responds by shrinking, although sometimes it seems as if he thinks he *should* be hit (hence the sometime hints of abuse); on other occasions, he answers the threat with excessive, but ultimately empty, bravado. Apart from physical threats like these, Dean is prone to watching his partner in exasperation, or in extremely charitable consideration, as Jerry's antics and/or struggles bedevil the limits of human patience, as though the poor flunky will flounder unless Dean protects him. However, Jerry was a lanky fellow, as tall as, or indeed taller than, Dean, the man to whom he addresses his childish pleas for mercy in such exaggerated fashion, contorting himself to shield his body from the anticipated blows he expects will soon rain down on him, squeamishly imploring Dean not to hurt him in earshot of anyone nearby (in the show or, more crucially, in the audience). It may have been difficult for viewers to fully accept and sustain a sense that the rough undercurrent persistently challenged the boundaries of acceptable behavior at the time (even in a society far more comfortable with corporal punishment), not to say the boundaries of comedy. Yet the audience howled with laughter.

Howling with laughter could indicate a great deal, including approval. Within the parameters of their partnership, Dean could seemingly do what he wanted with Jerry, even if that meant brushing him aside, stepping on him, or castigating him. On April 3, 1949, Lucille Ball voiced an exaggerated "complaint" about this dynamic as a guest on their radio show:

> You've got some nerve, Dean Martin, asking me to come down here and be a guest on your radio program after the way you beat up that sweet, adorable little Jerry Lewis! Why, if I weren't a perfect lady, I'd slug ya. The idea! Beating up that darling, cute lambie-pie. . . . He's behind you, where he'll be safe. He's not going to stay out here where you can knock him down again . . . and kicking him, and throwing dirt in his face, and trying to drive your car over him.

Indeed, Dean often treats Jerry like an object that can be abused with impunity, even, in two different *Colgate Comedy Hour* sketches, packing him into, respectively, a suitcase and a golf bag.[1]

What they had was certainly a strange and in some ways inexplicable partnership, not quite master/slave, not quite king/subject, not quite bully/weakling, yet clearly and continually a "wedding" between assertion and confidence on one side and trepidation, anxiety, and trying too hard on the

1 February 4, 1951, and April 27, 1952, respectively.

other. Yet the strong man/weak man connection is in itself broadly based in the culture. With Dean & Jerry, two riddles are provocative. First, what was unique and ineffable about them—ineffably unique and uniquely ineffable? Second, why in order to enact their vertical dynamic did they so repeatedly voyage to the South? To be sure, Dean & Jerry constitute in themselves no rebirth of, or outright allusion to, the American slave system of the mid-nineteenth century and onward; we would never make the argument that they do. But again and again we do see a clear playing out of a certain stereotype of dominant/submissive relations that most certainly also characterized the continuing American popular imagination of slavery. It is not that Dean owned Jerry; but he surely often gives the impression that he thinks he does: directing Jerry's movement, paying no attention to what Jer' says, in the end always showing up to redeem Jer's weaknesses. Dean, after all, did come to assess a decade-long partnership with the words, "To me, you're nothing but a fucking dollar sign" (qtd. in Lewis, *Dean* 277).

Picturing Jerry under Dean's thumb makes it hard to avoid thinking about Stepin Fetchit in *Steamboat Round the Bend* (1935), Butterfly McQueen in *Gone with the Wind* (1939), or, exactly contemporaneous with Dean & Jerry's performances, Amos 'n' Andy. For several years when the *Comedy Hour* was broadcast on NBC, *Amos 'n' Andy* (1951–1953) was broadcast on the competitor CBS, with African American actors Alvin Childress and Spencer Williams taking the roles that white radio performers Freeman Gosden and Charles Correll had popularized on the long-running radio show of the same name (1928–1955).[2] At the peak of the radio show's popularity, movie theaters paused film screenings in order to broadcast the latest episodes to theater audiences unwilling to miss them. The television version was filmed with a multi-camera setup at the Hal Roach studios (a technique borrowed from Lucille Ball and Desi Arnaz's *I Love Lucy* shot at Desilu from 1951 to 1957),[3] but it left the air just a few years later in response to protests from the NAACP and others.

The older/younger, stronger/weaker, smarter/goofier dynamic is always central with Martin & Lewis. In *You're Never Too Young*, Dean plays an older, quasi-paternal protector figure, but the gag is that Jerry is only pretending to

2 The radio program spawned the film *Check and Double Check* (Melville W. Brown, 1930), which starred Gosden and Correll in blackface.

3 Principally by Karl Freund, who had photographed, among other features, *Metropolis* (1927) for Fritz Lang.

be a youngster. In *Living It Up*, Dean is a protective (but fake) doctor figure watching over the vulnerable (and "sick") Jerry. In *The Caddy* (1953) Jerry is the subservient "helper" trying to make Dean a tournament winner. The two were cast as ostensible father and son in several *Comedy Hour* skits, and it was not strange in their movies that father-son dynamics came into play, albeit not between them. The duo's behavior sometimes devolved into a clear simulation of physical violence, enacted as more or less justified paternal "discipline" dispensed upon a recalcitrant child—in "spare the rod and spoil the child" fashion. From Jerry, in fact, there is a constant expressive demurral, a shrinking back, a casting of the self as a creature about to be physically assaulted: a crying out that is half enunciation, half whine. The painfully ingratiating smile, the painfully strained, tweeting voice, even while making declarations. Even more significantly, situations in which that voice is *unable* to make declarations, tries hard but doesn't have the equipment to achieve success, as in the numerous "takes" on delivering the phone message we find in the bathtub sequence of *Artists and Models* (discussed below in "Up the Ante"). The Jerry mouth gapes open to speak, showing readiness and intent (that is, situational appropriateness), but at the same time he can stammer only a half syllable here and there, because although he makes utterances he is again and again bereft of the knowledge to support them.[4]

Yet why does this odd dynamic position itself in the South?

[2]

Since they knew that he was never a Southerner in truth—Dean hailed from Steubenville, Ohio—how did audiences understand his slide into a Southern drawl when he spoke, or that in his repertoire he fell back so cozily on "Southern" songs? Since he was one of the first members of his family to speak English rather than Italian, was drawled English the only English Dean heard outside the home, somehow? Or, was he later on affecting a speaking style to match his laconic persona? And what was Jerry, a New Jersey native, doing when he covered "Southern" songs?

The beginning of NBC Radio Network's July 26, 1949, *Martin and Lewis Show* begins with Dean singing a medley of minstrel songs that includes a few

4 On Jerry's "linguistic incompetence," see Pomerance, "The Errant Boy," in *Enfant Terrible!* 255 ff.

bars of Stephen Foster's "Old Folks at Home," better known by its lyrics as "Way down upon the S'wanee River." The May 20, 1951, *Comedy Hour* broadcast closes with Dean and Jerry "dancing a Charleston to [Shelton Brooks's] 'Darktown Strutters Ball'" (Hayde 99). Dean's 1955 Capitol Records release *Swingin' Down Yonder* includes numerous songs that were expressly Southern in their lyrics, including "Sleepy Time Down South" (Clarence Muse, Leon René, and Otis René, 1931), "Mississippi Mud" (Harry Barris, 1927), "Dinah" (Harry Akst, Sam M. Lewis, and Joe Young, 1925), and "Georgia on My Mind" (Hoagy Carmichael and Stuart Gorrell, 1930).

After the pair split, Jerry recorded a number of his own solo records, including among them minstrel favorites like "Mammy" ("My Mammy," Walter Donaldson, Joe Young, and Sam M. Lewis, c. 1921) and "Rock-a-Bye Your Baby with a Dixie Melody" (Jean Schwartz, Sam M. Lewis, and Joe Young, 1918).[5] In *Scared Stiff*, Dean breaks into a minstrel song, "Carry Me Back to Ole Virginny" (James A. Bland, 1878), during one of his character's stage performances within the film.

Why these frequent melodic voyages south of the Mason-Dixon line?

And in their twin excursions, why is Dean's "South" so much more naturalized, so much more believable, than Jerry's? Jerry picks the songs but sings them like a newspaper boy from New Jersey; Dean, the Steubenville grifter, becomes the crooner Elvis Presley so admired.

[3]

The Mason-Dixon Line can be crossed—Northerners can visit the South—and it can be straddled.

Charles Mason and Jeremiah Dixon, c. 1765, surveyed, etched, and defined it. Henceforward America could have the North and the South and all that could come thereafter. If during the Civil War one crossed that line to one's peril, in times of peace it was a zone of flotation, and moving up and down the country was easy as pie. At times, Dean affected everything but the stick of hay coming out of the side of the mouth: lazy phrasin', a tricklin' river drawl, the words thick with molasses (just dig into that Plantation Unsulphured

5 The latter song inspired the title of *Rock-a-Bye Baby* (Frank Tashlin, 1958), though the film was a remake of *The Miracle of Morgan's Creek* (Preston Sturges, 1944).

Blackstrap Molasses, $55 a cup) and as few in number as would do the trick. If you kept it short, you'd have plenty of time and space for havin' yer druthers. Nothin' on earth more important than havin' yer druthers. Check out Li'l Abner (Peter Palmer)[6] in the Broadway musical of November 15, 1956:

> If I [ahhh] had my druthers
> I'd [ahhh'd] rather have my druthers
> Than anythin' else I know . . .
> (Gene DePaul and Johnny Mercer)

Jerry certainly did check that show out, doing a cameo as Itchy McCrabby in the 1959 film version (as a favor to Norman Panama) (Levy 243). Itchy was a long way from Abner, Dean's avatar: Jes' plunk yerself on a branch leanin' over the stream, with yer line and hook dropped in, yer eyes half closed, sun meltin' down, leaves flickerin' a kaleidoscope o' green over yer face. Nothin' that has t'be done. Nothin' pressin.'

> I'm just breezin' along with the breeze,
> Trailin' the rails, roamin' the seas,
> Like the birdies that sing in the trees,
> Pleasin' to live, livin' to please.
> (Haven Gillespie, Seymour Simons, Richard Whiting [1926])

Like Abner, Dean never allows himself to be pressed. It is not hard to understand his unremitting irritation (usually blanketed by sweetness) at the "hyperactive neurotic" he is chained to.

If we watch Dean in performance we note that he says little, takes little time talking, so that he has time at his disposal, time to dispose of. The words ooze out like sap, and mean, in almost every case, "Let things be as they are." But letting things be is a conservative way of playing, and Dean's lyrics, his sung sentiment, is almost always conservative, almost always focused on working hard to keep things going and heterosexual coupling, the standard pith of American pop songs. Dean's bright-toothed smile is readable as a heteronormative trademark and in itself part of his language. He smiles in lieu of speaking. His smile is speech, alluring speech.

Viewers are not inspired to regard this drawler as a calculator, an interpreter, or even as basically intelligent. His good looks will carry the day, if

6 Also to be seen lounging in Tim Burton's *Edward Scissorhands* (1990).

his glorious voice doesn't. All this comforting belief that breezin' along with the breeze really is ordained as mankind's noblest aspiration is based in a perduring anti-intellectualism, the conviction that there must be something wrong with somebody whose brain works too fast and too slickly. Jerry is North by Northeast just as Dean is South and West. Money, the crowd; the crowd, hustle; hustle, make a buck; make a buck, hurry up; hurry up, do a lot; do a lot, say a lot; say a lot all at once; all at once, all at once, all at once. (Try saying all that out loud very quickly without taking a breath.) Jerry is caught on Madison Avenue, caught in the Village, caught on the Upper East Side, caught behind a billboard, caught in a hotel room, caught, caught, caught, a cat wanting out. The body won't be navigated, not assuredly, but the mouth will transport it. What comes out of Jerry's mouth is babble, at racing speed.[7] And his vocal cords are in constant use to shape and constrain the tones so that they rise and fall in pitch, both expressing a huge range of frustration and need and imitating a plethora of instruments. Jerry was not so much the vocalist as the band. The *whole* band. And the dancers. And, as he made himself watchable, the audience watching him.

[4]

The regular *Comedy Hour* appearances of The Four Step Brothers, "a quartet of dancers who combine swing with jive and a touch of gymnastics" (Hayde 154), contain what may well be Dean & Jerry's most spirited interactions with dancers—which is to say, rhythmic movers. Consider the athletic dance performances in which Dean & Jerry got involved with the Brothers on the April 27, 1952, May 31, 1953, and February 13, 1955, broadcasts.[8] The members

7 "Babble," as in the *Tower of Babel:* a corrective to informational communication.

8 The Four Step Brothers were not actually brothers; they began in 1925 as a trio, but became a quartet and danced in Harlem's Cotton Club, in theaters on the Keith-Albee-Orpheum circuit, at Radio City Music Hall, and in a number of Hollywood films. In 1950, they were the first African Americans to appear on US television, performing on Milton Berle's *Texaco Star Theater* despite the objections of sponsors (Berle threatened to walk if they didn't go on), and thereafter on *The Ed Sullivan Show* (Martin & Lewis's direct competition notwithstanding that

of the quartet were unrelated—brothers in name only[9]—and group members rotated over the years. By the time they appeared on the *Comedy Hour*, The Four Step Brothers were Maceo Anderson, Rufus L. McDonald, Prince C. Spencer, and Alfred T. Williams. Their dance routines involved synchronized steps performed as a group and individual steps performed by one member at a time while the other three watched, clapped, and stomped. This was what they did near the end of several *Comedy Hour* broadcasts. After one dancer had completed his bit, the next dancer "upped the ante" by performing something more difficult and/or acrobatic, typically ending with one dancer doing multiple somersaults. The dance routines were not only highly athletic, but also more than a little bit sexualized, with undisguised pelvic thrusts (a tick not collected by Elvis Presley until at least 1954). One gets the sense of "ants in the pants."

But on the *Comedy Hour*, there's a switch: after each of the four dancers has had his turn, first Dean and then Jerry get a turn also. One surmises that Dean's and Jerry's participations were at some level rehearsed (despite the feel of spontaneity one gets from the end of these broadcasts, when time is either running low—or more frequently—needs to be filled in order to get to the end of the hour without dead airtime). But their joining into the performance always comes as a not-entirely-welcome intrusion on a carefully choreographed and scrupulously polished dance routine, an intended upstaging of the Four Step Brothers. And, given Dean and Jerry's comparative lack of skill as dancers, their anticlimactic dancing is always a dose of comic relief. The hosts of the show get to finish the routine—honorary "Step Brothers" as it were—even though their steps are clearly not up to "brotherly" snuff.

What, however, is *in* these awkward moments? Dean and Jerry both trying hard to be "two of the guys," to be "on the team," but apparently without any real hope. Dean and Jerry both showcasing the ultimate good faith by clapping along enthusiastically as the Brothers dance—"We're big fans, too!" Dean and Jerry both being "good sports," since obviously the "name of the game" is "everybody has to do something" and they don't want to be insulting by saying no. It may be that these athletic metaphors are far from random, that in the dance Dean & Jerry were watching with such stupefaction one

---

they had guested on Sullivan's first television broadcast). At this time, The Four Step Brothers appeared in *Here Come the Girls* (1953).

9 Unlike the Nicholas Brothers, Fayard (1914–2006) and Harold (1921–2000), of *Stormy Weather* (1943) and a number of other films.

could see the most supreme athletic ability; Jerry could hold his own on any dance floor (see the jitterbug scene, with Sheree North, in *Living It Up*), and he worked his physical comedy with astonishing athletic skill. If a longstanding American racial dynamic was bluntly in play here, no explicit signals were given, as they are often not given today.

Just as Dean & Jerry absorbed a little mojo from The Four Step Brothers, the effect was strangely reciprocal. Just a few months after the last of their three *Comedy Hour* broadcasts with Dean & Jerry, when The Brothers appeared at the Ebony Room in Chicago a reviewer noted, "Prince Spencer looking just like his man Jerry Lewis" ("Zig Zag with Ziggy Johnson," *Chicago Defender*, May 21, 1955, 18).

As happened with much American popular entertainment culture in the 1940s and 1950s, albeit with a special zest and weirdness, Martin & Lewis partook of an underpinning received mythology of the Old South. "Nostalgia was the norm," Edward Campbell informs us, and

> by 1900, the image of the South put forth in stories, novels, and theatricals had done much to heal the war's wounds and rekindle an interest in the region's ways. In fact, the literature and plays drawing upon the newfound spirit of reconciliation were to continue, thus reinforcing the myth. Within this climate of accord, it seemed only natural that the theme would emerge in the new and increasingly wide-ranging form of popular entertainment, the film. . . . To provide the most appealing image, the film companies drew heavily upon the literature of Southern local color and the minstrel shows so recently prevalent. Though unknown to many of the customers, the body of writing provided just that touch of romance, splendor, and diversion they craved. (10–12)

When Martin & Lewis gestures and set-ups were "southernized," when they showed off their comparatively limited talents against the dancing genius of The Four Step Brothers, the myth came alive.

MOUTH TO MOUTH

[1]

No serious study or even serious admiration of Martin & Lewis can proceed far without coming to the mouth. The mouth, portal for the soul's voyage. The mouth, weapon of the hunt. The mouth that sings, the mouth that devours, the mouth that whimpers, the mouth that declares.

In silent cinema and in mime, the performer's mouth is useful for a repertory of expressive gestures (surprise, anger, pensivity, irritation) but as an instrument of sound it is, by definition, "on hold" (except in the "auditorium" of the viewer's imagination).[1] Dean and Jerry, whose work was entirely in the sound era, use their mouths expressively, even extravagantly, just as though they are in silent performance, while at the same time making sounds that would be a challenge to orchestrate.[2] The *sound of Dean & Jerry* can be put on the page only approximately, and with some degree of difficulty. Coobling, droobling, spoobling, cajoobling, noodling, spoonling, and broodling . . . or whinnying, mumbling, chiding, chortling, snorfling, gagging, wheedling, sneedling, pumphing, strumphing, gasping, schlasping, distorting, screeching. . . . The mouth as the center of an insatiably hungry monster, for whom we might become the next meal. But this monster eats by making sound.

Jerry Lewis has (understatement!) an animated mouth—ready to talk his way forward even when he can't see where he's going; even when he's not talking. The point in appreciating Jerry's mouthing is to stop trying to find cogent meaning on the surface of it.

Just as there are plenty of singers who do not emit melody the way Dean does, there are plenty of comedy performers who do not *mouth* the way Jerry does. Tight-lipped Charlie Chaplin, taciturn Buster Keaton the "great stone face," mouthless Harold Lloyd, shy Stan Laurel, zany Lucille Ball, big-mawed Jim Carrey, glib Jerry Seinfeld, and ultra-snarky Joan Rivers: none of them do it.

With Jerry, the mouth is alive.

[2]

Beyond the fact that in many performative moments we find Dean & Jerry with open mouths both, many of Jerry's screen and publicity images show him in particular as a man with a prominent mouth. Not: a man in whose face a mouth is prominently to be found, a gorilla-man, but: a man whose being can readily be associated with mouthiness. Existentialism of the mouth. Mouthiness, as in talk, blather, soundings, comprehension and incomprehension, musicality, teeth, the dark vacuum, proportion, the tunnel, the mine. Even in some of his very last work, the July 6, 2018, extended interview with

1 In sound cinema, it is in that "auditorium" that the connection is made between the mouth we see and the voice we hear. See Chion.

2 In his 1960 film *The Bellboy,* Lewis in fact is mute.

Jerry Seinfeld for *Comedians in Cars Getting Coffee*, we see moment after moment of the aggressively open-mawed and soundless, but also totally yielding, mouth, the mouth that has so much to say it cannot speak. Not simply the mouth that is speechless but the mouth that screams its inability to speak. A soft mouth. A flexible, even shapeless mouth, forming every conceivable sound and sculpting every conceivable syllable . . . at once.

The Jerry Mouth suggests, most superficially, ravenous need, impoliteness, immaturity, aggression, and rudeness. What it can be understood more profoundly to mean is empty openness, forward vulnerability, truth. And then we have the way it played against the glorious, sculpted face and ineffably crooning mouth of Dean Martin—Dean who crooned even his displeasures. It was only rarely that Martin opened his mouth wide, a technical move—call it a "vocalizing open mouth"—that was part of a vocal routine already in progress and already displaying him, concertedly and intentionally, as "swank" and "reserved" and extremely "capable," except that, given Jerry's painfully awkward participation, "poor Dean" could do nothing to be completely smooth. Dean's mouth opens wide on call: that is, Dean can open his mouth wide, when need be—all the great singers can. Jerry's mouth opens even when there is no call for an open mouth. There is something animal about it, animal in the sense that it has a throbbing vivacity of its own, an urge for fulfillment and release. Not the mouth *of* an animal but the mouth *as an animal.*

[3]

Dean's mouth is nothing if not socialized. When he was not singing or scolding Jerry—which he did repeatedly on radio, stage, and screen: the Great Caviler (and Cavalier)—Dean often appeared to be keeping his mouth shut, cognizant of the fact that if words can get one into trouble, silence rarely has such consequences. Perhaps he thought that from words trouble would come to him more than to anybody else. A perfect vehicle for this closed-mouth ethos was the western, and of all his screened moments Dean was perhaps most laconic in Howard Hawks's *Rio Bravo*, where he is contrasted with the only slightly more loquacious Chance (John Wayne); but even in his late-career celebrity roasts, by which point his experience had given him plenty to say, he typically left the talking (and the biting critical commentary) to others, and one had the feeling his own biting critical commentary was being held in.

To watch Dean smile is to consider a man biding his time, until there arises something worth using words on: for accomplishing or obtaining, for making an opening or closing one off. At that point—then and only then—words issue forth, whether spoken or sung. (Very often sung.) Sometimes in the fact of Jerry's antics Dean cannot help himself and starts to snicker—evidence for us of the unrehearsed nature of their performance, or else evidence that even the "unrehearsed nature" is being performed—but most often he just looks on, sometimes smiling, sometimes holding his breath, the perfect stand-in for the audience, the ultimate spectator who has the best spot in the house (and not by accident).

[4]

What's inside of a mouth, whether open or closed?

Not only a tongue, which allows for the shaping of all manner of sounds, spoken, sung, mumbled, garbled, and otherwise externalized, but also *teeth*, which macerate words and food. The teeth can also be weaponized as Jerry is sometimes inclined to do, often biting himself without appearing to notice. The mouth was not only central to Lewis's and Martin's personae—the former by jiving; the latter with poise and artifice—but central as well to the economic structure that helped mold the Martin & Lewis career.

Interestingly, in the popular imagination the toothed mouth was virtually inseparable from cleanliness. At the moment when Martin & Lewis were emerging as Hollywood stars, they were frequently aired on television programs sponsored by the Colgate-Palmolive-Peet Company. The duo worked to promote the company's line of cleaning and personal hygiene products including, perhaps most importantly, Colgate toothpaste. The opening of the December 19, 1954, episode of the *Colgate Comedy Hour* showed both stars backstage in a shared dressing room putting a series of Colgate products to use, immediately after the credits. In quick succession, Dean and Jerry take turns at the sink demonstrating items as an offscreen announcer (George Putnam) calls them out by name: first, Dean brushes his teeth with Colgate, then Jerry washes his hands with Palmolive soap, then Dean washes a cloth with Fab laundry detergent, and then Jerry cleans the sink itself with Ajax, "the foaming cleanser, ba-ba-ba-ba boom-boom boom!, floats the dirt ... right down the drain!" Dean had a "natural" toothpaste smile, a bodily gesture and propriety ideal for commercializing a cleansing product. Jerry was always as if being chased by a racing toothbrush (as we see in one of the animated Colgate commercials that punctuated the show) that couldn't run fast enough to get into his mouth.

But beyond hygiene products, there was much else that could go into the mouth. On the November 4, 1951, *Comedy Hour,* during an especially frenetic game of hide-and-seek that he was playing with the camera operators while ostensibly introducing one of Dean's songs, Jerry blurted out, in syncopation, "Brush your teeth with Ajax!" This entirely nonsensical sing-songy jingle was at once utterly unexpected and totally improbable, a perfect transposition between two potentially interchangeable consumer cleaning products and between two potentially readable versions of Jerry. Was he being a completely improvisational soul or a zany performer carefully scripted? In the following broadcast, however, he used his mouth to publicly offer both Colgate and his audience a sincere apology. Or was it sincere? The mouth is not always sincere.

For its much-celebrated toothpaste, Colgate had patented and continually touted The Colgate Protective Shield, an "invisible and impenetrable barrier," like something extruded by a flying saucer, that would coat the teeth after they had been scoured with the company's product. No bacteria would ever get through this shield, said Colgate. And the Shield would make not only every tooth-brusher in America but, especially, the company's two super-spokesmen *bacteria free*. For all their on-camera nonsense, all their brazen loudness, all their cacophony, all their delirium, all their obnoxious interruptions—there would be no dirty or "harmful" residue from Martin & Lewis.

Jerry's smile is as toothy as Dean's, and he often exaggerates an expression by protruding his (on film often prosthetic) teeth beyond the border of his lips. This was a gag Jerry had used since teaming up with Dean, and perhaps before. One 1946 reviewer thought, "The most hilarious sequence of all is ... [when] Lewis props himself with a set of huge, protruding teeth" (qtd. in Hayde 5). Jerry would likely have had a large variety of oral prosthetic devices eventually. He later recycled the tooth gag many times, including as Julius Kelp in *The Nutty Professor* and as a disguised Gerald Clamson in *The Big Mouth*, not to mention some post–World War II pseudo-Asian takeoffs including those seen in *My Friend Irma*, *Living It Up*, the prologue to *Hollywood or Bust*, and *Rock-a-Bye Baby* (1958).[3]

3 A notably more thoughtful and respectful portrait of Asian character is presented through Miyoshi Umeki and the great Sessue Hayakawa in *The Geisha Boy* (1958).

He also made a habit of leaning his face uncomfortably close to others, to Dean unendingly but also to non-intimate others, in this way brazenly penetrating what Edward T. Hall called "intimate social distance" (see 175ff.). In live, three-camera television, forward-leaning moments of this kind are exaggerated by the use of close-ups, suggesting an unexpected (as well as, often, "improper") intimacy that would have brought to mind precisely those senses that neither film nor television can convey, namely touch, smell, and taste, all of them involving organs the Colgate-Palmolive-Peet line of products was laboring to reference and clean and odorize, to activate and render pleasing to consumers. Did kissing inspire Colgate-Palmolive? Or did Colgate-Palmolive produce a demand for kissing? Makeup artists had to make especially sure that Dean and Jerry's teeth were bright white on camera, especially for their frequent close-up shots, smiling, singing, or mugging.[4] The Shield was a mythic invention, to stir the brusher's energies, but not a bona fide additive. As additive, they had (the chemically inert filler) "Gardol." *"No other leading toothpaste contains Gardol to give you long-lasting protection against both bad breath and tooth decay . . . with just one brushing!"* the advertisements eagerly promised.

Paul Goodman spoke at the University of Toronto in 1965 about advertising hype such as Colgate's, pointing to companies touting rival toothpastes that all, said he, had differently named chemically inert ingredients added to their formulae. These would do nothing but give the company's advertising agents the license to claim wondrous uniqueness. Crest (a competitor) had "GL-70"! The consumer, wrote Goodman, "must be persuaded to buy" by advertising that "draws less and less on the direct relation between the excellence of the produce and the cost of its making—the word 'cheap' is never used—but more and more on the comparative estimates of social opinion, emulation, fear of inferiority or not belonging" (182). Did both Dean and Jerry actually have the "cleaner, fresher breath" that Colgate and other marketers emphasized and promised for everyone? When we see their mouths in such close proximity to one another—Jerry leaning in so he'd go cross-eyed watching Dean from one inch away—when we see them implicitly modeling for countless toothpaste advertisements while they are speaking to, or yelling

4 A demanding task in a way, since in early black-and-white television (programmed color television did not invade the USA until 1953), white would produce an irritating glare and often performers had to wear blue in order to seem to be wearing white.

at one another, we may be apt to wonder whether either of them wearied of inhaling the other's breath.

[5]

A mouth to be washed out with soap?[5] Jerry was insistent that he and Dean kept their comedy clean. Needless to say, the problem of interpreting the word "clean" comes up, but we can take him to be meaning, *No smut, no filth, no salaciousness, no dirty sexual implications*, and of course he is exactly right. Lewis was *horrified* to discover during the 1970s that, despite a family-friendly commitment to programming only "G" and "PG"-rated films, at least one theater in Staten Island, New York, associated with the "Jerry Lewis" theater chain, was screening pornographic films to try to counter flagging box-office numbers.[6]

The mere *thought* of sexually explicit material screening in a theater bearing his name was completely intolerable to Lewis, a taste he refused to have in his mouth. After the institution of the MPAA ratings system (c. 1966), X-rated films damaged the eponymous Jerry Lewis brand of good clean family fun. Mouth wide open, but no *Deep Throat* (Jerry Gerard [pseud.], 1972). Jerry Lewis's were paroxysms of laughter, not of sexual ecstasy, administered safely at a mediated distance. Screaming, bleating, honking, wonking, irritating, and besmirching verbally, but as clean as newly dried laundry. And Dean, for all the rubbing and culminating he might well have conjured *hypothetically* for his onscreen female "companions" (always inevitably and unalterably female), was never less than prophylactic in the story.

5 The idea of treating a person who had used the mouth for profanity, foulness, or incorrect behavior by "washing the mouth out with soap" had been current since at least the early 1830s.

6 Summary of unpublished primary-source research findings based on the *Staten Island Advance* newspaper conducted by students enrolled in CIN 220 at the College of Staten Island during the fall 2005 semester. The Jerry Lewis Theaters was a chain of venues created by Lewis in 1969. These were to be franchised out, offering potential buyers small auditoria (two or three in a venue, prefiguring Cineplex) projection that could be operated automatically (to lower overhead). The Lewis logo, name, and cachet were expected to boost sales. On the Jerry Lewis Theaters, see Melnick and Fuchs 153–58.

[6]

Dean's mouth was very rarely featured onscreen *as such.* He did not have a repertoire of oral gestures, and at a key moment in *Artists and Models,* indeed, his screaming mouth is given emphasis by crossed eyes. There were no macro-close-ups when he was in the middle of a song. Indeed, he tended to be shown in medium-long, so the carefree swing of his arms and tilt of his head could design a composition. Dean is therefore not really working through *orality* in the performances, aside from the fact that when he sings obviously the song comes out of his mouth. The song supplants the mouth, as it were. The song has its own character. The song is his mouth.

Kissing is something else: While kissing, the mouth disappears underneath the standard pose. And Dean could be caught *being kissed by* Jerry, without warning, and the mouth would retreat.

[7]

James Williamson (1855–1933) made *The Big Swallow* in 1901 in England. A man wearing a three-piece suit and hat is seen in full shot carrying a cane. Gesticulating, he hoists the cane over his shoulder for emphasis. He approaches the camera and as he moves closer and closer to the lens, his face fills the screen. Soon we have only his mouth. And then . . . the mouth opens and comes forward still more! Great swelling cavern of black! The mouth appears to devour the camera entirely. The screen turns black. We are with Jonah inside the Whale. Then in a shot taken from behind him, the photographer with his camera on its tripod tumbles forward into a dark void; into that mouth his whole body falls, legs last. The film's final shot shows the man seen in the first shot chewing as he backs away from the camera, then smiles and bares his teeth laughing as the film ends. (Was the cameraman especially tasty or especially tough?) It is terrifying to watch this mouth chew.

Not infrequently, in his television appearances, Jerry steps forward aggressively and makes to eat the camera (and perhaps also the cameraman). In Jerry's lifetime, no one was likely seeing *The Big Swallow,* so the gestural explosion on camera appears distinctive.

Mouthing is important in *At War with the Army* (1950, the first Martin & Lewis movie filmed but held back from release for a year or so). Early in the film, Alvin Korwin is on food duty, ladling out chow to the men of the platoon while belting out, "The navy gets the gravy while the army gets the beans!" Is it the young man's enthusiasm for his sentiment, or the fact that he has a big mouth?—but every other word comes out at a point when Lewis's jaw is wide open, as though, cook's assistant, he's personally going to eat everything there is to eat instead of feeding it to the others. In Frank Tashlin's *Who's Minding the Store?*, Lewis's Norman Phiffier is a gun salesman (at a *faux* Abercrombie & Fitch) encountering a big game hunter. Anxiously (Lewis's characters are neverendingly anxious, and that is the source of the mouthiness, since they would wish to explain and rationalize the anxiety but are too anxious even for that) he refers to "a boa constrictor with the open mouth that ate the cameraman and the camera and part of a rug." Again, and from *The Big Swallow,* the trope of swallowing. The chewing as a prelude to swallowing. The chewing as dismemberment and dislocation. A disturbing curiosity: how relieved we are to see this big mouth swallow, to know that the process has been completed, the act finished, the violence brought to a proper close. Immaterial it is now that the photographer has been dismembered and disassembled, has morphed entirely into protein sliding into the darkest recesses of the abysm.

[8]

A swallow implies *incorporation,* and a big swallow, a big mouth, a big hole in the middle of the face, implies *devouring.* Polyphemus the Cyclops glaring at Odysseus his possible meal. The Giant above the Beanstalk glaring at Jack. Goya's Cronus devouring his son (see *Saturn Devouring His Son* [1819–1823]). But in this devouring is also cinematography's incorporation, the incorporation of viewing, the incorporation of the viewer, the whole audience aggregated into a morsel: all of us imperiled, who thought we were living in exclusive safety on this side of the lens. But the feeling as we watch is less of actual danger than a disconcerting sense that our spatial coordinates might come unmoored, that we might well topple into and/or become absorbed into something larger and more abstract than ourselves, as happens to the cameraman who is swallowed by the void (and along with him the viewers of the film) in *The Big Swallow.*

[9]

Lewis did his own version of *The Big Swallow* gag on the October 15, 1950, *Comedy Hour*. In a brief opening skit the actual mayor of Steubenville, Ohio, and the actual mayor of Newark, New Jersey (who have traveled to the NBC Studio in New York), welcome (their native sons) Dean and Jerry to a triumphant homecoming before the crowd, recall their respective misdeeds, then turn on them and run them both out of town, as it were. The two race to the front of the stage as the curtain is drawn behind them.[7] An irritated Dean then utters a series of seemingly ad-libbed and almost entirely unconnected sentence fragments, leaving Jerry alone looking somewhat bewildered:

> JERRY (batting his eyelashes, and turning to directly address not the studio audience but one of the cameras as he starts walking toward it): It's true. Ladies and gentlemen, our writers Ed Simmons[8] and Norman Lear,[9] who write the entire show, said that we should make our show as informal as possible. We'd like to do that so we'd like you to relax and I'd like to come right into your living room and join you folks. . . .

By the time Jerry finishes this sentence, his grimacing face is in full close-up and getting even closer, mouth wide open. What happened next is unclear from the available video, but there appears to have been a cut to commercial, which in the viewer's mind neatly fills the space created as he or she is digested by the creature onscreen.[10] The cut to commercial relaxes us with the thought that the sponsor, too, is keeping a wary eye on this hungry mouth.

7 Scorsese's *The King of Comedy* (1982) with Jerry Langford and his high school principal; also in the skit is Victor Borge." TO "Scorsese's *The King of Comedy* (1982) with *The Jerry Langford Show*, where Lewis surprises Rupert (Robert De Niro) with his high school principal. Also in the skit is Victor Borge.

8 (1919–1998). Began by writing Danny Thomas's monologues with Norman Lear. In the 1970s, he was head writer for *The Carol Burnett Show*.

9 (B. 1922.) Lear is most famous not for his early gag writing but for creating and producing numerous A-list television comedy shows, including *All in the Family, The Jeffersons, Good Times, Maude, Mary Hartman, Mary Hartman, Sanford and Son,* and more.

10 John Caldwell describes moments like these as examples of how "early television . . . showed off its technical limitations," citing Martin & Lewis's live television

What else might fit into his maw? A microphone? A camera? Toothbrush and toothpaste? Well into the 1990s, Lewis often performed a particular gag: putting an entire drinking glass—whether tumbler, goblet, or stemware—into his mouth, the circumference of the lip prying his own lips open. In August 1962, in a famous guest-host appearance on Jack Paar's *The Tonight Show,* he at one point very abruptly "attempted" to eat the camera, which is to say, of course, eat all of us who were looking at the show *through* the camera. Surely the idea of Jerry devouring us with that mouth, here and now, for real, is only a troubled speculation. "Oh, but this is *so abnormal!* Oh, *what is he going to do with that mouth now????*" Surely the Powers That Be cannot possibly let him eat the audience! But is anyone really in control?

[10]

And what of the thirsty mouth? "Lips that touch liquor shall not touch these." This was reputedly one of the lines suffragettes used to convince their male brethren of the evils of drink and the dark consequences that would ensue. The same proscription did not—at least ostensibly—hold true for Dino, who can be seen sipping (what looks like) liquor, or at least having a thought to where the bar is, in so many of his screen appearances. On the January 25, 1953, *Comedy Hour*, he goes over to Jerry's "house" and Jerry offers him a drink. Seated comfortably on the couch, about to watch a 16mm film of some of their previous shows, an early instance of television's use of flashback episodes, he asks for a glass of . . . milk. Both Dean and Jerry pause, then look at the camera incredulously and chant in unison, "Milk!?!"[11] Dean's bottle quests

---

performances on the *Comedy Hour* as a prime example of "this celebration of technical limitations and performer volatility" in which "Lewis constructed and exploited his uncontainable volatility by playing it against TV's technical inabilities" (46–48). Caldwell notes, "In early television, recognizing these technical limitations was part of the fun, too. Pointing out how the apparatus worked or failed to work, even as one watched the performance" (370n45) was part of the shtick.

11 Not to forget that in the 1950s, in stereotype or not, many Jews restricted their drinking to Friday night's Sabbath wine and let loose only when they went to the Catskills (to Grossinger's or Brown's). More liberal attitudes were for goyim. (On stereotyping and comedy, see the section immediately below.) Remember, from Talmudic scholars in the yeshiva onward, the Jewish personality was associated

were as implied as openly shown, and he soon came to be able to "indicate" inebriation just by drawling with special length or walking with a slight tilt (in the time-honored pantomime that audiences had learned to recognize).[12] No matter what the diegesis had Dean doing onscreen, walking, singing, talking, or flirting, the feeling was that out of the corner of his eye he was bottle scouting. Every offscreen look was matched to some implied liquor cabinet.[13]

But mouths are also for kissing, and both Dean and Jerry appear to have done their share. Jerry's style was full on the mouth, almost doglike, with plenty of tongue, and he gives his mouth to males and females alike. In the latter case, he usually swung the woman low to administer the osculation with great theatricality. There's a whole bit in *Artists and Models* whenever Eugene Fullstack kisses Bessie Sparrowbush (Shirley MacLaine): his response is physical and extends to his entire body—an extreme close-up shows his toes curling up in his shoes, calling up the conventional Hollywood twist of the lifted female foot meant to signal sexual stimulation! Meanwhile the kisses proffered by the svelte Soviet spy Sonia (Eva Gabor) leave him cold. Dean's style was subtler, but much practiced in its forcefulness and apparent resistance to defense. We may choose to think of kissing as a statement: "I love you," "I miss you," "I'm glad to be with you." Or as a prelude or an adjunct to nudity. But with Dean and Jerry the kiss is more basic and more emphatic: "I MOUTH YOU!" Or: *I am to you, for you, and with you, AS A MOUTH.*

[II]

What can mouths hold that is more densely material than a cigarette? In countless shots and still photographs, we find Jerry with a cigarette in his mouth. Indeed, the very iconography of the Rat Pack—both offscreen and, to a slightly lesser extent, on—is oral fixation on smoking and drinking. While actors rarely drank alcohol on set, instead performing the act of imbibing by means of non-intoxicating substitutes, producing smoke cannot really be

---

with verbality (see the matching Christian-and-Jewish dinner-table scenes in Woody Allen's *Annie Hall* [1977]), and verbality was Jerry's kind of shtick.

12 *Ocean's 11* (Lewis Milestone, 1960) is just one of the more blatant examples of Dean's ostensibly unending bottle quests.

13 In Yiddish terminology, casual with viewers aplenty at the time, Dean Martin was the absolute paradigm of the shikkur (the alcoholic).

faked although many performers today insist on using cinnamon cigarettes in lieu of tobacco. One somehow has the striking impression with the Rat Pack, though, that smoke is smoke, the real shebang. Smoking on television or in a film was in some sense an act, a character gesture (and a time-filling piece of stage business), but it was also physiologically real for the performers, and as such it is a revealing micro-example of just how thoroughly the very personas of Dean Martin and Jerry Lewis (along with their semi-improvisational approach) troubled the usual divide between performed fiction and lived reality.[14] Dean & Jerry may not have been getting drunk onscreen (although many of Martin's later television performances seem to have been calculated to bely that hypothesis), but they had to have been feeling the effects of nicotine as they smoked cigarette after cigarette: irritation, abdominal discomfort, desiccation, nausea and accompanying disorientation, mucus depletion . . . (recall Jerry pantomiming various patients' complaints in *The Disorderly Orderly*).[15]

Smoking emigrated from America to Europe in the early seventeenth century but, Wolfgang Schivelbusch points out, without a name until years later. "Drinking smoke" was fashionable for some time, as was "Drinking tobacco," which supplies a healthy centuries-old foundation for the equable balance between inebriated Dean and smoking Jerry. Smoking was long associated with contemplation (Schivelbusch 105) but had another effect peculiarly associable to both Jerry as a performer and the Dean & Jerry team: "Smoking creates both a feeling of activity in leisure and one of leisure in the midst of activity" (107). Consider how the filmed person sitting calmly by a window and smoking as the daylight drops in seems to be *doing something.* The smoking would seem to give the character an intensified consciousness of time passing, and, we surmise, being conscious of time this person would be striking a thought, making a plan, thinking back on something unresolved. Or, especially in Jerry's case, engaged in some thrust far less meditative and more nervous, as in seeking out his interlocutor's weak points: "I don' understand!!" . . . "Whaddaya mean? Whaddaya mean???"

Think of that frenetic style of action Jerry always wore—doing, twitching, doing, twitching, doing, doing, twitching, twitching, even when not doing. The relentless wanderings, direction-reversals, loopings, jumpings in

14 Cigarette commercials were not banned from American television until 1970.

15 On the "pantomime of complaint" see Miller 32–34.

place that lead to no perceptible change in the state of affairs. As to wholesale political-cultural-economic effects, beyond smoking being an *ersatz* action, as Schivelbusch calls it (pointing to the possibility of eventfulness even in tranquility), there was a major shift in play: "The common goal both [tobacco and coffee] were used to achieve was the *reorientation of the human organism to the primacy of mental labor. The brain is the part of the human body of greatest concern to bourgeois civilization*" (110; our emphasis). In the celebrated boardroom mime of *The Errand Boy* (1961), Morty S. Tashman conducts an invisible band while puffing frantically on a cigar (see Clayton 99). Smoking accelerates, Schivelbusch observes, as time goes by and the process becomes simpler: pipe >>> cigar >>> cigarette. "Acceleration, of course, may well be *the* phenomenon of modern times" (111; emphasis original).

[12]

Consider the crane shot that pulls back from the open mouth on the billboard in *Artists and Models*. Open mouth, giant female lips, and gleaming white teeth to which Dean applies a paint brush. Martin, as struggling New York artist Rick Todd, is a sign painter, but Todd wants to paint canvases that will hang in frames on gallery walls.[16] Todd's "portrait" of the moment, however, is on a massive brightly colored billboard advertising Trim Maid Cigarettes: a work far too big and too garish for any New York gallery, however fictionalized and hypothetical.[17] The head is nearly twice the size of Martin's whole body. Had she a body, she would have been as large as the title character in *Attack of the 50 Foot Woman* (Nathan Juran, 1958), but the Trim Maid Cigarette model cannot move and lacks all volume—she is a two-dimensional advertisement, a monstrous feminized manifestation of fifties consumer culture.

The opening of *Artists and Models* in some way suggests Frank Tashlin's *Will Success Spoil Rock Hunter?* (1957), where we linger on the "oh-so-kissable

16 Recall that sign painter was the original profession of Antoine Lumière before he took up photography and founded the Lyon firm of Antoine Lumière et ses fils, which brought the Cinématographe into the world.

17 In 1954, pop art was still in the future. At that point, Andy Warhol was a commercial artist known mainly for drawing shoe advertisements. On *Artists and Models*, see also Hilsabeck 127–29.

lips" of movie star Rita Marlowe (Jayne Mansfield)[18] among other parts of her body, lips that singlehandedly save the job of ad man Rockwell P. Hunter (Tony Randall) by preserving the Stay-Put Lipstick account. This suggestive passage (it is not a "blue" one) is very much in keeping with cigarette advertisements of the period. Countless full-color magazine advertisements for brands like Camel, Chesterfield, Lucky Strike, and others depict attractive women—including a number of Hollywood stars—clasping cigarettes between their fingers, just beyond the pale of their brightly colored lips. This is the pose in which the Trim Maid billboard model is fixed, an oversized cylindrical ersatz priapic cigarette (but the phallicism is distinctly *not* played up in the scene) protruding in three dimensions from the two-dimensional surface of the billboard just below her painted chin. Both Dean and Jerry use it as a step to climb into her mouth, as she swallows Dean and, later, Jerry whole, inhaling each in turn like a drag on a cigarette.

[13]

That graphic, immobile, gaping female maw appears in inverted miniature in *Scared Stiff* when Larry Todd (Dean) hides himself in a trunk to avoid being apprehended by the police for a murder he did not commit. He uses a knife to cut a hole in the side of the trunk, a hole that just happens to coincide with the mouth of the female face on a sticker advertising "Sunshine Cruises to the West Indies and South America." Given that there is no diegetic reason for Larry to be cutting that hole—he is already capable of breathing and being heard on the pier where the trunk has come to a rest—we can imagine it happening just so that his fingers can come out exactly here, and exactly this way. (Again: nothing definitively "blue"; recall that the Production Code was still operative.) Certainly getting the little hole to coincide so closely with the tiny mouth without Larry's being able to actually see it took some amount of planning when the film was shot, even if the finger we see emerge from this makeshift orifice was not in fact Dean's.

But what if Roland Barthes, thirty-seven at the time, had gazed at this poster-finger-trunk combo as part of the meditation that led four years afterward to *Mythologies*? It is not difficult to see how the female eyes in the ad,

18 (1933–1967), star of Frank Tashlin's *The Girl Can't Help It* (1956), partner of fighter Mickey Hargitay, mother of Mariska Hargitay.

gazing upward and off, broadcast one kind of meaning in themselves and in context, and another kind of meaning when the finger is there beneath them. *Or are there two fingers? BUT NO*—one of the "fingers" is but a shadow of a finger, a picture of a thing that is not the thing itself: recursive reference, the doppelgänger shadow lingering in the light. And is this woman the potential cruiser? Or a resident of the West Indies (and South America) waiting to be found?

In *Artists and Models*, the mouth of the blonde on the billboard is Brobdingnagian, capable of ingesting whole entire male human bodies in one swallow, but this tiny dark-haired woman's mouth is correspondingly Lilliputian, large enough to accommodate only a single index finger. What is that index finger indexing?

[14]

The billboard mouth in *Artists and Models* is metaphorically Jerry's bleating mouth, a carnivorous and insatiably hungry maw ready at every succeeding instant to devour those who gaze at it, meaning us, the audience. As an indication of Jerry, this mouth has ceased movement for the briefest moment, only to dramatize by contrast the incessant twitching, gurning,[19] grimacing, teeth-gritting, yawning, puckering, beavering action we can imagine and remember before and after. So frenetic, so hungry is this mouth that when we catch a glimpse of Jerry standing quietly, backstage, onstage, at a doorway, on a road, we fear instantly that something is wrong.

Jerry's mouth is typically a factory for sound, but it modulates the quality, engagement, feelingfulness, and desperation of the mouther so that again and again we do not decode what Jerry is saying at all. That, standing at his side, Dean should not decode Jerry either seems entirely appropriate.

[15]

Plenty of things—handkerchiefs, pills, other people's fingers (Dean's especially)—frequently end up in the Jerry screen mouth, but it's something

19 See Ricky Jay, "Grinners, Gurners & Grimaciers," *Jay's Journal of Anomalies*, 45–52.

of a surprise to see him insert a gun, handle-first, when negotiating with a group of gangsters as Gerald Clamson in *The Big Mouth*. This is not the life-threatening act of forcefully inserting the barrel of a gun in someone else's mouth—almost always an act one man does to another man—but an act of infantile frustration that inverts the aggressively phallic cliché of the crime film. Completely unable to exert his will on others, Gerry turns the gun on himself, but not suicidally—another cliché.[20] Instead, Gerry takes firm hold of the barrel of the gun and bites hard on the grip. To "bite the bullet" is a figure of speech describing a physical act of enduring something physically painful, with the bullet safely removed from the gun, but to bite the gun rather than the bullet is a uniquely Lewisian mode of expressing frustration. The grip is the interface between weapon and hand, and to bite *it* is an expression of even greater frustration and powerlessness.

One frequently characterizes a speaker of having "rapid-fire delivery" (as in a "rapid-fire" machine gun): Jerry is a paragon, especially in his grammatical inversions that make for daunting confusions when he speaks quickly. Dean's emphatically slower speech accentuates Jerry, dramatically. But "rapid-fire" is a weapons descriptor, detailing the number of rounds that can be sent off per second. Jerry putting a "gun to the mouth" is self-indicating.

Incidentally, Lewis seems to have loved guns, and not just as movie props for genre films in which they were seemingly indispensable like *At War with the Army*, *Scared Stiff*, and *Pardners*. By the 1950s, according to biographer Shawn Levy, "He'd begun amassing guns . . . and enjoyed firing them . . . with his neighbor Danny Kaye. He'd even taken to sleeping with a gun beneath his pillow, though this was less a sign of materialism than of his innate insecurity" (111). Lewis accumulated quite a large personal arsenal through the years. When his belongings were sold after his death, the auction included a concealed weapons permit issued by the Las Vegas Metropolitan Police Department for 1989–1990 and nearly eighty different firearms: more than a dozen shotguns, as well as more than fifty pistols of all shapes, sizes, and calibers, including a Colt .45 revolver with his signature inscribed on the

20 Perhaps most notably depicted in the asinine blague M. Beudet (Alexandre Arquillière) mimes in Germaine Dulac's *The Smiling Madame Beudet* (1923) when he withdraws the unloaded revolver he keeps in his desk drawer and aims it at his head, pretending to commit suicide, as a way to express his pique. The gesture is sometimes mimed even now in everyday life with the index finger as a gun barrel.

handle, a Colt .45 "John Wayne Commemorative Single Action revolver . . . in presentation case," and, perhaps most mysteriously, a historical shotgun with a "silver inlaid plaque engraved 'JEW' . . . stored in a luggage case adorned with Jerry Lewis films sticker" (*Property from the Estate of Jerry Lewis*, 29, 35).

[16]

The taciturnity central to Dean's presentation of self, the closed-mouthedness fully formed and performed, is certainly helped on some occasions by the familiar "cover" of him apparently having drunk too much. He tended to stand as an observer, thus as a simulacrum of the audience member stunned by the routine; and the more obstreperous and physically energetic Jerry's dance the more Dean's gaze upon it would seem not only observant but also, at turns, judgmental, to some degree disapproving, if not subtly amused and trying to hold that in. It was often difficult to determine which way his reaction went, because he was not showing it. Central here, and the alcohol consumption entirely to the side, is Dean's *closed mouth*. We have the sense with him, this active watcher, that he is not only forming comment but also reserving comment. That after the show is done (certainly after their initial five- or six-year honeymoon), when we have been sent to bed, he might well have something to say, most probably to Jerry directly; and what he says would be blunt, sharp, pointed, and possibly cruel. When the singer isn't singing, then, the songful mouth is a locus of reservation.

Jerry's performative mouth is an expressive one, lips broadly parted, eyeballs gawking as though to direct the throat to speak. He does not restrain his felt response to situations; he announces it instantaneously and fully. Often, the Jerry mouth is so bent on announcing feeling that it speaks before there is anything to say—anything rational, cogent, well formed—and we hear vowel-heavy syllables in a babbling rant. This non-restraint—call it refusal to restrain; or inability to restrain—gives a direct pointer to taciturnity as a specific feature of social life; indicates taciturn Dean as a neurotic of a particular kind, notably the kind of citizen who would find expressive Jerry a problem. *The world is hard for all of us—keep it to yourself!* Jerry doesn't keep it to himself. Like the physical comedians who came before him, he expresses his condition, but in this case, notably, expresses without hesitation, without consideration, without evaluation, without checking the consequences.

Let us say that Jerry's mouth is a consequence itself, and that Dean's mouth is waiting for consequences. Dean is ready to pounce on Lucille Ball's "darling, cute lambie-pie" Jerry, but pounce like a puppy or pounce like a bear?

KEEP GOOD RECORDS

[1]

Before he came together with Dean, Jerry's act was called "Panto-Mimicry," as an advertisement in *Billboard* indicates (November 17, 1943, 44). *Pantomimed Mimicry?* By 1944, he was in a notable part of ritzy New York, among the new acts at The Glass Hat restaurant (in the Belmont Plaza, at 49th and Lexington)—a "novelty" act that ran about eleven minutes:

> Zany kid, who synchronizes mugging and motions to recordings played by an electric phonograph, is an amusing turn that had the patrons beating

their palms for more. He does a slaphappy version of an operatic baritone doing "Largo al Factotum" from *The Barber of Seville* but really clicks for top returns with a sunken-cheek version of Sinatra doing "All or Nothing at All."[1] Lewis closes the act with the now standard bit for all such pantomimes, Danny Kaye's version of "Dinah."

The reviewer who wrote this in *Variety*, signing, "Turo.," concluded that however amusing Lewis's act, it was "identical to that done by a number of others" ("New Acts," August 9, 1944, 35), a slam that could hardly offend a seventeen-year-old earning $650 a week (roughly $11,000 in 2023 dollars) from doing this ("Behind the Riot Act," *Photoplay*, September 1952, 150). Although it shows up in *Scared Stiff* and on the *Colgate Comedy Hour*, the "record act," a super-specialty routine, was not to be counted on for the future, however, and even if he hadn't joined with Dean the act would have found its limits. In April 1952, *Variety* pronounced the form "almost passé," albeit in a review of another "record act," the Pantomaniacs, a "pair of newcomers to [the] footlights" who were then appearing at the Flamingo in Las Vegas (Will., *Variety*, April 2, 1952, 68). The stretch for Jerry, and the heart of the gag, was juxtaposing a particular recorded voice with the "wrong" body, or the "wrongly" costumed body, or the body that moves "wrong." Another way to conceive this: the voice separated from the body out of which it is thought to flow.

But back to Turo.'s comment: . . . just imagine Jerry Lewis being decried *i-d-e-n-t-i-c-a-l!!!!* Is this an objective calculation from the reviewer, or a show of dull sensibilities, even disattention? If for Turo., Jerry's shtick at The Glass Hat did not amount to much, he also found the show "slow-moving . . . with little cohesion"—*Oh, that Jerry who cannot make cohesion!!!!*—and blamed Tommy Dowd, the magician who shared the stage with Lewis and three other performers, doing a "straightforward emcee job in addition to his legerdemain" ("Night Club Reviews," *Variety*, August 9, 1944, 34). A far more auspicious pairing was soon to appear on The Glass Hat stage, and the "emcee job" would be anything but "straightforward."

In September 1944, Lewis took over emcee duties in addition to "pantomimicries in unison to phonographic playbacks," although a reviewer again noted, "Of course, this type of act is nothing new," but conceded, "in some

1 Frank Sinatra didn't work with Dean & Jerry until the 1951 Muscular Dystrophy Association telethon (Levy 196).

of the things he does Lewis really is seemingly better than the originals." Reviewer "Kahn." noted, "Rest of bill includes Dean Martin, swooner," but opined, "Martin, with a new nose bob, is the show's weak spot; he's got a fair voice but lacks the feel necessary to reach the customers" ("Nite Club Reviews," *Variety*, September 13, 1944, 40). *No feel!!!!* As noted, Dean had gotten a rhinoplasty the year before he got together with Jerry.

Jerry was wholly capable of throwing mimic gestures into his routines, but strictly speaking miming was usually a marginal specialty (again, until *The Bellboy*). The mouth had to be part of the business, the mouth as escape valve.[2] Dean, as a singer the more likely of the two to resort to mouthing, often settled for silent (critical) takes, however understated was his minimalist approach to the typically broad act of pantomime. With Jerry mouthing off, Dean very often stood and stared, lips sealed, like an astronomer gazing in wonder at a shooting star or a high-paying customer gazing with dismay at a waiter who has dropped the food.

[2]

If there was truth to the story Dean told his son Ricci years afterward—in show business, there are no absolutely true stories—the Martin & Lewis pairing happened because he made bold one night to ruin the record act:

> Dad said he happened to be sitting at side stage [*sic*] one night while Jerry was doing his act. Dad looked to his right and saw the phonograph that provided the songs for Jerry to mimic. "Rico, I just took my finger and moved the needle on the record," Dad would grin in telling me the story. "The record skipped and the kid just flipped." Jerry was stunned, glancing back at Dad with a look like, "What the hell do you think you are doing?" But the crowd loved it and Dad continued to bounce the needle periodically through the rest of Jerry's routine, the audience going nuts with Jerry's exaggerated look of alarm at each snafu. (29)

2 In the boardroom scene in *The Errand Boy*, Jerry rapidly toggles between inhaling a massive cigar and pantomiming the "voice" of the jazz band on the soundtrack (that he is using the cigar as a baton in conducting).

Notably, in sharing the story with Ricci (nicknamed "Rico"), Dean never used the word "ruin," as in "ruining Jerry's act." Instead, he says Jerry "flipped," implying an exaggerated topsy-turvy physical move. Dean's spontaneously inspired gesture was, as viewed by the audience gazing at Jerry, nothing short of brilliant; and he would have heard the audience's growing delight from offstage.

Jerry got back—or "got back"—at Dean while the crooner was crooning, stepping up with a waiter's platter and blocking the audience's view of him. Jerry, then, had neither modesty nor shyness with this impertinent stranger, and the stranger himself was happy-go-lucky, catch-as-catch-can, a spontaneous (and brilliant) improviser with a situation suddenly at hand. The "what the hell do you think you are doing" look Dean recounts Jerry giving him can be a reprimand, but it can also be a dumbfounded question, aimed at some klutz who can't see an act in progress. The audience reacts as though it is neither of these, but in fact a calculated shtick in the act. Jerry has a perfect vantage point for looking at that audience, and can pick up directly the way they are positively responding to the "interruptions." He can immediately build what Dean is doing into the act.

With a simple finger move, Dean Martin opened the door to Martin & Lewis, and without hesitation Jerry Lewis walked through that door. The door to Martin & Lewis and movie history, in a momentary flash. Everything changed, not unlike the way late-1970s disc jockeys in the South Bronx changed popular music and invented hip-hop by putting their fingers to rotating turntables, repeating short passages of long-playing records, cutting and scratching, transforming a playback technology into a musical instrument.

The boys went beyond mere interruption. They noticed their interruptions, and noticed the effect of them, both on the responsive audience and on the resulting modifications to the act. There would later be very little of the Martin & Lewis comedy that didn't spring from interruptions of ostensibly coherent acts-in-progress.

A way to understand Dean's pranks—and in his recollections he does not own up to this—is that he was struck by "the kid's" extraordinary talent at improvisation and wanted to see just how far it could go. This pushing the athlete to break yet another record—pun intended—became a trope between the two of them, each one taking a kind of pride in giving audiences the impression he was trying to dismantle the partner's routine when in fact egging the partner to a more and more redeeming salvation.

Here—let me see you get out of this trap!!!

[3]

Reading reviewer comments, one gets a strong sensation of what might be called "conventional expectation," essentially a generic view of performances. For example, a record act was to be seen and understood as a record act, as flowing from the history of record acts, partaking of their fundamental nature, no matter who was performing and how. The form defined, identified, and constrained the actual event in every case in all the reviews. Almost all American entertainment at the time stood upon such received forms: the comedian form; the singer form; the conversationalist form; the host form; the dancer (tap-dancer) form. Thus, any typical television singer looked very much like every typical television singer; there was a role, it had a form, it had a look. This kind of circular logic determined the similarity of so much of conventional entertainment in the Martin & Lewis years. We find much the same kind of generic "containment" in the ways newspaper and media reviews circumscribed "westerns," "science-fiction," "melodramas," and the like. All these are fixed types, even for critics who write about genres merging and being revised. An early trouble of Jerry's, then, was that no matter how he stretched himself to do a peculiar record act onstage, he was seen as doing nothing other than a record act, and his gesticulations flavored the essential formula but did not eclipse it. How could he distinguish himself? How to get work? How to find, or make, an identity? Advertently or by pure chance, Dean was helping in this identity quest, and reciprocally revising his own status as a romantic crooner.

[4]

Mouth, voice, sound, and ear. The "record act" relied on one of the fundamental properties of sound cinema, that the sound/image relationship (as Michel Chion describes it) is essentially arbitrary. When sound and image are synchronized, the viewer—through what Chion describes as a longstanding perceptual habitus of "audio-vision"—assumes a logical and necessary relation between whatever are the juxtaposed sounds and moving images. *Assumes:* takes as *already* established when in point of fact the relation is only now, here, at this instant being established for the first time. (Chion points out that the sound of a punch, or of a tap shoe striking the stage, when heard on the soundtrack of a film, is in neither case an acoustically faithful recording of the associated sound event, but a conventionalized sound that has affective resonance through the mere fact of synchronicity and the accrued force of repetition [60–62].[3])

We hear a truly interesting sound/image *mismatch* in *Scared Stiff* when Myron M. Mertz (Lewis) performs a spirited impersonation of Carmen Miranda[4] as part of a "record act" when the singer herself is "indisposed." As Dean manipulates a hand-cranked phonograph playing a Carmen Miranda record, Jerry dances in drag in spangled dress, platform heels, and fruit-festooned headdress while lip synching the plaintive, infantile, demanding Portuguese lyrics to Miranda's song, "Mamãe eu quero" ("Mommy, I want it"), a cross-dressed performance that becomes even more difficult when the record skips or rotates too quickly or too slowly. Abrupt shifts in tempo are matched to cross-cutting between Dean cranking the recalcitrant phonograph offstage while Jerry shimmies onstage, munching on a banana he pulls from the headdress at one point. The punch line comes when, as the record ends, a Miranda voice that sounds suspiciously like Jerry's, screaming "Hey Ma!" (in English) is heard, causing both Dean and Jerry to do a double take.

In this case, even a performer's star character is wedded into the performance form: a *Carmen Miranda number.* Another, slightly more subtle instance in the film is when Mertz, startled while on the deck of a ship on a foggy night, seems about to scream. But he does not make a sound, and instead we hear coinciding blasts of the offscreen ship's foghorn as he opens his mouth wide once and then twice.[5]

Arbitrariness, as in an arbitrary association between a sound and a figuration, is a longstanding feature of animated cartoons, at the root of the somewhat pejorative term "Mickeymousing": a musical sound is provided the viewer for every action onscreen. Dick Stabile and the *Comedy Hour* orchestra made extensive use of this principle by having percussion sounds punctuate

3 Viewers love nothing better than taking for granted the tap dancer's acoustical extravaganza as they hear it, but very often (in the case of many of Gene Kelly's routines, for one example) "taps" were added in post-synch by a sound editor.

4 (1909–1955). Renowned for song and dance numbers performed with elaborate—even preposterous—head coverings and a Latina swagger.

5 This little trope had been used more than once by Alfred Hitchcock. It would be a signal mistake to guess that Jerry Lewis was unfamiliar with the cinema of his time.

and accentuate whatever physical blows were thrown onstage—and we might well wonder to what degree these slap/boom connections were pre-rehearsed: once a band and band leader become very accustomed to working with a performing duo, these mickeymousings, as it were, can be virtually spontaneous. It is as though the Stabile drummer—very likely Stan King—became attached to Dean & Jerry's nervous systems. Interestingly, what almost always resulted from the felicitous synchronicity of performed fisticuffs and well-timed percussive notes was audience laughter. THIS HIT + THIS BOOM = LAUGH. Was it the content of the shtick that moved them to laughs, or the perceived sound-image synchronicity?

The fundamental incommensurability of recorded sound and image was a characteristic of sound cinema more broadly. Lewis was born in 1926, the year of Vitaphone's *Don Juan*, and would spend much of his career creating sharply discordant combinations of sound and image. This is part of the DNA of what Lewis does as a performer. And what Martin does as well, although in a different mode; for him, already an accomplished vocalist in front of the audience, critical was understanding how in movies his singing sound and the "look of Dean singing" needed careful interweaving. His costume, his facial expressions, his body language, his business with cigarettes, glasses, and microphones, the direction of his gaze had all to be curated and modulated, since no one could assume that the mellifluous, easygoing, almost naturalized voice audiences would hear would translate into postures and gestures of Dean's body.

Lewis's version of the record act includes several fundamental elements:

[1] *Lip synch.* This is the most recognizable and ubiquitous part of the record act, and it plays an integral role in sound-film recording practice. Since so-called "wild" sound recorded on the set or on location—extraneous sound, room tone, distracting and uncontrollable location sound—is almost always unusable, actors are called upon to rerecord all of their lines of dialogue in a soundproof setting while synchronizing these recordings to their own lip movements which they watch onscreen in playback. This is called ADR: additional dialogue recording.[6] With the record act, Jerry reversed and decoupled this process to produce comical results, by lip-synching to the sounds

6 No better textbook illustration exists than the "dubbing room" sequence of Lewis's *The Errand Boy*.

of a deep operatic voice or to the high-pitch of a female voice that the audience was to suppose could not possibly be his.[7]

[2] But Ricci said his father told him, "*The record skipped*"! The perils for lip-synchers in such a situation are multiple. The record as a technical item suddenly takes over the spotlight. The singer finds it a matter of blind luck to "cover" the skip believably, since skips are random and unpredictable in most cases (until, by repeating the act, one has learned where the skips are). The act is vulnerable to collapse, which is exactly what occurs in *Scared Stiff* when the Carmen Miranda record playing onstage with Mertz starts skipping. Martin & Lewis adopted and played with performative collapse.

[3] *Mugging*. Either following what is going on in the song through facial expressions in an absurd way, or working toward other ends, the performer "acts out" the meaning of the lyrics, or a response to that meaning, thus turning a sound (a song) into a sound effect for a full-fledged dramatic scene. Acting out can be exaggerated, warped, made absurd, made histrionic to change high drama to pure comedy.

[4] *Dance and so-called hysterical performance* (see Rae Beth Gordon). The record act will fall flat on its "face" if it does not seem that the performer is wholly wrapped up in the sounds he hears (and we with him). "One writes what one hears *within* one, not without" (Leonard Bernstein to John Adams, January 27, 1966). The sounds or words in the air must go far beyond mere semantic pointing, actually apparently entering the "body and soul" of the listener, "moving" them, urging, cajoling, pressing, and seducing muscular (bodily) response. In a case like this one, the response is a reverse indication of the acoustic effect for Jerry; if he twitches, he is hearing. And if his motions are to be visible at a distance, without question, they must be dramatized through exaggerations of extension and size. Jump once again, and quickly, to mime: if we look at Jean-Louis Barrault's contemporaneous and quite marvelous marketplace sequence in *Children of Paradise* (1945), we note how the camera continually swoops in for medium- and medium-close shots to facilitate our vision, whereas in Jerry's earliest "record act" appearances, there was only fixed space.

7 Orson Welles did too, but in an entirely different way, recording the soundtrack first and then acting it out in what he called "playback."

What Jerry tends to project is the frantic mouth, the desperate mouth, unable to keep up with—to synchronize with—the (albeit artificially imposed) reality of the moment. What Dean projects is the fluid, comprehending mouth, its anxieties barely perceptible, its effort seemingly automatic.

[5]

Stilled in photographs and posters, the melodic Dean Martin has a mouth that seems to have no earthly need for action. I don't need to speak, I'm not singing, I don't need to tell you anything my posture isn't already telling you. Synching with what is around me is irrelevant, as far as I see it. Even without sound, or that peculiar, riddling silence that can be produced in a sound production and that can confound the synch, the Jerry mouth is iconic and central to his character. In a poster for Tashlin's *Disorderly Orderly* we find an angled photographic Jerry Lewis head perched atop a cartoon body in doctor's outfit, stethoscope sprouting from his ears. The mouth is wide open—but static—in what can easily be taken as a scream of despair. A perfect Wherever-I-am-I-have-something-to-say pose. This could have been a picture of a character thinking, but even here, with no movement and no sound, Jerry can be, can only be, in full evocative mode. Synching with everything.

Both Dean and Jerry are reduced to caricatured off-beats in the visual culture surrounding their nightclub and television appearances during this period. The line caricatures work as equivalents to publicity stills. To some extent, those iconic line-drawings are the images of these two entertainers that have survived, used in DVD and other branding. It was even possible for these caricatures to migrate, as though on their own steam, out of the Dean & Jerry universe to new climes: see the Lewis cartoon in Martin Scorsese's *The King of Comedy* (1982) or, for Dean, Al Hirschfeld's etching, "The Summit" (2002). But the record act invoked neither sound nor image alone, and in a strange, evocative way, not the marriage of sound and image either. The record act made sound float inside the picture like a UFO.

UP THE ANTE

A defining principle of Martin & Lewis comedy was *augmentation*. Part of their performative back and forth involved a continual upping of the ante, like a high-stakes poker game in which all but two of the players have folded: bets increase in turn as the inevitable end of the game gets delayed and more money amasses in the pot—a cumulatively greater payoff promised at the end. This principle of augmentation follows a definite sequence, with each shot followed by one that builds on the previous, every move followed by a countermove. This suggests a winner-take-all mentality as well as the confidence inspired by the postwar American growth economy, in which plenitude supposedly begets greater plenitude, with old limits continually surpassed.

Note that in augmentational structures the culminating moment will likely have its own idiosyncratic built-in laugh; but this is nothing compared to the effect produced when the moment comes at the end of a mounting chain. In most gags, the payoff is bluntly and of itself an immediate and complete reversal, like the finger poking through the trunk in *Scared Stiff* discussed above in "Mouth to Mouth." Here follow four scene analyses to reveal systematic augmentation, much in the way that in "Can You Relax?" we did scene analysis to reveal improbability.

{A} Entrances

Scared Stiff

[a]

The gangster film has a visual and aural signature that is immediate and unmistakable: nocturnal, high-contrast, night-clubby, thuggish. *Scared Stiff* is no exception. It has an exquisitely paced "pinball" beginning that nicely shows the importance of augmentational structuring in Martin & Lewis comedy:

[i] We are looking at a mid-town section of The City at night, in a major nocturnal thunderstorm as a massive lightning bolt hits. Camera tilts down to the street to watch a black car glide up to the neon-fronted Chit-Chat Club. Two thugs step out and stand for

a moment next to a lit poster advertising tonight's entertainment, Larry Todd (Dean).[1] One thug gets his pal to hold his coat and hat, and "politely" enters the club. Transition to:

[ii] Backstage, where Rosie (Dorothy Malone), a showgirl in a revealing spangly outfit, grabs a passing waiter, Pierre (Henry Brandon), and plants her lips on him before he heads out to serve drinks, augmenting the act of giving over your hat and coat.

[iii] Pierre is quickly waylaid by the visiting thug, who lets him know the Big Guy wants to see him . . . NOW! The two of them exit, and Pierre is pushed into the thugs' car. Car zooms off and rounds a corner, just at the instant a taxi comes *from* that corner toward us, dropping Dean off at a stage door. (Dean's entry is a rebound from the exiting Pierre; and Dean is an augmentation of Pierre.)

[iv] "It's rainin' cats and dogs out there!" says the stage door manager in his cozy office, watching Larry enter sopping wet. "Sure is," says Dean, withdrawing from one trench coat pocket a tiny kitten and from the other a tiny puppy, both of which he deposits on the manager's table. The actual kitty and puppy are rebounds of the door manager's small talk; and being alive and adorable they are augmentations of his stale metaphor. Larry is told he's on (upping the ante as well as the urgency), and makes an entrance to:

[v] The stage, where with a snazzy band accompaniment he swings into a fabulous opening number, "I Don't Care If the Sun Don't Shine," accompanied by four different showgirls in revealing, spangly outfits:

> I don't care if the sun don't shine
> I get my lovin' in evenin' time
> When I'm
> With my baby . . .
> (Mack David, 1950)

Big Dino voice, big brass, big finish (note, the "I" of the song is bigger than, more important than, "the sun"). Cut abruptly to:

1 Which may suggest Italian Dean's (and maybe also Jerry's) "affiliation" with the underworld. Six years after *Scared Stiff*, Billy Wilder's *Some Like It Hot* (1959) beautifully captures the visual and acoustic signature of the thug encounter.

[vi] The kitchen area, where a maître d' (Alphonse Martel) is screaming (in distinct European dialect) at the head waiter (Manuel Paris) that Pierre has vanished, *so who is going to serve the customers*? The answer?: Myron (Jerry) is out there filling in already, he's just taken a spaghetti order out. *Desperate panic* from the maître d' (Myron much more dangerous than Pierre). He strides out of the kitchen, instantaneously slipping to the floor, a sudden reversal of his determination. Spaghetti on the floor all around him. Meanwhile, in the main room, Larry is still blissfully singing: "I don't care . . . ," his words literally true at this very moment despite the mounting chaos.

[vii] Getting up and cagily following the strands of spaghetti strewn around him, the maître d' enters the dining room where spaghetti has been stuck on tablecloths and table legs, forming a kind of pathway of indications; the camera slowly moves through it ahead of him.[2]

It need hardly be said that the spaghetti trail can lead only to Myron, soon to be seen clumping between the tables with a huge platter piled high with spaghetti.[3] When the maître d' creeps up behind him and screams, the spaghetti flies up into the air and—we can hardly be shocked—lands like a monster wig on a diner's head. "I'm nervous," Myron says, "I'm not well."

See these comedic moments in a flow chart. Rain >> thug entrance >> thug exit. Thug departure bouncing off Dean entrance >> Dean's little animals >> Dean onstage, "I don't care" >> Dean's insouciance and the freaked out maître d' >> the maître d' and the spaghetti trail >> the bigger spaghetti trail >>>> even more spaghetti >>>>>> more and more spaghetti piled up >>>>>>>>>>>>> spaghetti cascading down >>> Jerry.[4]

2 A little trick reprised respectfully by François Truffaut in *Baisers volés* (1968) when we silently track up to a bedroom and see pieces of clothing dropped on the floor to make a kind of blazed pathway in the "woods"; and later by Steven Spielberg with the celebrated trail of Reese's Pieces in *E.T.* (1982).

3 A comedy bit to be reprised in the restaurant date scene of *The Disorderly Orderly* (1964).

4 In *My Friend Irma Goes West*, Jerry also struggled with a recalcitrant plate of spaghetti, eventually resorting to the role of a snake charmer to coax it into submission.

[b]

The aggregating spaghetti in *Scared Stiff* calls up a fundamental principle of comedy, reflected in the argument of *unlimited development* explored by Chaïm Perelman and L. Olbrechts-Tyteca in *The New Rhetoric: A Treatise on Argumentation*. The *unlimited development* argument poses the possibility of always going further in a certain direction without being able to foresee a limit to this direction, and this progress is accompanied by a continuous increase of value. As a peasant woman says in one of Jouhandeau's stories: "The more it is good, the better it is. . . . It is possible to defend behavior which the [watchers] would be tempted to blame, were it not assigned a place in the protraction of that which they approve and admire" (287–88).

This observation of Perelman and Olbrechts-Tyteca, brought to our attention some time ago by Vivian Sobchack, seems potently applicable to numerous Martin & Lewis comedy routines but none more pungently or succinctly than the spaghetti spill.

- Taking over for the defeated (fallen) maitre d', the camera wends its way along the floor, and each discovery of spaghetti leads to both minimal satisfaction at having successfully caught the problem and promise that what is still missing is about to appear. The undeveloped nature of the movement along the floor is a constant promise of development.
- The successive discoveries of spaghetti pose variations, and can thus be read through the logic of augmentation. We move from (i) spaghetti in the maître d's hand to (ii) one, two, three strands on the floor as he comes to the kitchen doors and moves through them, then (iii) still more on the floor but one strand wound like a giant worm around the foot and shin of a woman's leg, then (iv) long strands looping over the back of a chair from the shoulder of a man, and (v) a trail of strands leading away several feet between tables. The maître d' is confounded looking at all this. The spaghetti vision (his attention) pulls back a little to where (vi) a side trail of spaghetti has opened to the right—Robert Frost's "Two roads diverged in a yellow wood." As we move forward we see legs, dark shoes and trousers, feet slipping in hesitant motion. Now, closer, (vii) the feet coming down gracelessly, like those of a novice trekking through deep mud, (viii) the feet

> turning and wrapped in spaghetti still until (ix) the camera focuses upward and we see the back of Myron, in a clean white jacket, as now he gingerly steps his way through a turn and we note that (x) he is holding a platter heaped sloppily with spaghetti. Ahhhhh!!! HIM. THIS! *Here* is the reason.

But we always knew Myron would be. Who else could cause a mess of this magnitude and cause it in this artfully maladept way? In our moving from (i) to (x), we knew we would be seeing Jerry and Myron, Myron and Jerry, who have both behaved so badly they don't merit being seen.

As he holds up the spaghetti platter it is difficult to tell whether Myron's nervousness and strain comes from *holding the material in the air* or from *being seen in a graceless pose* or *from being alive in the first place.*

Meanwhile—Larry continues to sing, "I don't care if the sun don't shine . . ." If Dean were less casual, less hyper-relaxed, and less ridiculously professional at the microphone (that is, in our ears), Jerry's antics (visible at the same time) would be much less funny.

It is worth noting that the procedure of unlimited development, the accretion of aggrandizements step by step, not only builds the humor but also endangers the comedian in one respect. With every step up the "ladder" of the joke, he is raising the ante on himself, making his upcoming appearance a greater surprise. Any person holding himself up as a great surprise about to be revealed to a hungry public will naturally enough worry that the structured approach has built up a punch line much larger than he is capable of delivering.

{B} Sober at the Country Club

The Caddy

[a]

Joe Anthony (Dean), on the verge of winning the Santa Barbara Country Club golf tournament, must not be allowed to drink too much; indeed, to follow his erstwhile pal Harvey Miller Jr.'s (Jerry) advice, must not drink at all. The organizer of the tourney is Kathy Taylor (Donna Reed), canny, attractive, and eager for Steve. She and her parents (Marjorie Gateson; Lewis Martin) are hosting a soirée at the country club with the anxious assistance of their butler Charles (a frigid Clinton Sundberg) and his temporary assistant, Harvey, who is moonlighting as a server because Joe insisted he "earn some money" rather than help him practice on the golf course. Still in this film, as always and virtually everywhere, the Lewis figure is, or is on the cusp of being, something of a nervous wreck. While the sociable Taylors would like their guest Joe to have a drink, Harvey is working against the universe to make sure no martini glass ends up in his buddy's hand, lest he blow the game tomorrow. Inside joke: glasses full of martinis must keep vanishing behind Joe's back. A full glass metamorphoses into an empty glass, is replaced by a full glass that metamorphoses into an empty glass. A question comedians ponder: how long can this cycle go on? *The liquid evaporates . . . the liquid evaporates again . . .*

[b]

The "back home" from which Joe emerges to play this tourney is Mama Anthony's pizza place in San Francisco, where down-home spaghetti dinners are served.[5] (Italian boy whose mama runs a pizza parlor competing in the Santa Barbara golf classic: upward social mobility, if ever there was.) The pizza joint is typically casual, there are checked tablecloths, circular tables, simple, affordable, filling meals, nothing fancy. The epitome of a family-owned Italian-American restaurant with a bar in the back where they treat every living person like a member of the family.[6] Contrast this with the world Steve hopes to squeeze into: a spacious and well-lit cavern, filled with people in formal dress seated on overstuffed furniture, with waiters bringing around trays of hors d'oeuvres—"You might as well take a handful," squeaks Harvey, "I don't know how you can fill up on these tiny sandwiches."

Given that the hors d'oeuvres are plainly visible to camera, no viewer would have trouble grasping Harvey's comment at face value: you *can* take a handful; they *are* very small. But Martin & Lewis are going further than pointing to objects clearly on the scene. They are teasing and stretching the cultural awareness of an audience that itself doesn't inhabit the country club. If they are not entirely unfamiliar with hors d'oeuvres, they may perhaps at least be a bit befuddled by the concept of miniature sandwiches offering any kind of meaningful sustenance. Getting anything resembling a satisfying repast would surely require at least a handful, as Harvey suggests not entirely in jest. He is both saying and not quite saying that he and Joe are also not familiars to this social set, and in this way pointing with only some subtlety to Joe's eagerness to climb the ladder.

5 About Dean's mother back in Steubenville, biographer Michael Freedland writes, "Mama Crocetti's meatballs and spaghetti were well enough known for people to try to obtain invitations to her table whenever possible" (3).

6 Compare, as a model of intergenerational conviviality, the bistro scene in *An American in Paris* (1951): also venue for a significant song and dance, and similarly nostalgic for a "smaller" American scene.

Mama's heaping plates are in the back of Harvey's mind (that's *amore*) and, he would seem to think, should be in the back of Joe's, too.

These boys certainly don't fit. But this is America, after all: in America, nobody, or almost nobody, doesn't fit (according to the Official Memo). Dean wants to fit *so baaaad!* (Escape that pizza family and its convivial warmth. That's too much *amore!*) His deep motive is to augment his social presence, and the "superior" nature of the club set will be announced again and again, with greater and greater amplitude. Everybody who is nibbling morsels in such a place as this club is hyper-conscious of being the sort of person who would be in a place like this club nibbling morsels. No more steaming-hot plates heaped with pasta brought to table by the owner's daughter, Lisa (Barbara Bates), as would be found back home in the Italian enclave of San Francisco, that tight old-country cluster.[7] The country club is populated by unctuous servers in white bow ties, one of whom, our butler-headwaiter friend Charles, loves to growl at Harvey, especially at a moment when he is taking a call from his girlfriend Lisa—Joe's sister—back at Mama's. CHARLES: "You can't use that phone!" That is, *these* telephones are not for the country club staff to use for personal calls; but disregarding such arbitrary rules Harvey upends the social hierarchies they enforce—you *can* use a telephone. He even has the audacity to end the phone call with an open expression of personal affection that is "completely out of place" in the cold formality of the country club: "Lisa, this phone call is SWAK," he says, explaining to the angry, puzzled headwaiter, "S.W.A.K.: Sealed With A Kiss." The waiter slams the receiver of the phone down and sends him back into the party with another tray of hors d'oeuvres: "Take this and get in there with it!" In a world where everyone knows their place and performs their assigned role—a world Joe cannot wait to join by dressing and acting the part—Harvey is the disruptive force of kindness, caring, and genuine feeling whose emotional authenticity and candor is bound to detonate the airless, sterile pretense.

Charles's seizing the telephone handset and slamming it down is not only one-upping poor Harvey, it is degrading him by announcing that Charles occupies a distinctly superior position, even though he's a waiter.

7 The San Francisco/Santa Barbara division is a subtle play on historical class and organizational differences between Northern and Southern California. See on this Didion and Davis.

[c]

On the surface of the screen here we find Dean's apparently unrehearsed savoir-faire in up-class situations like this one accompanied by Jerry's impossibly gauche, hopeless, and klutzy interruptions, all of which are technically *obscene:* ob + scena: out of place; inappropriate. Beneath this surface is a powerful class critique, especially a pointing up of the country-club crowd as a whole, people who are none of them on home turf (in fact, socially they're out on a limb), none behaving as they would really like to, obsessed indeed with "giving an impression." Harvey Miller Jr. is genuinely himself, albeit by way of the sometimes-alarming physicality of Jerry; more than a character, he is also a model of genuineness.

But for augmentational purposes, Harvey self-indicates as genuine with increasing warmth, in this way expanding his separation from the club set.

[d]

These country club denizens are hyperactively inert. Their body language screams out: poised languor on the over-stuffed furniture, casual service from an underclass in starched whites that has the explicit charge of catering to their every need and never having the temerity to interrupt their oh-so-precious "conversations" or their oh-so-clever "observations." The clubbers make a spectacle of how little they need to do, but with utter disregard for all of the infrastructure—human and material—that exists only to prop up their class illusions: never-used swimming pools, shelves lined with high-priced consumer goods never to be consumed.

A tiny theoretical intervention upon this party: we are watching people who have nothing to do, yet time is passing and the film traps them and their desire for self-aggrandizement in a single setting. It would help the illusion if they could *seem to be doing something.* Put a glass in your hand, the waiter is passing; or snatch an hors d'oeuvre. Or both. Now if you have a glass, put something in it and drink. Then put more and drink more. This is an excellent loosener, a good way of ensuring that everybody can continue pretending everybody is having a marvelous time. But it's also a way of keeping your hands in the action in a progressively augmented way, albeit the action is trivial.

All around Harvey are sedate, cocksure, heteronormative couples with more money than they can spend. Merely by being there they contradict the spontaneity and genuineness of Harvey and his authentic bonds with Joe and Lisa, who together form their own odd nuclear family. But a fraternal ménage won't work for the Joe who wants stability and position; he needs a girl on his arm. The augmented heteronormative posture Joe is preparing for, and that is counteracted by Harvey, is one more privilege of the uppers. In his instinctive, persistent rule-breaking, Harvey punctures illusions all around, and offers a distinctly other—some would say, more sensible—mode of operating in the world: take a dip in the pool! Indeed, in the scene immediately previous, although Harvey is affectionately committed to Lisa, he ups the ante on his misbehavior with a spectacularly fey performance at the swimming pool, cavorting around the twinkling water with obvious delight, wearing a white robe, an ascot, and a beret, and singing "The Gay Continental" with all the bravura of a person who does not see any contradiction between being a devoted boyfriend to Lisa and a gender-free entertainer:

> Continent-continent-continental,
> And I got this way quite accidental.
> All my people have riches and velveteen britches and
> White ties and tails and top hats on,
> And top hats and top hats and top hats on,
> And they breakfast in bed with their spats on.
> (Harry Warren and Jack Brooks)

Plenty of disapproving glares from the priests, hidden beneath Oh-so-socially-appropriate-but-empty smiles.

[e]

Dean's martinis are disappearing because Jerry is squirreling them away to make sure his chum is in the best possible shape to compete in the tournament. First he creeps up from behind and delicately draws away the glass when Dean's head is turned toward Kathy. Soon, a glass or two later, he is downing the drink. Finally, Charles delivers an entire pitcher that Harvey must get rid of, so he apparently drinks the whole thing and we get a Jerry-Lewis-as-drunk character bit. Extending arms and legs at uncomplementary angles, staggering, rolling eyes. Only Jerry could be *this* drunk . . . ! But he cannot be this drunk without having built up to the moment with anticipatory gestures.

Raised here is the specter of Jerry Lewis married to alcohol, a trope addressed in *The Nutty Professor*, to be sure, but also something of a rarity, since usually the Jerry character is at least chemically sober and in a powerful augmentation the Dean character is not. Michael Caine wrote usefully about playing drunk that "a real drunk makes a huge effort to appear sober. A coarsely acted stage or film drunk reels all over the place to show you he's drunk" (6). Here, we may think of young Harvey as someone unused to hard liquor and now overcome by the martinis. But see at the same time young Jerry Lewis (twenty-seven years old), whose performing style broadly speaking is a kind of open rejection of staid sobriety. The exaggeration of the behavior, "officially" in line with "showing that Harvey is drunk," merely affirms the *already-inebriated* nature of the actor playing him. Harvey knows, surely, that here in the country club he must "make a huge effort to appear sober," an effort we can see that he cannot manage. But Jerry knows he is not at a country club, he is on a movie screen. And, too, in being "over"-drunk this way he is mocking not only country clubs but also skilled actors hard at work pretending to be drunk much less emphatically.

[f]

Aristocracy manifests as a mode of control, bodily and otherwise. The ability to bend others to one's will, the capacity to hold one's body (though not necessarily one's member) erect, the former with the assistance of furniture and clothing (starched shirts, stiff collars, in both of which the wait staff and many of the guests are dressed). Soldiers stand at attention as a show of their self-control and their simultaneous submission to the control of another. Thus, non-conforming bodily comportment is a performance of resistance, an unwillingness to submit to the codes of socially acceptable behavior. We see it in the way Jerry walks, we see it in the way he holds himself so loosely. For others, we see it on the dance floor—think Henry Fonda dancing "in the worst way" with Marjorie Weaver in *Young Mr. Lincoln* (John Ford, 1939). Dean's slouching and relaxing postures are, in *Scared Stiff*, preparations for standing up at the altar.

[g]

The Pretzel (because every Dean and Jerry routine must have one):

Kathy likes Joe and Joe likes Kathy but soon enough, romanced up and down, she comes to believe that he is affianced to Lisa back home. She gets stiffish, hostile, cold. But it's not Joe affianced to Lisa, it's Harvey. Lisa is Joe's sister. Will Kathy come to realize Joe is free for her? And will Joe ever be able to be really free for Kathy or anybody, since family bonds are family bonds and to make things more confusing his sister is coupled to the impossible Harvey? Joe & Harvey chained together, a foretaste of Stanley Kramer's *The Defiant Ones* (1958). Are they defying the system, or defying one another, or both? Unbreakable chain, a chain of love and devotion, but also a chain of unmatched attitudes and behaviors. Perhaps Mama will make a giant pizza for Joe & Lisa & Harvey & Kathy, and the lovers will all sit around being happy ever after. Especially if onscreen it can look like the best pizza in the universe.

{C} Room Service

Living It Up

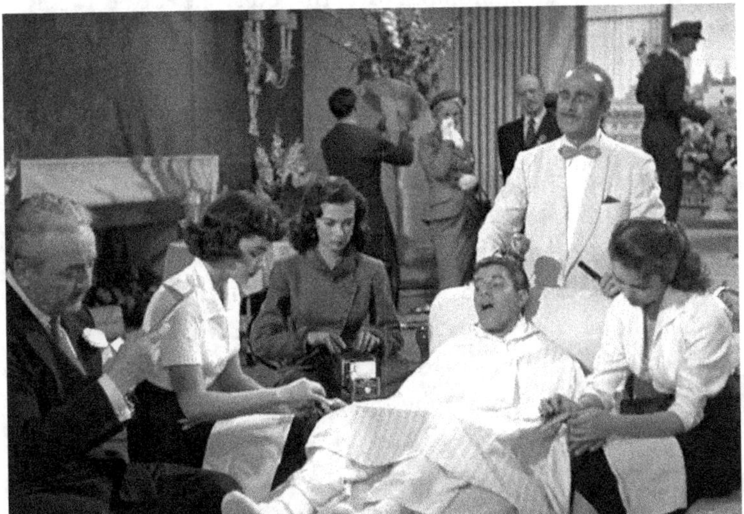

[a]

"I wanna have FUN!"

Homer Flagg (Jerry) is shouting at Dr. Steve Harris (Dean) in defense against the "doctor's" prescription for discipline and rest because Homer has been having way too much fun, with all the attention he's getting. As a "poor young man dying from an incurable disease" Homer has been ensconced in a three-bathroom, bigger-than-big hotel suite in Midtown Manhattan (at no cost to him). Tone it down, Steve wants, not in the interest of your health (after all, you're not really dying), but because too much enthusiasm on your part will destroy the illusion we have constructed together in order to wangle a free trip to New York from arid and unexciting Desert Hole, New Mexico. Desert Hole is shown as a rather charming, if backward, sunny southwestern anti-utopia; the antithesis of New York as the center of modernity. Homer's "sick boy" enthusiasm is unbridled. There is a generosity and all-inclusiveness to his fun, and it is available to just about anyone who wants to participate, including the viewer, since wherever in the massive place he trots the camera dutifully races to follow. As does his minder and personal physician Steve, who is a total wet blanket.

No sooner have they been shown to their suite at the Park Ritz than Homer is throwing an impromptu party that everyone else believes is a sort of pre-mortem wake. He goes out onto the balcony and shouts down to the city streets below, "Hello, New York! I love you!" and then invites everyone up for dinner. This is no empty offer—he shouts down the (correct) room number, 3608; makes a quick head count; and places a room service order for 3,000 shrimp cocktails to make good on his invitation. Realizing that Homer's enthusiasm can be contained only by restraining him physically, Steve locks him in one of the suite's three bathrooms: "You wanna have fun, go ahead and have fun." All by yourself.

The implication would seem to be that Dean will be entertaining the perfectly costumed and neatly coiffed Janet Leigh in the palatial penthouse suite while Jerry goes about his business in the elaborately appointed third bathroom.

[b]

Homer is tended as well as attended. A masseur is using a vibrator to relax the top of his head (his brain?!), smoothing down the infamous Jerry Lewis topcut. At the same time there is a weeping "nurse" on either side of him, and a wooden-faced stenographer taking a letter to the owner of Saks Fifth Avenue:

HOMER (dictating): Dear Mr. Saks, How's the family?

STENOGRAPHER: Dear Mr. Saks, How's the family?

HOMER: Is that what I said?

STENOGRAPHER: That's what you said.

A lovely conversational gesture and a very beautiful example of the manufacture of a comedic moment out of the thinnest possible materials, using simple musical repetition. Here, there is almost nothing to work with beyond the opening line of a ridiculous letter and the stenographer set-up, but the dictation is spun out almost half a minute, humorously, just by the take/match-take tactic.

READER: The dictation is spun out almost half a minute?

MATTHEW AND MURRAY: Is that what you heard?

READER: That's what I heard.

One could always take a further step:

MATTHEW AND MURRAY: Are you *sure* that's what you heard?

READER: You said it. I'm sure.

MATTHEW AND MURRAY: But, are you *sure* you're sure?

READER: Well, sure I'm sure I'm sure!

On and on, building, augmenting, blowing up the balloon called Funny. Their radio show was full of this artful plasticity, of which Dean and Jerry became accomplished masters. Stretch shtick.

One of Dean's favorite televisual gestures was the two-handed stretch, pantomiming as if he were stretching an invisible piece of chewing gum for camera operators and production personnel who might be wondering what unscripted byplay he and Jerry were engaged in at the end of numerous broadcasts. *We're stretching. We're killing time.*

Like this sequence with Homer and the stenographer, moment after moment in *Living It Up* runs on and on, one line disconnected from another, one instant disconnected from other instants except by Homer's excited scurrying around with Dr. Steve dragged along behind. "Lemme show you this!"—"Now lemme show you this!" Homer is most amazed at the bathrooms: So shiny, so clean, you gotta wash up *before* you go in there." A moment germinated out of nothing.

The ledge invitation to the crowd follows a well-known formula. One cannot put a character on a ledge if there is no chance he might fall, and the fall should be from a pronounced height. Best way to illustrate the possibility of falling: have a second character lose balance and slip over so that he's hanging by a fingernail. First character doesn't notice. This is exactly what occurs here, with Dean hanging from the ledge momentarily. In *The Sin of Harold Diddlebock* (1947) Harold Lloyd is the second figure, slipping and sliding at the edge, with a really marvelous matte shot of the traffic way below; the first character, who doesn't pay him any heed, is Jackie the Lion, way too cool to be worried about a stupid human. Homer in *Living It Up* (the scene is a direct homage) is the lion. When he yells down to the crowd, he is reprising one of the opening moments of *The Caddy*, when (essentially playing themselves) Dean & Jerry yell down to their adoring crowd and toss them photographs, all based on a real event. But here again is the slightest wisp of material stretched into a jolly strand: 1. Look down, 2. See the crowd, 3. Address the crowd, 4. Catch their response and respond to that. There is no need for a crowd at all, and surely not for a ledge, except that a hotel room would have a window and a window could lead to a ledge and for comedy a ledge is good. Not the diegetic story, then, but the movie as a way of telling it; good for the movie = good for movie comedy = Jerry conscious of himself as a comedian.

As to Dean the vocalist—his Steve has cornered Homer in a bedroom to give him a lecture but suddenly the phone rings. When he picks up he stands with full postural dignity, puts back his head, and gives the textbook sonorous and deeply serious doctor voice. "Yeeesssss?" By contrast, Homer has been screeching like an ape.

[c]

Here, as in so many countless places within the Martin & Lewis oeuvre, Dean is the Fun Police. Society's Voice of normality: "Calm down . . . you gotta calm down." Yet at the same time, a cop in love with the robber he nabs.

Calm down. You gotta calm down. (Really? Why?)

When Dean tells Jerry to calm down—this is perpetually happening—we know instantly and unequivocally that of course Jerry won't, and can't, and wouldn't. So the two words take on a kind of mantra humor, the humor you get from any simple words uttered over and over until they separate from context. "Calm down. *Calm* down. Calm *down. Calm down. Calm down!* CALM DOWN . . ."

Our Dr. Steve is presumably the Paragon of Tranquility. Homer's sickness, his true illness, the real one lying beneath the fakery, is that he is having too much fun and too clearly having a good time doing it: that he can't, won't, and wouldn't stop having fun. Thus, in *Living It Up,* Steve is invested in getting Homer to bed, and keeping him there . . . alone, like one of the patients on the television program *Ben Casey* (1961–1966), an episode of which Lewis directed nine years later, resting quietly under the covers, supine and helpless, while doctors and nurses actively minister to their medical needs, or at least jiggle them around.

Calm down. You gotta calm down.

Not only to minister to needs of the patient in bed . . . but to take a boisterous and perfectly healthy person and turn him into the patient you will minister to in bed. But no malice. Nothing intending to hurt in any way. Only care and protection.

Calm . . . down!

Arrogance and protective love blended inseparably and inextricably. Control and desperation in one flash. Yet inside Dean's figures as they *calm* Jerry is a certain *agita,* an anxiety or fear, not of Jerry the person but of some horrible tempestuous force that threatens to be unleashed, and with it the powerful feelings it can or will induce in the self and the other. *Calm down* as prayer.

Homer's true sickness, which is expressed in the film's title, is highly contagious—indeed, the virus could infect several thousand more people in the film by the end of the day. Wait. Wait!!! What about outside the theater?!! *Calm down.* The effects on movie spectators, as some media effects researchers (like Paul Lazarsfeld, in his "Limited Effects" Theory) were wont to note, might well have been plenty calming, or at least minimal rather than expansive. In the face of this monomaniacal and potentially infectious malady, however, Dr. Steve performs the role of cautious, risk-averse supervising practitioner—already dressed in a literal and metaphorical gray flannel suit, he puts on his horn-rimmed spectacles to take that telephone call, saying, "Hello. Yes, this is Dr. Harris . . . I told you Mr. Flagg is in no condition to receive visitors. He needs all the rest he can get."

All the rest one can get.

Calm. Down.

[d]

Living It Up raises the question of the nature in "reality" of the space in which Martin & Lewis move. Is that hotel suite part of the civilian hospitality structure; or is it a carnival?

One power of Martin & Lewis was that their antics remained on the far side of the glass, on the far side of the fourth wall, so that even when that "wall" was broken, the breakage was temporary and harmless—a wink at the camera, an acknowledgment of the profit-driven core of the whole enterprise, a temporary conga line for the studio audience. Not a "break," indeed, but a slight "warp." The movie audience could feel free to get on with their day—of shopping, recreation, work perhaps—or their evening. The television audience could turn off their set at 9 p.m. or change the channel for *Toast of the Town* or Sid Caesar's *Your Show of Shows* on CBS or NBC. The Martin & Lewis phenomenon was only "the boys" up to their high-jinks, no harm done, just a good laugh. Back to work. "Real life certainly doesn't look like *that*, at least not for us. Maybe for Dean & Jerry, after all, they're rich. Did you hear that Jerry has fourteen cars, parks 'em all in the driveway, a regular parking lot. He could drive a different one every day of the week and only drive the same car twice in a month! I betcha he and Dean don't worry about how much it costs to fill a tank with gasoline, or how they're gonna pay the mortgage, or the dentists' bills—I betcha Colgate takes care of *that*."

Didja hear, didja see? Didja see, didja hear?

Our view of celebrities is fundamentally ambivalent. We love them and we hate them, sometimes simultaneously. They are like us, but not like us. Or not *enough* like us; as we are not *enough* like them. We want to be like them, but then again we don't. We'd like to maybe be their friends, but probably not. Nice homes, new cars, and new clothes sure do sound nice, but nervous breakdowns and messy divorces, not so much. While they were flying high, no celebrities roused us more, stirred, stewed, pruned, and spooned us, than Dean & Jerry.

Didja hear they're best friends in real life? They go everywhere together, eat together, share an office, have the same secretary, have a little apartment on the fourth floor of a walk-up, love to share pizza, even wear the same clothes—and at the same time!—compete for the same girl . . . ! Real life. Real life. Calm down.

[e]

The hotel suite/room service bit begins in the corridor outside, with a platoon of uniformed bellboys marching enormous bouquets into the room. When we go inside we find something that could *conceivably* pass for a hotel suite turned into a hospital room, gaily dressed cohorts milling around, bright gildings of sunlight, an air of severely affected gaiety as though there is a secret hanging in the air that no one should breathe. It could *conceivably* seem this way. But in fact the place much more resembles a famous diva's dressing room, right after the show, jammed with sycophantic hangers-on, managers, family, admirers, the press, anybody and everybody hanging and milling, twitching and nodding their hundreds of thousands of heads. Flowers everywhere. The place a veritable garden—flowers of congratulations, flowers of celebration, flowers of adulation, Get Well flowers, Stay With Us flowers, We Love You flowers. Homer is not only the sick boy, he's the super-famous sick boy, and this is a beautifully constructed double entendre. As Jerry, Homer is "sick," in that he doesn't behave like a normal. But also, as both Jerry and himself, Homer is a major star (of the moment), and Dr. Steve is the controlling force in this backstage nirvana. A film about celebrity masquerading as a film about mortality.

[f]

The previous scene opens with an extreme and telling close-up on the front page of the *New York Morning Chronicle*, bearing the headline, "HOMER'S

END NEAR" above a photograph of Homer's backside, his body slung over Steve's shoulder. The gag, of course, is a double entendre connecting the visual proximity of Homer's posterior to the photographer's camera and his purportedly imminent demise. Like moments in *Artists and Models* when we see newsprint (Rick, jobless looking at the want ads), this static, monochromatic black-and-white world of newsprint and newspaper photography (albeit with a block of red on the banner)—a familiar piece of ephemeral material culture for viewers of the film—prepares one for what is to come, by opposition. (The very trope of the celebrity's arrival at the airport is itself a black-and-white vignette, straight out of 1950s newsreels, a trope that we see in the *Comedy Hour* "Martin and Louis [*sic*]" skit, and in the arrival of Rita Marlowe and "Lover Doll" Hunter in *Will Success Spoil Rock Hunter?* [which his niece watches on a black-and-white television in his apartment]). What follows in *Living It Up* is a vibrant, moving, Technicolor world of sumptuous colors, none more sumptuous perhaps than the periwinkle blue dress that Janet Leigh wears in the party scene—a stark contrast with the black-and-white photograph of her that was published in the January 1954 issue of *Photoplay* (p. 65), in the very same issue as an article on Dean Martin the family man, who had recently added a sixth child—a boy, Ricci—to his already-large brood (Maxine Arnold, "The More the Merrier," 38–39, 80). In a world of grey suits (light or dark, take your pick, see below), dark wood paneling, and tasteful polished marble surfaces, this periwinkle blue V-neck dress with upturned collar, which she wears with a matching periwinkle blue headscarf and matching periwinkle blue elbow-length fur-lined gloves (set off by a tasteful pearl choker necklace and understated pearl pendant earrings that get their own over-the-shoulder close-up shot when Martin is gazing soulfully into Leigh's eyes), are a sheer visual delight, matched only by the cornflower yellow pajamas Lewis changes into for the second act of his big illness scene, now fully rehearsed with Steve's help. Living it up means dressing up, even if one remains in bed the entire time. And dressing up for "living it up" means one thing above all else: color.

Not only color: Technicolor!

Nothing could be more liberating for designers, cinematographers, directors, and studio publicity folk, and for the Technicolor Corp. itself, always obsessively concerned with marketing its wares, than a picture in which the color was liberated from realistic use and able to fly spontaneously in any and all directions: the Dean & Jerry picture. Here, as nothing was really to be taken seriously, color could reflect itself rather than things as we know them. Flowers, pajamas, painted walls, billboards, farmyards, whatever material the script called for could be designed for maximal display of coloration. Every frame could be a wonderland.

[g]

The story of Janet Leigh's dress in *Living It Up* has not yet been told (we know it was an Edith Head), nor has the story of the rest of the fabric colorations we see in the Martin & Lewis pictures. Records might exist in the Paramount archives, or in performer correspondence, and/or within the contents of a performer's estate. Frequently at Paramount, for example, a star would be given the option of purchasing her garments after shooting, at a substantial discount (men tended to wear their own suits). Color not only struck the audience's eye, then, not only worked as an ad for Technicolor Inc., but also helped an actor strain or relax into a role. In their color films together, Jerry is uniformly more spectacular to look at, in terms of color, than Dean, who is dressed to seem proper, somber, businesslike, and "straight." Jerry's solo films later play with color in an exceptionally daring way, but even here in *Living It Up* he is locked inside fern-green paisley pajamas as he lies "sick" against a dusty rose headboard; or jiving madly on a dance floor in a black tux surrounded by kids in rich turquoise, spring-apple green, floral fuchsia, and peach yellow (while Leigh is in a vibrant David-Hockney-swimming-pool aqua gown); or stuttering around his suite/cell in an optical-illusion bathrobe of white, black, and blood red globs that oscillate with his every twitch.

One more word about color, design, and consumer fetishism of the time. Consumption was not just a habit in the 1950s, it was a piety. And viewers of a film like *Living It Up* could not only be tickled but made hungry by the forms and colorations they saw. A man, for instance, could crave that robe Jerry wears over his banana yellow pajamas and might wonder where he could buy such a thing. A woman might want that periwinkle dress, or the aqua one, letting slide away from her consciousness that when Edith Head made these, the items were one-offs.

Think of Technicolor as an augmentation of the look of the everyday.

[h]

One of the classic tropes of nineteenth-century stage magic is the container with a capacity that is far greater than its exterior dimensions suggest, including the inexhaustible bottle (from which could be poured any kind of drink, in unlimited quantities, for any number of spectators) and the magic portfolio (out of which were produced objects and living things of every description, even though the portfolio was apparently flat and was folded up and carried offstage after the illusion was carried off).[8] Georges Méliès gave the portfolio trick new life while reversing it in *The Devilish Tenant* (1909), playing an impecunious boarder who manages to pack away his entire apartment, including all of the furniture and another of the tenants (played by his real-life son André) into an ordinary carpet-bag before spiriting away himself and its contents prior to the arrival of the landlord to collect the rent. Let us say that the interior of the cabinet is an augmentation of the outside view.

In staging the *Comedy Hour* for live television, Dean & Jerry (with help from set designers and concealed assistants) performed variations of "the inexhaustible bag" on several occasions. In the theatrical hotel sketch that was part of the February 4, 1951, broadcast, Jerry emerges from a suitcase in which Dean has packed him to avoid paying for a double room. This gag was reprised in the ocean liner sketch that was part of the April 27, 1952, broadcast, when Jerry emerges from a golf bag in which Dean has concealed him to avoid paying transatlantic fare for two. In the library sketch that was part of the April 29, 1951, broadcast, Jerry places a small satchel on the checkout desk, and then produces no fewer than twenty books as the laughter of the studio audience increases book by book—a stack that ends up taller than the librarian (Dean)—followed by a string of frankfurters. Like Méliès' *The Devilish Tenant*, the former two gags point to scarcity—impossible compressions performed to conserve limited monetary resources. Yet the fantasy of the inexhaustible cornucopia was the fantasy of consumerism, the possibility that infinite and infinitely appealing consumer goods could be conjured out

8 For a relatively contemporary take, see the standard clown-car routine, where an apparently unlimited number of clowns pile out of a tiny car in the center ring of a circus; or *Dr. Who* (1963), where the Tardis is much bigger on the inside than on the outside.

of the most ordinary articles of everyday life once those containers had been imbued with magical powers.

Beyond being a clear symptom of the expansive heyday of consumerism and postwar optimism, of the glee that infected American culture at the time, was the hotel suite in *Living It Up* an especially salient example of the Pandora's Box that held the universe of Dean & Jerry? Did this space—did all of their spaces—offer a terrifying specter of boundlessness? Was Jerry the magical force, and Dean the controller, inside Pandora's box (the cell that very soon—at the end of *Kiss Me Deadly* [1955]—would explode on the beach of good behavior, spreading its fun-filled nuclear holocaust to the ends of the earth)? An obverse way to put this: in that posh hotel suite, when Homer is speeding around all these busy people, screeching and squealing and whining and pining, why doesn't a single one of them feel the liberty to run with him?

Nobody runs with him.

This is to raise the crisis of the boxed-in Martin & Lewis audience. Does the viewer of a film like *Living It Up* feel the desire to spread herself around this hotel suite, check out every bathroom, jump on the sofa, race out onto the ledge—the camera will do most of this, but does the viewer feel content and joyful about this camera? Or is the viewer, like Dr. Steve, fighting the tide? Order, calmness, calmness, order, order, calmness, calmness, order. "This film will be over and I will be able to walk sedately onto the sidewalk and tell everybody what an abject fool Jerry is. Why, he can't even enjoy a proper hotel suite without treating it like a playroom!"

Or would the viewer think, "O, how liberating. To be free from the obligation to treat this playroom as a hotel suite!"

One aspect of the "inexhaustible container" bit is its magical property—that in its use it defies scientific logic. But this "magical property" is precisely, in tone and effect, the power that Dean & Jerry bring together to the situations they contrive. Every Martin & Lewis scene, in every medium, is a "container" that proves inexhaustible and inevitably spills over into the mental—if not the physical—space of the viewer.

Enacted in a comic register, "inexhaustible container" illusions are an index to the plenty that postwar American culture seemed to offer. (The uncountable bodies leaping into the swimming pool in *Hollywood or Bust*; or even the uncountable postures and gestures in Jerry's body and tonalities in Dean's.) The delights were not mere immaterial illusions, they were tangible, even sensual, like Anita Ekberg's petunia-pink dress in *Hollywood or Bust*, or Janet Leigh's swimming-pool-aqua gown in *Living It Up*, or the *Artists and*

Models ball with the makeup painting, the gay costumes, the fluttering colors of all kinds in a climate of triumphal ecstasy:

> The public virtues of democracy were woven into the fabric of private life, into the brand new, 1959-model textures and colors and shapes of the suburban kitchen. Pink porcelain, ersatz copper, or "the Platinum Look—the cool billion-dollar look" of brushed aluminum and everyday elegance: style meant leisure, pleasure, convenience, and the USA. (Marling 279)

When Pandora's Box is exhausted, so too is hope.

{D} Dean Takes a Bath

Artists and Models

Space not only situates but also circumscribes stories, and can fundamentally determine what happens within them. *Artists and Models* is consistent with what Pamela Robertson Wojcik calls "the apartment plot," which is "any narrative in which the apartment figures as a central device." This mode thrived in American cinema between 1945 and 1964:

> This means that the apartment is more than setting; it motivates or shapes the narrative in some key way. . . . The apartment plot comprises various and often overlapping subplots, including plots in which lovers encounter

> one another within a single apartment house or live in neighboring apartment buildings . . . and plots in which aspects of everyday life are played out and informed by the chance encounters and urban access afforded by apartment living. Most, but not all, examples of the apartment plot are set in New York. Most, but not all, revolve around white, middle-class characters. (3)

The story of *Artists and Models* turns on two sets of same-sex roommates living on two floors of the same building becoming romantically involved to form two heterosexual couples—Dean and Dorothy Malone; Jerry and Shirley MacLaine—but Dean & Jerry transform the stairway between those two floors into the setting for a protracted comedy of miscommunication.

The extension of a gag beyond its logical conclusion, stretched to its absolute breaking point, is epitomized by the series of missed connections when Eugene (Jerry) relays an urgent telephone message to Rick (Dean), who is languishing in a bath. The simplest communication, one line of dialogue that Mr. Murdock (Eddie Mayehoff), for whom Rick is desperately eager to work, dictates to his secretary Bessie Sparrowbush (MacLaine) in but a few seconds, is comically distended into an extensive and elaborately cross-cut sequence of some forty-five shots spanning some five minutes and forty seconds of screen time transpiring in six separate locations: (a) Murdock's office at the Murdock Publishing Company; (b) the bathroom of Rick and Eugene's third-story apartment; (c) the third-floor landing; (d) the public telephone shared by everyone living in the apartment building in a hallway two flights down on the first floor below; (e) the second-floor transition space between (d) and (e); and (f) Rick and Eugene's bachelor kitchen. Here is an absurd sequence that suggests a mashup of classic D. W. Griffith–style parallel montage with the maddening circumlocutions of a Rube Goldberg device or drawing.

Parallel editing (bouncing back and forth between spots that are fragments of the overall story space of the moment) was often yoked to the narrative device of a telephone call[9]—so much so that some film historians have speculated that the challenge of representing telephone calls cinematically (and the simultaneity which a telephone call invokes) may have stimulated early examples of crosscutting by filmmakers at Pathé-Frères and later by Griffith, replacing other cinematic devices like split screens (Gunning, "Heard"; Young). In this sequence in *Artists and Models*, the telephone links Murdock's

9 The telephone was patented by Alexander Graham Bell in 1876.

office to the apartment building through a series of crosscut shots. But nested within the shots inside the apartment building setting is another, much more furious set of alternations. These follow Eugene's trajectory as he bounds up and down the stairs to serve as a human relay for a telephone line that cannot stretch into the apartment itself (the house phone is affixed to the wall).[10] Cheap apartment rental; shared phone, as in a prison. Where vocal communications fail (one cannot hear someone shouting when separated by two flights of stairs; one speaker can be so out of breath he can no longer make words; or the listener may be Eugene Fullstack, obsessed by only his chewing gum and his comic book), they are eventually replaced by mime. All the jabber augments toward pure gesture.

If parallel montage usually represents efficiency in storytelling, this sequence highjacks that device for opposite ends. Indeed it dwells in the interstices, in the numerous instants (each, taken alone, with little or no ostensible narrative importance) that show Jerry going up and down the stairs—the exact material that typical parallel editing would avoid. Eugene's entrances and exits and racings up and down are not filmed on the kind of set that Pathé built, a staircase leading from nowhere to nowhere, for the numerous cases where actors were called upon to enact such transitions in very early film. These are the kinds of shots that irritated film viewers of the 1910s (Tsivian 146), shots that later Hollywood cinema was eager to eliminate, but here they are designed to captivate the viewer. Also, interestingly, like Griffith (see *Intolerance* [1916] especially, but also *The Sunbeam* [1912]), Tashlin favors cross-cutting between three narrative threads—Murdock in his office; Rick in a bathtub; Eugene on the stairs—rather than two.

Tashlin also lingers on what looks like a purpose-built staircase set, to emphasize the circuitous and cyclical physical relay that impedes direct human communication (and its technological extension via telephony). Tashlin turns what in another film might have been a simple three-shot sequence (in which staircases—not just one but two flights of stairs!—need not appear onscreen, only the interiors of the rooms, connected by the stairs, in which the ostensible dramatic action occurs) into fifteen times as many shots and considerably more screen time. This is a virtuoso counter-example of montage as accrual and augmentation rather than economy, a big middle finger (and a rather hilarious one at that) to the purported efficiency of the classic Hollywood style and all it represents.

10 Cell phones coming much later, telephones were always connected by a cord.

Here is Tashlin's sequence as a shot list:

(ADVICE TO READER: As you move through these shots, you will likely feel you know what's coming next and have a tendency to skip through the routine. If you would like to have a tiny taste of the excruciating extension involved here, instead read this very carefully, word for word, and let the frustration build.)

Artist and Models: The Telephone Call

[1] *Apartment Building First Floor.* Kathleen Freeman (the LANDLADY)[11] picks up the ringing telephone on the first-floor. (Bright red lipstick; dark red sweater; green-on-green Chinese key-pattern wallpaper behind her.

[2] *Murdock Publishing Company Office.* BESSIE (MacLaine) in an apricot open-neck shirt-waist with headset on and Murdock standing behind her.

[3] *Apartment Building First Floor.* LANDLADY drops the telephone receiver, leaving it hanging on its cord, looks up the stairs, and screams, "Rick . . . TODDDDDD!!!!

11 (1923–2001). Her 301 screen appearances included *Singin' in the Rain*, *Batman* (1968), and, with Martin and/or Lewis, as a principal supporting player in *3 Ring Circus*, *Artists and Models*, *The Ladies' Man*, *The Errand Boy*, *The Nutty Professor*, *Who's Minding the Store?* (1963), and *The Disorderly Orderly*.

[4] *Murdock's Office.* MURDOCK checking his watch, speaking his message, "Could Mr. Todd meet me at the Stork Club for lunch in half an hour?"

[5] *Apartment Building Third Floor Landing.* Looking toward bannister, EUGENE comes to door chewing gum, comic book glued to his face. *(Same green-on-green wallpaper; EUGENE in a pale blue and red checked shirt.)* He hears the voice beckoning from below and replies, "Telephone, okay, just a minute . . ."

[6] *Rick and Eugene's Bathroom. Long shot.* RICK is in foreground humming as he bathes, EUGENE approaching from some way off, through the bedroom. He is chewing gum frenetically, eyes glued to his comic book. EUGENE doesn't stop chewing and gawking at the book, while RICK eyes him. EUGENE catches sight of RICK.

EUGENE: Oh Rick! Oh, hello, Rick —There's a telephone call.

RICK: From who?

EUGENE: What?

RICK: Who is it!?

EUGENE (ingenuously): Oh, I don't know.

RICK (voice lifted): Well, go find out!

EUGENE (back to comic book): Oh, all right.

[7] Medium-close portrait of RICK.

RICK (screaming): Now!!!

[8] *Long shot, as in* [6]:

EUGENE (near bedroom, which abuts the bathroom): Oh, check check. (*He leaps back over the bed and runs out.*)

[9] *Apartment Building Second Floor Landing.* Apt. 2A in the background. EUGENE is running down the stairs from the third floor, a few efficient little dance steps. He turns, runs past 2A, heads for:

[10] *Apartment Building First Floor.* EUGENE runs down from the second floor, goes straight to phone:

EUGENE: Hello?

BESSIE (on phone): Hello?

EUGENE: Yeah, who's calling?

[11] Murdock Publishing Company. Portrait shot of BESSIE SPARROWBUSH.
[12] (as in 10): EUGENE: Oh, okay. Just a minute. (Lets phone drop, dances his way up the first flight of stairs.)
[13] Apartment Building Second Floor Landing. EUGENE is flagging a little; he heads up the next flight of stairs.
[14] Rick and Eugene's Bathroom, as in [6]. EUGENE runs in excitedly

EUGENE: It's the Murdock Publishing Company!

RICK: We'll go places. What'd they want?

EUGENE: Uh-oh, I didn't ask.

[15] *Portrait of Rick,* as in [7]. RICK: "Well, go and ask!!"
[16] *Portrait of Eugene.* EUGENE: Oh! Check-check! Okay! *(Heads out.)*
[17] *Rick and Eugene's Apartment. Long shot,* as in [6]. EUGENE runs through the bedroom while Rick turns his head to watch.
[18] *Apartment Building Second Floor Landing.* EUGENE is heading for the stairs to the first floor.
[19] *Apartment Building First Floor.* EUGENE is descending the stairway more slowly. He goes to the telephone. EUGENE: Hello. What do you want?
[20] *Murdock Offices.* BESSIE is reading a blazing red ASTROLOGY magazine. BESSIE (into phone): "Uh, Mr. Murdock would like to know if Mr. Todd can see him."
[21] EUGENE (into phone): Just a minute, I'll find out. *He drops the phone, heads up the first flight of stairs a little less energetically.*
[22] *Apartment Building Second Floor Landing.* EUGENE struggles to, then up the stairs leading to the third floor.
[23] *Rick and Eugene's Bathroom,* as in [6]. EUGENE stumbles in, arms flailing.

RICK: Well? WELLLL?

EUGENE (gasping some): Can you see . . . Mr. Murdock?

RICK: Can I see him?! Of course I can see him! When? WHENNN?

EUGENE (gasping): I don't know.

[24] *Portrait of Rick,* as in [7]. RICK: Well, go find out!!!

[25] *Portrait of Eugene,* as in [16]. He throws his head up and down affirmatively and breathlessly.

[26] *Long shot,* as in [6]. EUGENE exits, stumbles over a bed, goes out. RICK is scrubbing his shin.

[27] *Apartment Building Second Floor Landing.* EUGENE is almost falling down stairs from the third floor. He turns.

[28] *Apartment Building First Floor.* EUGENE needs the handrails to help him down the stairs. He goes to the telephone. EUGENE (gasping): H'lo. When? When?

[29] *Murdock Office.*

BESSIE: When, where? Oh. Mr. Murdock would like to know if Mr. Todd can have lunch with him at the Stork Club in half an hour.

[30] *Apartment Building First Floor.* EUGENE (holding phone): He'll . . . he'll be there. *(He hangs up; struggles up the first flight of stairs, half-crawling.)*

[31] *Apartment Building Second Floor Landing.* EUGENE struggles along and up the flight to the third floor.

[32] *Apartment Building Third Floor Corridor. In extremis,* EUGENE comes up from the stairwell.

[33] *Rick and Eugene's Bathroom. Long shot,* as in [6]. As RICK washes his neck we see EUGENE's hand in the far distance reaching around a doorjamb. He struggles forward, collapsing between the beds, then further forward, collapsing between the near bed and the bathroom (all the while RICK is blithely washing himself). EUGENE lifts himself up with the aid of the sink and the bathroom doorknob.

RICK (gesturing with hand): What they say? What'd they say?

EUGENE (pointing behind him, then pointing at RICK)

RICK: What'd they say, speak up!

EUGENE (out of breath)

RICK: I can't hear ya, tell me, give me a signal, something! WHAT DID THEY SAY?

EUGENE: (gesturing: "hold on")

RICK: Eugene—what'd they say?

EUGENE: (Trying to speak, in vain)

[34] *Portrait shot RICK,* as in [7]. RICK (helpless): Give me a signal. Something!

[35] *Portrait shot EUGENE,* as in [16]. RICK's head is in the right foreground. EUGENE raises his right hand to make a bird. He wiggles it. RICK: What!? *(EUGENE shakes his head.)*

[36] *Rick and Eugene's Bathroom. Long shot,* as in [6]. RICK is attempting with his left hand to gesture incomprehension. EUGENE is bending over the tub with his right (bird-) hand "squawking."

RICK (playing charades): Duck?

EUGENE (flabbergasted): Duck!

RICK: A duck, right?

EUGENE: (Trying to make a signal)

[37] *Portrait shot RICK,* as in [7]. RICK (playing charades): A duck. A duck!

[38] *Rick and Eugene's Bathroom. Long shot,* as in [6]. EUGENE shakes his head, flicks his ear, twists his hands together.

RICK (playing charades): Sounds like? Sounds like ____ Murder! Murder! Sherlock! (EUGENE makes signals) Murder? Murder? (EUGENE makes sign for "flat/stretch") Murdock! Oh, Murdock!!! (EUGENE grins in spasms of ecstasy, slapping hands together in success). Oh yeah, Murdock. It was him on the phone.

[39] *Portrait shot RICK,* as in [7]. RICK: Well, what's he want? WHAT'S HE WANT? What's he want?

[40] *Rick and Eugene's Bathroom. Long shot,* as in [6]. EUGENE is standing, making vertical pumping gestures with his arms. RICK (playing charades): A cow???? (EUGENE's eyes are wide open, mouth agape, hands outstretched.) Murdock wants a cow??????? (EUGENE points into Rick's face.) What's he want a cow for??? (EUGENE chews his own forearm.) Want to MEET a cow! (EUGENE folds his

hands together, begging.) Wants me meat, right? (EUGENE touches RICK's face urgently.) What???

[41] *Portrait shot* RICK, as in [7]. RICK (playing charades, with extremity of facial gesture now and hands flapping in front of his face): WHAT DOES HE WANT?!!! (Eyeballs turned inward) What?

[42] *Rick and Eugene's Bathroom. Long shot,* as in [6]. EUGENE is leaning half over the tub, pointing to Rick. He slips into the tub with Rick. RICK (playing charades): M-m-me??? (Then popping out of the "game"): What are you doin' in the tub!!?? Meet . . . he wants to meet . . .

[43] *Rick and Eugene's Bathroom. Closer on the tub.* EUGENE AND RICK are filling the screen. EUGENE urges RICK on by hand. RICK (playing charades): Oh! Murdock wants to MEET ME! (EUGENE embraces RICK's head with a fully explosive grin.) Where, where? Where, all right! (EUGENE points off.) WHERE DOES HE WANT TO MEET ME? (EUGENE still pointing.) Out there? Does that mean now? (EUGENE flaps his hands imitating a bird.) Where? He wants to meet me and fly? (EUGENE seizes a hanging white towel and exits the tub, dripping.) Where?

[44] *Rick and Eugene's Kitchen. Medium shot.* EUGENE goes to the refrigerator, withdraws a cantaloupe from the middle shelf, stumbles away with it toward the camera.

[45] *Rick and Eugene's Bathroom. Medium-long shot from the end of the tub.* RICK is wrapped in a towel and wearing slippers, drying his ankle. EUGENE enters rear left, stumbling some. In his mouth is the white towel like a diaper, with the cantaloupe inside it like a baby's head. He lifts his near leg at the knee. RICK (playing charades, pointing): Oh, you're a stork, that's it! Mr. Murdock wants to meet me at the Stork Club. Right? (He rushes out, and EUGENE falls into the tub.)

The movement structure of the finale could not be simpler:

1/ Rick (Dean) is in the tub.
2/ Eugene (Jerry) is near or in the tub with Rick.
3/ Eugene is in the tub alone.

Now, how is icing spread on this cake?

[a] If Rick is bathing why would Eugene be in the bathroom with him? To what end? Answer: to help his buddy retrieve a telephone message from elsewhere.

[b] Why would Eugene not simply grab the message and convey it? Answer: because the humor flows from the extension of the bathroom/bathtub contact, not its simple purpose. Eugene must take as long as possible to get the message through.[12] We know this is Martin & Lewis's need, because they are working out a staged routine for a camera; but in what way is this Eugene's need?

[c] Why is Eugene so inept at giving over this message? Answer: Eugene isn't inept, he's utterly sincere: out of breath means OUT of breath. But the only thing he thinks about is comic books, or the gum he is chewing. He's *doing two things at the same time, obsessing with his comic and bringing to Rick words that have nothing to do with the comic at all.* Analysis could go even further . . .

But there is a pressing question underpinning all this:

Why of all places does Tashlin propose the bath as setting? Surely Rick could be at the dining table absorbed by the daily newspaper. Answer: because if Eugene "falls into" the newspaper it's not half as funny as (i) having him in the tub with Rick; (ii) having him play charades with Rick beside the tub (of all places, Rick being naked and Eugene being oblivious to that); or (iii) Eugene falling into the tub by himself.

What immediately follows this sequence is a more properly efficient use of a staircase as a movie set, some moments having elapsed since Rick emerged from the bathtub. He is now outside, bounding down the stairs leading from the apartment building to the street in a natty blue suit as five little kids are playing on the steps. He can't avoid catching his love interest Abigail (Dorothy Malone) just as she is about to enter the building wearing a light purple ensemble: all shown in one long shot that is also a long take of about forty seconds that settles on a medium two-shot engaging Rick and Abigail in unimpeded, open, smooth face-to-face conversation. This coda, set in a

12 This sequence is a flip on the "traditional" game of "Telephone," which we see enacted by James Cagney and others in the prison dining scene, in *White Heat* (1949). There, the problem is handling (natural) alternations in the message content as words pass from idiosyncratic person to idiosyncratic person. Here the message is intact as a message, but in fact broken up into meaninglessly ambiguous phrases because Eugene brings only part of it each time.

similarly transitional architectural space—another staircase game—is both a condensation of the game that we have just seen enacted across the previous forty-five shots and a concise rejoinder to its spectacular inefficiency. The ease and simplicity of this sidewalk back-and-forth, fitting comfortably within the space of a single shot and temporally within a single take, could not contrast more greatly with the excruciating narrative and communicative ineffectiveness of what has preceded it.

Why, anyone might wonder, are we atomizing the telephone call sequence here, rather than just passing over it?

We atomize the telephone call sequence not only because of our fondness for Raymond Bellour and, say, his scrupulous attention to the intricacies and convolutions of Hitchcockian montage (see *The Analysis of Film*), or for V. F. Perkins and his guide paths to close reading, but also because such attention to individual shots and their sequential arrangement reveals other kinds of alternation within the mise-en-scène of the constituent forty-five shots.

There is an alternation between shots involving the horizontal depth of the apartment and the shallower depth of the staircase (which extends into space vertically). The apartment is filmed first *through* its doorway and then *through* the doorway to the bathroom, while the adjacent walls in the staircase shots allow no depth. Eugene is fixated by the flat surface of the comic book he holds in his hands. But his movements—his bouncy energetic tone—are played out in deep space as the sequence starts and by way of his gradual depletion as he gains more and more fragments of the "sacred" message. We also see Martin composed, lackadaisical, blissful in the tub morphing into a frustrated maniacal monstrosity when, in the charade game he (magically, automatically) thinks is in progress, he can't get the punch line of the message quickly enough. There is also a contrast between MacLaine's somewhat distracted but thoroughly businesslike neutrality of vocal tone *as she delivers the key message,* and the comparatively abstract nature of Eugene's deliveries.

Beyond Tashlin's exquisite symphony of camera positions: an exact spotting for each shot, not always precisely replicating earlier positions in this same spot but calculated nevertheless to reveal space and objects in a tellingly weighted way (see for example his different ways of showing the second-floor landing or Eugene at the phone); beyond Lewis's extraordinarily sensitive appreciation of his own body as a performative tool, the stairs that must be "climbed" again and again and again and again so that his legs finally give out (although at the start he virtually dances along); beyond the way the lungs must cease to serve their function as well: finally he can only point, there is no air, no oxygen, but he has worked it out with Martin that at exactly this moment Martin should be bellowing at him, "WHAT?????"—it is the bellowing that helps make the silences funny; beyond all this is something still more meaningful. These alternations—of movement, of gesture, of shifts across deep and shallow focus, of spaces obstructed and unobstructed, are nothing short of kaleidoscopic, Technicolor greens, reds, and blues shifting before one's eyes against the more neutral backdrops, the aqua bathroom, Rick's golden skin, Eugene's baby-blue and red checked casual shirt, the green wallpaper, Kathleen Freeman's World Series red lipstick, and so on. Dana Polan comments sharply on this:

> In 1950s America everyday reality itself is presented as already artificial, already a paint-by-numbers world on which colors are applied extravagantly. For instance, one kitschy yet omnipresent and quotidian symbol of the 1950s is Jell-O, and I suggest that, more than just a food, it is a visual phenomenon that sums up the age. Through its vivid artificial colors it replays the period's fascination with the brightly colorful (it is a kind of Technicolor food, with exaggerated and excessive brightness and artificiality). . . . The films of Tashlin and Lewis are "Jell-O movies" that speak of the technical marvels that brought them into being. (217)

If every generation has its own kaleidoscope, the pre-cinematic wonder machine with the flickering colors and twisting lights that engages viewers in absolute pleasure, *Artists and Models* is, in a way, the kaleidoscope of the 1950s just as *Spider-Man: Across the Spider-Verse* and *Barbie* help make up the kaleidoscope of the 2020s thus far. Instead of bits of glass inside of the mirrored cylinder as in the classic toy, *Artists and Models* offers shreds of comic books, bits of torn-up advertisements, frames of Technicolor movies,[13] blobs of Jell-O, fragments of consumer objects—was that a shard of a tail-light of a 1956 New Yorker?—all shifted around, never the same image twice. And, far from an avant-garde film that looks like a kaleidoscope image, it comes in the guise of a story so hackneyed, so cliched, so predictably silly, that viewers can just sit there and revel in the images with mouths hanging open. Images not as representations of a reality but as visual arrays constituting a reality themselves.

13 *Artists and Models* was one of the last films shot with the Technicolor camera (on Kodak recording stock) before going through the three-strip Technicolor processing and printing. Once Kodak ceased production of that stock in 1955, the camera was mothballed.

AN AMPERSANDED TRUTH

[1]

"We're not a team," said Dean Martin, "we work together" (*Colgate Comedy Hour,* November 4, 1951). Two men, born almost a (crucial post–World War I) decade apart in two different parts of the country. What is it that kept them together: their faces side by side; their attitudes fencing; their bodies as though grown on different planets? A ligature bound these two very distinctive personalities, every whole being greater than the sum of its parts. This ligature—like a pair of cursive letters running into each other—united feeling and action, and was at the same time a shorthand, a capsule for experience, time, memory, and hope.

Looking at Martin & Lewis, consider that connecting *ampersand*. In Dean & Jerry's case at least, the ampersand is more than a signal of conjunction, a stamp of partnership; it *is* the phenomenon, an ornate and always unintelligible glyph, a sign without sound. As a graphic form the ampersand originated as a quickly written cursive "ET" (Latin for "and") with the E and the T partially and distinctively superimposed so that one did not have to lift the writing utensil off the writing surface. Ampersand = *and per se* (1820). A delirious squiggle recognized quickly.

Martin & Lewis: one can translate the & as "and" but to be more honest one must face the totally unpronounceable, the quivering litany that bears remarkable similarity to some of the babbles we hear from Jerry's mouth when Dean prods him & to Dean's irritated prods when Jerry babbles. Slapdash evocation. Mystery. One & the other.

& is a word that turned into a punctuation mark—Latin language transmogrified into punctuation, an interstitial *substance*, a filler, neither subject nor object nor verb but integument. Nothing—not even the word "and"—more powerfully raises to thought the very issue of conjoining two-into-one. Conjoin: not formally unite, not legally merge, not physically overlap. Join together, a branch grafted onto a branch.

Originally handwritten only—and done so hastily as to become a symbol—& is later integrated into the typographer's typecase (some excitingly florid examples can be found in the history of the art: type designers go to town when they come to the pleasurable challenge of creating an &). At one point, its usage was so frequent that it appeared as the twenty-seventh letter of the alphabet, right after "z." . . . w, x, y, z, &. Dean & Jerry, Jerry & Dean.

Audiences took for granted how, when they yukked together—or later, when they yukked solo—their comedy never depended on a connection made rational, on some exploration inevitably gone wonky or some proposal turning back on itself. The comic moments had no temporality. Dean & Jerry's "being together" never truly had a beginning, a middle, or an end. Think of beginnings, middles, and ends as nothing but arbitrations.

[2]

Because the ampersand was a shorthand, ampersanded comedy could be shorthand, too. Here invoked and displayed, never twice the same way, is the lost language of stenography that was invented (sometime around the days of Xenophon) and oriented to speed up transcription of the heard voice (very long before computerized voice recognition in the last days of the 1970s). To the uninitiated, shorthand looked like chicken scratches. These "chicken scratches" were well known in offices, actual and represented, during the 1950s. Martin & Lewis routines sometimes included secretary and/or stenographer characters, but their comedy was also designed to speak to the stenographic mind, the mind that seizes and copies in speed and that was shared all across the corporate world of their time.

Without being able to read and decode a stenographer's shorthand notes,[1] one could get the feel of the process, appreciate the design, just as, watching a Martin & Lewis routine, one could break up in uncontrollable mirth, even sweat and flow with tears and gasp—without really *comprehending* what was going on or why one was reacting this way. If someone asked you what you were cackling about, you would not really be able to explain; and if somebody wanted to know why you liked this duo, explanation would be a challenge in the same way. The routine, the behavior, the climaxes, and also the audience's reception, were shorthands for complex human experiences tossed off or quick-coded by a pair of cultural scribes who were "taking down" the dictation of their world.[2]

1 For a filmic example of shorthand technique look at Hitchcock's *The Wrong Man* (1956), the moment when the Balestreros (Henry Fonda, Vera Miles) are meeting their lawyer (Anthony Quayle) for the first time, and the camera slides away from them to show us the steno pad in use on the secretary Mrs. Daly's lap. As Prince Ali (Omar Sharif) says to Lawrence (Peter O'Toole) in *Lawrence of Arabia* (1962): "It is written."

2 In many cases shorthand was used as an alternative—not only a prelude—to typewriting. During the 1940s, dictaphones were introduced, siblings of, not quite replacements for, shorthand. The dictaphone, a device by which a speaker could record, say, a letter for later transcription into shorthand then type, was in use after World War II using a plastic belt, but it was not until the 1970s that the magnetic-tape dictaphone came out, much more commonly found in offices. Many early machines (using wax cylinders) were produced by Edison, whose Kinetoscope was among the earliest instances of commercial motion picture exhibition. One such dictaphone shows up in Billy Wilder's *Double Indemnity* (1944)—Walter Neff (Fred MacMurray) cannot necessarily confess his crimes to a human being, but he can speak freely into the receiver of a dictaphone.

That Martin & Lewis were short-handing their culture can be understood in two importantly different ways:

First, most obviously, on its surface their discourse was largely unintelligible to the bulk of their audience—unintelligible as in, *not at all like Dick and Jane*[3]—cryptic bleats and squeals and groans and facial extensions and stutterings and hesitations and disapprovals and interruptions, ellipses that easily seemed socially "out of place" in polite society but that also seemed to lack placement or appropriateness altogether. The actions didn't seem to quite fit the situation. And the situations were so warped to begin with that appropriateness went out the window, except within the very artificial confines of the dramatic set. Interruptions galore, apparently without end, going both ways, heading in two opposite directions at once: one correcting the other, one modifying the other, one canceling the other, one putting icing on the other's cake.

Second, in a broad way they synopsized, contracted, sharpened, and articulated the racing pace of culture at the time, the sense of experience not quite understood but flashing by nevertheless, the hope and the promise and also the blocking out of historical memory. Let us say that all comedians' routines are difficult to remember and recount to others; but Dean & Jerry's routines are more than difficult, they are quicksilver.

Sometimes, Dean & Jerry's shorthand looked exactly like an artist's quick sketch, but penetrated to a depth. It suggested (a) the body as an organ of speech, (b) posture as commentary, (c) movement as design, (d) relationship as social critique, and—perhaps most importantly—(e) *speed.*

[3]

> Balzac claims that artistry itself is tied to a quick grasp.
>
> —**WALTER BENJAMIN,** *BAUDELAIRE* 41

The idea of Dean & Jerry's comedy as stenographic inscription could easily be relegated to the status of a convenient, even whimsical metaphor and nothing

3 Dick and Jane readers, for teaching young children, were widely circulated as of the early 1930s. This would have been too late for Dean, but not at all too late for Jerry.

else. But there are two things about their routines, live, on television, or on film, that one does well to remember:

[1] They played to an absolutely enormous audience—not only across America—and could certainly claim what was at the time equivalent to "global reception" as we think of it today. We note Martin & Lewis as the "biggest thing in show business" not as hyperbole but because *they were* the biggest thing in show business (and in an era where "biggest things" and other superlatives weren't so bottomlessly fashionable as to change every month).

[2] Their enormous audience was nothing if not ravenously receptive, a kind of tablet on which their every syllable could be—and was—inscribed, yet also a living tablet that reached out for more and worked to keep up with the patter. Dean & Jerry were literally dictating their angle on everything—experience, time, feeling, love, hunger, fear, urgency, sex, war, you name it—and in rapid-fire shorthand bursts. Key: *rapid* fire. The audience wasn't a cynical one (broad-based, culturally penetrating cynicism began only after the assassination of John F. Kennedy in 1963, and was exacerbated around a decade later through the Watergate scandal). The Martin & Lewis audience wasn't cynical, it was hungry.

[4]

In actual practical usage, shorthand was a way of joining a dictating voice to a page. Joins and joinery were all over shorthand. The ampersand was a cryptic but exciting way of joining what was on its left to what was on its right with a flourish. It brought the left hand and the right hand together in an orthographic applause. It drew one side of a universe into contact with the other. It made unity, as explained by Norman O. Brown:

> The unification of the human race: a mental fight, a struggle in and about men's minds. The rents, the tears, splits and divisions are mindmade; they are not based on the truth but on what the Buddhists call illusion, what Freud calls unconscious fantasies. (81)

And since the conjoining ampersand was an inscribed sign, a sign made by the hand, the joining together seemed indissoluble, at least fully human.

Always through time, Dean would be with Jerry, Jerry with Dean. The "break-up" was only a fable.

[5]

Civilization is propriety. What are the proprieties of conjunction? Can you join absolutely anything to absolutely anything else? And if you are joining, what *kind* of join should you use? It is sometimes "proper" to use the word "and" and sometimes an ampersand instead, since although, as one could claim, they "mean" the same thing, they are clearly *not* the same. And who has the power to choose; & who has the power to choose: the author, the editor, or the typesetter? Was the ampersand used only when a line of type would admit one character but not three (the economic logic underpinning social construction)? On modern keyboards the ampersand was retained as a supernumerary to the number 7, retained for future generations of typists to learn how to produce with the index or third finger of the right hand while the left pinkie hit the SHIFT. A two-hander.

But—: Since it was two-handed; and since it invoked doubling; and since it meant *this* + *this,* why not supernumerary to the number 2? (Who could or would have made a decision like that?)

Regarding the QWERTY keyboard (as it is called, because of the syntactical positioning of those exact keys on the top row beneath the numbers) we know that the very design was laid out *to slow* typists *d o w n* because otherwise their actual (early) typewriter mechanisms would jam or malfunction at the speeds which the best keyboardists could attain.[4] The resultant design was a "speed bump." Note that early typewriters had individual letter or symbol type, each piece of which rested at the end of a long metallic rod that acted with key pressure by lever action. We are experiencing something like that jamming at this very moment as we compose our text online, across an international border. When a typewriter becomes a computer and a telephone line becomes wifi, speed increases, but delays and malfunctions persist. Often in their comedy Dean & Jerry give a hint of this proclivity toward accident,

4 In the 1940s and 1950s, conventional Underwood typewriting machines had keys that were exceptionally heavy, so that one had to develop the muscles of one's hand and fingers just to type "Hello." Jamming and malfunctioning were not hard to produce.

showing how decorative, architectural, commercial, or creative designs were impediments (to us but not to them). Every jam, every malfunction, takes time. And time has value. But time is an element of the comedic routine as they played it.

Think for a moment of expression as production. When one actually types an ampersand one is laboring to compress three characters and two spaces—a sequence of five individual keystrokes—into a single simultaneous action involving both hands and the action of several fingers, manual contortions that many typists, becoming more and more adept over time, taught themselves to do so very efficiently, and so routinely, that they came not to notice. An invisible complexity. What could be a more apt typographical representation of Dean & Jerry's dual aesthetic, itself wound up in an invisible complexity? The gearings and intercalations of that aesthetic also came to be unnoticeable, once the pair had been conjoined in the audience's mind, once the idea of the Martin & Lewis routine was established. Dean & Jerry were like two chemicals thrown into a beaker.

[6]

> The office blues is a mildly depressive state that is mostly a result of deprivation and loneliness. It's characterized by . . . a sense of unreality—of merely existing rather than really living during working hours.
>
> —**CINDY GLOVINSKY**, *MAKING PEACE WITH YOUR OFFICE LIFE*

In the hustle-bustle 1950s, the office was the absolute laboratory of Western culture, the home territory of the ampersand. The ampersand join was an office matter (and, therefore, an official matter). (Dean & Jerry are forever finding themselves at one office or another.)

Office work is notoriously rote: hours spent in front of a keyboard (*not* an easy-touch keypad) beneath flat, uninspiring lighting, bonded into machine/human interactions that replace feeling, bodily movements restricted to repeated motions of the hands, wrists, and forearms, repeated stress injuries creating new disabilities that, if nowhere near as crippling as the muscular dystrophy Lewis spent his entire career trying to eradicate by funding the Muscular Dystrophy Association, still were rampantly widespread in the American population. The archetypal images of American office work—nearly the same in King Vidor's *The Crowd* (1928) as in Billy Wilder's *The Apartment* (1960) as in Alan J. Pakula's *All the President's Men* (1976) as in Terry Gilliam's *Brazil* (1985) as in Steven Spielberg's *The Post* (2017)—show rows and rows of desks occupied by scarcely individuated people keyboarding away on adding machines and/or typewriters, as though in pious reverence for a petrifying system: "All revolutions have followed on the breakdown of bureaucracies," Max Lerner paraphrases Brooks Adams, "and have in turn depended for the consolidation of their power on the creation of new bureaucracies" (409).

Vacuuming out the juices of the soul . . . . .

Needless to say, it was this "system" with which Martin & Lewis were at war as they performed.

Watch Jerry turn even rote labor into poetry and ballet, perhaps never more touchingly than in *Who's Minding the Store?* when, playing at being a typist, he boldly removes the typewriter altogether and performs a typist routine in pure mime (self-reflective mime, as his eyes continually give off "comments"). Exquisite method here, extremely rapid finger movements (there are no keys to resist). How many words per minute?[5] How good are you? What are you worth?[6] Dean was no less dexterous. See the brilliant moment in *Rio Bravo* when from a shot glass held high he pours a drink back into the bottle without spilling a drop.

The organized separation of laborious action from material product (rapid finger; no typewriter) allows us to conceive of a vast army of low-paid laborers spread across the world and busily engaged in making the same bodily gestures, all day long, *no matter what is being typed.* Bills of sale, lawsuits, letters of injunction, contracts . . . click clack click clack. The typist may often be as much a monkey wrench in the system as its dutiful slave, jamming up the works and preventing "work" from getting done.

5 See, for another cinematic take on speed typing, *Populaire* (Régis Roinsard, 2012).

6 Words-per-minute is a standard comparative scale. The value of the individual worker and her [*sic*] payscale is condensed into a single number—how much content can be mapped onto a line before tugging the carriage return, a mechanism made obsolete (unlike the QWERTY keyboard) in the age of word processing. A very competent typist could easily handle more than 90 words a minute (these are measured as perfectly correct words, no spelling or punctuation errors). The then-familiar (but now utterly retro) clicks and dings of the typewriter are fed into Jerry's routine quietly (as though in the typist's mind).

The *Who's Minding the Store?* typewriter bit was a variation of a routine Lewis had performed much earlier, on the January 10, 1954, broadcast of the *Comedy Hour* in the guise of "world-famous concert artist" and "guest virtuoso" Pietro del Canto playing "a new work by Leroy Anderson incorporating the very latest innovations in melodics."[7] As the "internationally famous" Del Canto, Lewis wears formal dress (white tie, tailcoat) and a shock of a wig, and seats himself at a typewriter with great—and false—pomp.[8] There is a candelabrum on the table next to the typewriter, as if he were Liberace[9] seated in his finery and ready to launch into a boogie. Then, suddenly, he engages in a series of exaggerated and physically violent "warm-up" actions with his arms and hands, notably slapping the hands down palms-up (a repeated Lewisian gesture), before "playing" the typewriter while simultaneously "conducting" himself and the offscreen orchestral accompaniment.

The hand bit: *WHAP! WHAP! WHAP!* We see this also in *Artists and Models* when Dean and Jerry have just finished an imaginary feast.

"The typewriter has, of course, been the woman's machine," C. Wright Mills, writing in 1950, reminds us, and in itself it has not led to factory-like effects . . . its operator, equipped with a stenographer's pad, has managed to borrow prestige from her close and private contact with the executive. . . . The typist works only with the machine; because her work is a straight copying matter, her most important traits are speed and accuracy at the keyboard. . . . She is usually closely supervised" (207–8).

[7]

There is no way to think of Martin & Lewis *without* some form of conjunction, *if not an ampersand then something*—as we see with Peter Wollen's use of the *slash* in "Cinema/Americanism/The Robot" (*Raiding the Icebox* 35–71). A slash can indicate "and also" but, as well, "or," and can join two words into a single noun. Sometimes we have dashing of two surnames in typographical

7 Composer Leroy Anderson's (1908–1975) *The Typist*, for orchestra, was composed in 1950.

8 A pomp that would be reprised after 1955 by Art Carney as Norton on *The Honeymooners*.

9 Władziu Valentino (Lee) Liberace (1919–1987), at the time a wildly popular and self-reflexively goofy jazz and classical pianist.

proximity (Martin-Lewis) or a standoffish hyphenation that puts distance between the two (Martin–Lewis). An "and" sandwiched between two dashes (Martin-and-Lewis) is like a made-up run-on word or an epigram (Martin-the-taciturn, Lewis-the-foolish), all blurted out without a pause to allow breathing room between words (Martin as in The-one-who-is-with-Lewis).

Three "great" hybrid joiners are recalled by Nicholson Baker, "the *commash* ,––, the *semi-colash* ;–– , and the *colash* :––," all now "extinct" (82). Imagine, if you will: Martin,––,Lewis. Or Martin;––Lewis. Or Martin:––Lewis. What arcane planetary configurations could these call up? And if they had been billed as any of these on posters and marquees, how might the performance have been or seemed different? No matter what was on the poster, the act specifically and dramatically fooled with proprieties, cast off perfunctory labels, shot beyond the limits of audiences' expectations. But would Dean & Jerry have been as they were, exactly, as Dean-Jerry, Dean/Jerry, Dean––Jerry, Dean,––,Jerry, Martin:––Lewis, whatever: followers of inspiration at the very moment?

At the very moment. That is, without a firm plan in place. Without an overall picture of the arc of development. Without words written and memorized. Without reliance. And, being instantaneous together, *twins.* Whether or not the Martin & Lewis bit was rehearsed and tightly choreographed—one is in no position to know—it seemed, once and always, improvised on the spot. Indeed, improvised on a number of arbitrarily or randomly connected spots, spots that weren't even spots because in effect they were blurs.

[8]

> Mutual giddiness, that's what love is.
>
> —**VIKTOR ROZOV**, *THE CRANES ARE FLYING* (1957)

Wherever you saw one you would see the other during the ten golden years from 1946 to 1956. Because in Western society we favor the discreet personality, the self-operating individual, the individual author who can be named, credited, and promoted as such, the conjunction of two persons always and already carried a certain strangeness. Who wrote this book? How much did Pomerance write? What parts? How much did Solomon write? What parts? Can you label those accordingly?

One sustained (a) the knowledge of being faced with two creative spirits, a crooner and a shrieker, *and* (b) the illusion that these two such incongruous personalities were somehow one. The deep problem underlying this "addition," as one might cavalierly think it, is articulated by Leslie Fiedler in relation to various conjoined twins who were exhibited as curiosities. After Chang and Eng were brought from the Kingdom of Siam to the United States (in 1829, he informs us, carried off "by a pair of Yankee merchant skippers" [*Freaks* 215]), conjoined twins were popularly known by the sobriquet "Siamese Twins." Can we think of Dean & Jerry this way, too, at least in metaphor? If we do twin them in metaphor, what is the resulting image that assaults and lulls us?

"At their most outlandish and terrifying," writes Fiedler of such conjoined twins, using words that could certainly be applied to Martin & Lewis, "they call into question not just the integrity of the body but the parameter of symmetry which bounds our notions of the beautiful and the human. It is as *mutants* we perceive and fear them, as threats to what we cannot help feeling is, or ought to be, the end of the evolutionary line" (203). Further, like Dean & Jerry, "Even before they became show Freaks, Chang and Eng were *already businessmen*" (215; our emphasis). They understood the economics of their exhibition and participated in their self-exploitation, even bringing their wives and children onstage and into posed photographs (which were sold for profit as *cartes de visite* and cabinet photographs). Such exhibitions and family photographs invited gaping onlookers to ponder the anatomical riddle of their conjoined bodies as well as the shared intimacies through which such progeny had been produced and were being reared.

Metaphor has a great power to linger and riddle, to run beneath the surface of rational thought like an underground river. Whatever they were biologically, Dean & Jerry were surely inseparable as a metaphor and then as a myth, at least until July of 1956 and, we argue, afterward, too. Inseparable, in that whichever one the viewer chose to focus on the other remained "attached" as a grounding. The figure cannot be lifted away from the ground. Dean & Jerry either appeared in constant companionship or else in solo turns wherein the absent one was all along predicted, foreseen, existent in the shadow, perpetually absent in negative space. Fiedler points to "the sense of the uncanny implicit in the notion of two humans so indistinguishable that one can usurp the other's place even in the arms of his beloved" (205). With Dean & Jerry, in a similar spirit (albeit more rationalized by the far-reaching logic of show business), were two inseparable bodies—four arms, four legs, two heads—bouncing some substitute for language between them like a pair of conjoined twins playing ping-pong with one another.

[9]

In films like *Artists and Models* and the entire run of *The Martin and Lewis Show*, viewers and listeners are invited to imagine Dean and Jerry sleeping in adjacent single beds and eating most of their meals together—prototypes, perhaps, for latter-day reality-television domestic competitions (like later television's *The Real World*) but surely partners to a symbiotic compact. One finished the other's sentences. A special kind of roommate, indeed. When one ate too rich a meal the other got indigestion. On a May 2, 1954, *Comedy Hour* skit in which the two are sharing a bunk bed in Atlantic City, Dean has the headache, but Jerry takes the aspirin, saying, "I guess you could call it sympathy pain."

Was Jerry *stuck on* Dean?

Or were they *stuck with* one another?

Were they constantly *sticking it to* each other?

Were they, like campers in a wilderness, *sticking it out?*

As the first generation of comedy filmmakers quickly realized—see Alice Guy's *A Sticky Woman* (1906) and Georges Méliès' *Good Glue Sticks* (1907), for examples—glue is a substance that can generate plenty of comic possibilities. (Originally made from animal collagen, the chemistry of glue, it is worth noting, was revolutionized—by researchers at Eastman Kodak—during World War II using ethyl cyanoacrylate, the product that was later marketed as "super glue.")

Super Glue can represent money above all things.

When, after a long period of sniping at each other behind the partner's back, Jerry wanted to dissolve the team in June of 1956, executive producer Hal Wallis was ready for no such thing:

> Our agreement with Wallis stipulated that we work as a team no matter who was producing the picture, and he was adamant we abide by the contract. Y. Frank [Freeman][10] reasoned with him. "For heaven's sake, Hal," he said. "These boys both want to stretch their wings. Can you blame them?"

10 (1890–1969). At the time, head of Paramount Pictures.

Amazingly, Wallis gave in—a little. He said he'd let us do one picture apart if we did three more for him as a team. If we wanted to get out of that, he told us, it would cost us. Big: a million and a half dollars, plus ten percent of the money we'd earned on our last two movies. (*Dean* 281)

In his memoir, Jerry notes the gossip he heard going around New York—*stick-um* gossip: "Are they crazy? Look at the money they're making." And "How would they get along without one another?" (281).

Nevertheless, "to stick with" has a meaning that goes beyond physical adhesion.

Lewis had a way of sticking with a gag until it eventually expired from sheer repetition. The prolongation[11] of a syllable: *LAIIIIII-dy!!!* The prolongation of a spit take, jaw dropped, eyes abulge, gawking into camera. The non-termination of spats, arguing and arguing and arguing and arguing and arguing and arguing and arguing, when the resolution was clear at the very beginning. If there was a resolution. If, in truth, there was a beginning.

[10]

Person and object, ventriloquist and dummy, is perhaps the most apt permutation of the Dean & Jerry dualism—but: which one is the ventriloquist and which one is the dummy? More operatively: which one was pulling the strings?

Martin & Lewis sometimes treat each other—and themselves—more like objects than like living things. In *Hollywood or Bust*, Steve (Dean) is able to get through the front gate of Paramount Pictures by joining a line of studio employees each of whom carries a stiff unwieldy mannequin. He carries his buddy Malcolm (Jerry) as if he too is an unmoving unwieldy simulacrum of a human being. "Really a real dummy," he tells the guard. Then he roughly drops Jerry onto the pavement like a sack of potatoes as soon as they have passed through.[12] In one of the more telling *Comedy Hour* skits (November 4, 1951), Dean is in the office of a theatrical booking agent and, hearing that the

11 Dribbling, drooling, spitting, or in some other way distinctively mouthing in response to a funny or weird moment. A comedic staple.

12 Analogous to Gloria Swanson and William Holden being driven through the Paramount gate by Erich von Stroheim in *Sunset Blvd.* (1950).

agent is looking to book a ventriloquist, he pretends to be one, using Jerry as his dummy. He pretends to manipulate him, affects to make him speak, but treats him less carefully than he would a finely crafted object made of wood: Jerry is dead weight. But Jerry's voice becomes Dean's "voice." Our suspension of disbelief is instantaneous, the play-acting spontaneous and easy. The setting behind the boys is a thin piece of fabric.

The real challenge comes when the agent offers Dean lunch and Jerry, just as hungry, remembers that dummies cannot eat.[13]

13 In *Stuck on You* (2003), by the Farrelly Brothers—perhaps the clearest cinematic heirs to the Martin & Lewis tradition—Matt Damon and Greg Kinnear play conjoined twins, however improbable that conceit, given that, in the true tradition of Arnold Schwarzenegger and Danny DeVito as *Twins* (1988), the two resemble one another not at all. Genealogy: Jonah Hill is born from the Farrelly Brothers. The Farrelly Brothers are born from Jim Carrey. Jim Carrey is born from Martin Short. Martin Short comes from Jerry Lewis.

AN INTERLUDE

POMERANCE
Matthew, how did you get into Dean Martin and Jerry Lewis?

SOLOMON
I saw a Tashlin retrospective in 35mm when I was studying at UCLA during the mid-1990s, and after seeing *Hollywood or Bust* and *Artists and Models*, I was hooked. The films were gorgeous and I loved the onscreen back-and-forth between Dean and Jerry. Bought both on VHS and watched them often. You?

POMERANCE
Well. At the age of six, I was taken by my parents to a local theater (if not a theater across the border in Buffalo) to see *Jumping Jacks.* I didn't have the slightest idea what it was or what was going on, but it sure did bounce. I know I saw *Living It Up* at Shea's Buffalo in 1954 when it came out—a total stunner. Color, you're right. But I'm eight, so I don't know any details.

SOLOMON
What drew you to the pair?

POMERANCE
I have a crystal-clear memory of them singing "Ev'ry Street's a Boulevard in Old New York" while ambling up an avenue dressed as street cleaners and sweeping their cares away. I had *not* yet seen other Hollywood musical films, except for one, *There's No Business Like Show Business* (same year), which entirely electrified me, so this Dean & Jerry moment was in the period of My Introduction to the Musical. I didn't see any actual, live musicals until years later.

SOLOMON
For me it's "Hollywood or Bust," with vocals by both Martin and Lewis, "VistaVision" and "Cinerama." My youngest daughter walked around the house singing it at one point. Always makes me smile!

POMERANCE
"Cinerama," you say?

SOLOMON
Those are the lyrics.

POMERANCE

That's a riot. Because in 1952 I know I saw the first Cinerama, again in Buffalo. I thought I was flying in parts of it. I remember it as an out-of-body experience.

SOLOMON

You were not alone. Douglas Trumbull felt the same way, for one. I'm still disappointed I missed the chance to see *This is Cinerama* in Cinerama in Bradford, England, in 1995. I overslept and missed the screening, a once-in-a-lifetime chance—jetlag.

POMERANCE

I thought you were going to say in the Cinerama Dome on Sunset, because my guess is, it would have been out of this world to go in there and see it. Funny how you came into all this by way of your graduate school experience, and in LA itself, while I came in at a very young age and on the other side of the continent. I know for certain that I imbibed Martin & Lewis a long time before being able to understand what they were, on any level. It was straight imbibition! The plasticity came through to me when I saw Jerry guest-host for ten nights in a row on the Jack Paar *Tonight Show*. I think the show ran 90 or 120 minutes, and he just had the stage—no other way to put it. Looping one thing into another, one outrage eating up another. It was like: neverending. This was in the fall of 1962, when Jack Paar had left, to be replaced later by Johnny Carson and get his own show. But the Jerry presence was like live Dada.

SOLOMON

Sweet nectar, indeed. Sounds addictive. I developed an affinity for films watching local UHF stations broadcasting from Tampa and St. Petersburg, but that consisted mostly of the Bowery Boys. Dean and Jerry weren't really on TV for me, except for the yearly telethon, which I never watched. I think I've appropriated the nostalgia of others to which I have no natural-born right.

POMERANCE

Funny. Appropriate away!

SOLOMON

More recently, since being diagnosed with multiple sclerosis—not muscular dystrophy, thankfully—I started taking more notice of Jerry's violent pratfalls.

Jerry later on suffered immensely from the falls. One can empathize with Lewis's desire to minimize his physical pain so that he could resume his daily activities. When walking becomes painful enough, one loses the desire to walk. When traveling requires too much walking, one loses the desire to travel. Such a condition must have been absolutely intolerable for someone like Lewis, who so much thrived on the thrill of performing and whose performances involved moving with energy and elan while responding physically in the moment to others. To move with ease, with energy, and with coordination, and without pain must have been worth it. Being thwarted continually and unrelentingly by one's body is unbelievably tiring, and makes one less ready to respond patiently or tolerantly to being thwarted by others.

POMERANCE

Just a little word play. *Thwart* comes from the Old Norse, pre-13th C. *Thverr* = transverse. One wishes to go forward, and in being *thwarted* one's world is at cross purposes to that. Jerry, falling, is thwarted by gravity, but also constitutes a gravitational force thwarting the conventional world. And earlier, when you said you were "hooked," I found a smile creeping onto my face as I thought of that bit in Kurt Vonnegut Jr.'s *Cat's Cradle* (1963) where he describes the punishment of being hung on a giant hook (the book is meant to bring a laugh).

SOLOMON

That's truly medieval. I love Vonnegut's *Sirens of Titan* (1959).
Jerry and Dean really foreground the issue of locomotion. Dean seems continually confounded about which way to go, and Jerry makes the allegedly straightforward act of taking a step (or steps) into a complex, labor-intensive production—a familiar feeling for me. Seeing the two in action makes me think: Why are people so intent on getting in one another's way?

POMERANCE

Once the population hits a certain point, and communication is global and swift, everybody is getting in somebody's way. Dean and Jerry are very modern.

SOLOMON

Lewis made falling down into performance art, despite—or because of—the very real challenge that falling can be for those who might have difficulty (or require assistance) getting back up. What happens when you fall down and cannot manage to contort yourself to get back on your feet?

POMERANCE

So: two odd things here. First, Dean just doesn't seem to fall, no matter the circumstances. Perfect poise. Secondly, when Jerry falls, *we never worry.* When we see Jerry fall—surely when Dean sees Jerry fall—there is a poignant sense that he is now out of the picture, for the count. He has fallen out of posture, fallen out of the moment, and will never find his balance again. But again, *Ping!, he's back!!* If we worried (at all), watching Jerry's antics would be torture, of the kind people endured later on with *Nightmare on Elm Street* (1984).

SOLOMON

The key is to avoid falling down in the first place. So, to see Lewis go from standing straight up to being totally horizontal in one virtuosic pratfall is a thing of beauty in part because we know that a little later he will appear to have popped up again, apparently none the worse for wear. But, it actually must have hurt like hell, especially because it was one of the refrains of his physical comedy and he did it repeatedly. His pratfalls are different from other comedians' because they can happen without warning, as an unexpected spasm of the entire body. He goes from standing straight up to completely collapsed, in an instant. A tree has fallen, but in fast-motion, and so quickly that you can't really perceive the way the trunk fell or have any memory of the falling. The way he appears to maintain bodily stiffness at the start and at the finish is also distinctive. Stiff and poised; then stiff and collapsed. Was there a jump-cut or some other ellipsis? How did he get down there so fast?

POMERANCE

Regarding falling, dropping out of gravity, and being *thwarted:* One sees in every routine they did, vocal or visual, radio, television, stage, or film, Dean trying very hard, and very assiduously, to *move forward.* Carry out a project, make a statement, get the attention of a girl, whatever. And Jerry is *sitting athwart* that process, placing himself at cross purposes. Becoming the insurmountable obstacle.

SOLOMON

He must have started having actual difficulty, both as himself and as the Jerry he was in front of audiences, getting back up, letting himself fall down less often, seeking narcotics, alcohol, or tobacco to ease the pain. The urge to move never waned and must have driven him to ever greater exertions. There is satisfaction in exertions, however futile. And Jerry is relentless. Where most other comedians would end a joke, just let it lie (pun intended), Lewis went a step further, then another step still further, then another, no matter how many trips up and down the stairs—onscreen, in outtakes, in rehearsals—(here I'm thinking of *Artists and Models*) may have been involved.[1]

POMERANCE

I had Bell's Palsy when I was about thirty, and for that I was given Percodan for about a week or ten days. Quite a relaxer, as I recall. You had to take Maalox, too, because Percodan eats away at your stomach lining. I didn't have any addictive or other side-effects at all, other than that, afterward, most of my laughter was internal; Jerry, of course, was on much heavier-duty stuff and for a considerably long time. This was given out as the cause of his "blowing up" in the 2001–2002 period. Like a balloon. Then he got back into his—I was going to say "true self" but the thing is, even blown up he looked true.

SOLOMON

One wonders if the "cure" is really worthwhile given all of that—I guess it must have offered precious relief for you and for Jerry, despite the side effects. I don't think he'd have kept taking it if it wasn't helping somehow.

POMERANCE

Maybe he would have, if a doctor had insisted it would take time to start working. It would be a signal error, watching Jerry hit the deck, to imagine that the fall represented genuine clumsiness. It spoke to a *state of imbalance,* which was precisely his message. But Jerry's is "clumsiness," not clumsiness, and is in fact enacted with extreme virtuosity. Look with care at the moment in *The Caddy* when he has placed himself carefully (with care!!) on the ground, his nose kissing Dean's teed-up golf ball. (1) The ball is his pal. (2) His head is the same shape as the ball, but bigger. Dean can hit him if necessary.

1 Notice that the home where Lewis lived for thirty years, at 1701 Waldman Ave. in Las Vegas, has a sweeping central staircase lined with mirrors and a second floor master bedroom, which would have probably obliged him not only to walk up and down the stairs during the conduct of his daily life but also to watch himself climbing up and down the stairs, reflected prismatically! Incidentally, his house had twice the number of bathrooms as were found in the suite in *Living It Up* (See Jerry Lewis House).

(3) He is attempting to communicate with the golf ball, and this is a sincere take on the shenanigans one can find on any golf course on any day: players "addressing" the ball, in their stance, but also whispering imprecations to it as it sails away. (4) Jerry is acting as though the ground (being grounded) is his rightful and natural place on earth. He goes to ground.

SOLOMON

What does this imbalance connote? If the world itself is out of balance, could one, ironically, be balanced, by being out of kilter with the rest of the world? What does the world look like from the golf ball's point of view? Spinning wildly out of control, completely off its axis, no up or down. How to regain verticality, or even horizontality when Cartesian coordinates have been nullified? Can we imagine what the body-cam footage in one of Jerry's pratfalls might yield? Dean serves not as a crutch but as a lamppost to lean upon, wrap himself around. The screen drunk requires it comedically, but Jerry even more, its melodic light shining down, its tempo-fixed pole providing rock-solid stability. The light, as it were, is Dean's voice, whether spoken with his distinctive drawl or sung with his soothing crooner melody. This is why Jerry drapes himself all over Dean so often as well as why he reacts so abruptly when Dean yells at him—the lamppost remains ever stable, but it is as if the light was flickering, in danger of going out. The lamppost provides great prospective stability, but one can gain no purchase on a pole—there is nothing to grab onto—one can only lean on it or try to use it to stabilize oneself and it remains in one place, firmly rooted to the Earth's surface, unmoving. This is fundamentally unlike a crutch or a cane which is expressly designed to assist mobility and perambulation.

POMERANCE

You have to wonder if Jerry watched Gene Kelly's "Singin' in the Rain" number and was dumbstruck to see the way he used that lamppost!

SOLOMON/POMERANCE & POMERANCE/SOLOMON

But the affinity of the man who couldn't stand up for the man who was a tower had a strange, inexplicable effect from the start. Levy recounts how in a 1945 booking each of them held at New York's Havana-Madrid club, they would ad-lib after the last show of the night:

> Bill Smith of *Billboard* caught this after-hours frivolity: "Martin and Lewis do an after-piece that has all the makings of a sock act. Boys play straight for each other, deliberately step on each other's lines, mug and raise general bedlam. It's a toss-up who walks off with the biggest mitt. Lewis's double-takes, throw-aways, mugging and deliberate over-acting are sensational. Martin's slow takes, ad libs and under-acting make him an ideal fall guy. Both got stand-out results from a mob that took dynamite to wake up."

"Martin and Lewis," Levy continues: "The phrase that would launch tens of millions of dollars had seen print for the first time" (65). But Dean as a fall guy—no. Dean was never a fall guy. Dean was a "stand-up guy" who glowed when Jerry fell, with "stand-out" results. And Jerry's results were "stand-in."

POMERANCE
You like that?

SOLOMON
I like it! I like it!

PART II

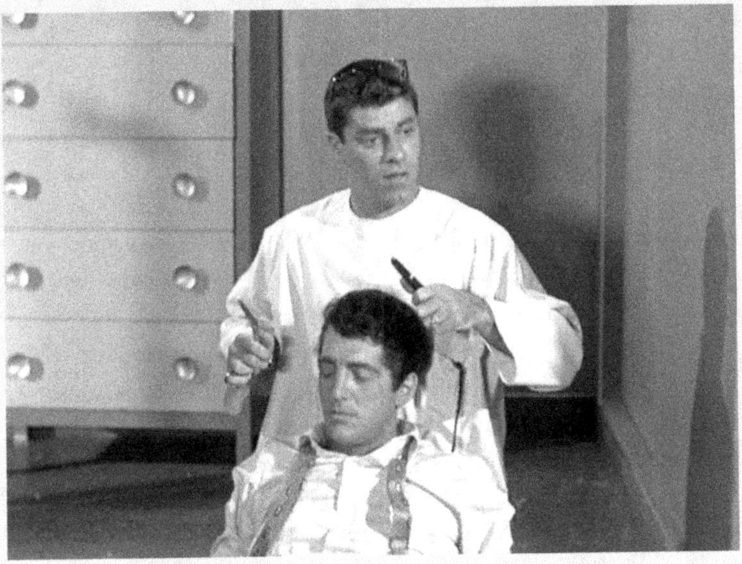

GIVE ME A HEAD OF HAIR

[1]

Dean Martin's father, Gaetano Alfonso Crocetti, was a "very successful" Italian immigrant barber in Steubenville, Ohio, according to Dean himself (qtd. in Freedland 3). It is no surprise, then, that Dino should be concerned with his hair, even unendingly aware of it, especially after he gained some degree of recognition as a singer and nightclub performer. In the 1950s, culturally speaking, there was nothing odd about young(ish) white males obsessing about their hair (see Edd "Kookie" Byrnes in *77 Sunset Strip* [1958] for a case that became virtually part of the language), nor does it seem unreasonable for us to assume that while Dean was young—younger than eighteen, certainly—it was his father who cut his hair. It would probably have been a matter of family honor for dad to do the job as long as possible, if the *ragazzo* was nearby.

Jerry Lewis's hair was a contrasting, and much more flamboyant, subject of jokes from the beginning, especially on *The Martin and Lewis Show* (1949–1953) on radio, where the verbal comedy was larded with "plenty of cracks about Jerry's hair" (Hayde 22). "What's that you've got your hair slicked down with, Mobil oil?" (May 29, 1949). "Well, personally, I like my hair exactly the way it is, pointing straight forward" (June 21, 1949). And so on. And on. Shawn Levy reports that in Chicago, "Dean applied scissors to his partner's greasy pompadour, cutting it into a juvenile buzz" about which Jerry initially wasn't keen; but he "realized how it affected the act" (78). Possibly, it dramatized the age difference between the two partners; and of the two, Jerry becomes the more streamlined. Levy is happy to recount that when he was performing at the Palace Theatre in Times Square, he imported his barber from California "at the cost of five hundred dollars so his hair would look perfect" (79). Lewis himself claimed that his main goal was keeping his hair under control. "I can't stand stuff in my eyes, so I used that shit to keep my hair out of the way." Levy concludes, "Where Jerry's hair once bespoke childlikeness and then represented a kind of cleancut hipness à la Harold Teen or Elvis-just-out-of-the-army, it has evolved into a mark of age, a symbol of a man at once out of touch and defiant about it" (79). We find ourselves being defiant about Levy's comment: rather than being "out of touch" with his age, Jerry, along with Dean, was prescient and profoundly in touch.

Once Jerry split from Dean, he had no stolid Lothario sidekick dropping his jaw and keeping a lookout. Now he turned the world around him into that normalized, lovable, tranquilly well organized zone in which, as an alien form, he could spectacularly land. The antics became even more unmanaged than they had been, more unshaped and amoebic, more outspoken and outrageous, more maladept, more vituperative, more self-regarding, more everything. Jerry was a living spring, ongoingly *letting his hair down* (at first playing the let-down who was letting Dean down and later playing the let-down who was letting down the memory of letting Dean down).

Dean had a million ways of showing how this guy next to him was letting him down, disappointing him, outraging him, just not fitting.

[2]

When consumer society blossomed at the end of the Second World War, the body and its associated "personality" became markedly saleable, a carrier and harbinger of fashion; and in the wake of the new fashion's sweep came a hair crisis. Men were doffing the fedoras that had characterized them in the 1930s and early 1940s. Women were becoming more discernibly businesslike. The male haircut became a vital feature of body upkeep, the barber being a king or doctor for personal style (as we find him in *You're Never Too Young*) and the hairdresser—as shown in Scorsese's *GoodFellas* (1990)—a magician, too. Long hair was especially unthinkable for men in the 1950s—at the sides of the head "long" meant trailing past the top of the ear; the exception was "long-hairs," by which epithet was meant intellectuals, professional musicians, or deadbeats. In the 1960s long hair meant "youth culture" (recall *Easy Rider* [1969]). During the golden age of Dean & Jerry's act, men's tonsorial concern wasn't just short but, how short? The buzz cut was both juvenile and military (à la Beaver Cleaver):[1] little boy pretending he's in the army, and usually beneficiary of a haircut arranged and dictated by parents, not by himself. The ornamental "wave" gave celebrity, especially if there were longish forelocks that could sweep toward or back from the face (a signal early case was Ricky Nelson).[2]

Hair products were triggering the postwar explosion of the cosmetics industry, the latter spearheaded by Max Factor on S. Highland Blvd. in Hollywood and made available to millions of consumers—female and, to a lesser extent, male—through sale in drug stores and department stores nationwide (see McLean). *Colgate Comedy Hour* broadcasts were punctuated by commercials for Colgate-Palmolive-Peet's Halo Shampoo—"Soaping dulls hair, while Halo glorifies it." Cleaning hair is one thing. We should *glorify* hair. Better still, find a magical potion that will do the trick.

1 Jerry Mathers played "The Beaver" on one of the most widely watched programs on early American network television, *Leave It to Beaver* (CBS 1957; ABC 1958–1963), starring alongside Barbara Billingsley, Hugh Beaumont, and Tony Dow. "The Beav'" became an American icon.

2 Eric Hilliard Nelson (1940–1985), younger son of Ozzie and Harriet Nelson, and co-star, with Dean Martin, of *Rio Bravo* (1959).

In standard practice, women had their hair "done"—a man's hair should never look "done"—and tended to keep it at medium length and sculpted. Shoulder length was generally out of the question. The more sculpted the "do," the more urbane. Desirable was a "fashionable style"—hair color not becoming crucial as a commercialized feature until the 1960s and hair length not for a few decades still. The man's terror: going bald, or revealing that he already was. Hairpieces and jokes to cover. The panic for women was a bad hair-do, something that would reveal all too blatantly that one had patronized [*sic*] the "wrong hairdresser" of the moment (Hal Ashby's *Shampoo* [1975] is a satire on this aspect of everyday culture). Many women had their hair "done" once a week, religiously, and with special concern on the morning before an important soirée. The woman of style had a hairdresser whose name she knew, to whom a special tip would be given at Christmas. Men's visits to the barber were routinized and operated on the basis of personal familiarity. Those who had white-collar managerial jobs had cuts or trims rather frequently, certainly every second week at worst. It would be remiss to think that Dean & Jerry were unaware of patterns like these in the culture they wished to copy, dissect, ridicule, and celebrate.

Most commercial hair-care products were directed at women through advertising, with hundreds of elegant advertisements appearing not only in women's magazines like *Ladies' Home Journal* but in the pages of entertainment magazines like *Photoplay*, *Modern Screen*, *Screenland*, *TV Radio Mirror*, and other similar publications during the decade within which Dean & Jerry were together. Jane Powell shilled Lustre-Cream: "It Never Dries, It Beautifies!" And then we had Breck: "Breck Shampoo brings out the shine in your hair. Like brushing 100 strokes." Or Helene Curtis: "SO YOU CAN ENJOY THE MOST BEAUTIFUL PERMANENT OF YOUR LIFE."

[3]

Facial hair is nowhere to be seen on either Martin or Lewis during the 1946–1956 period of their partnership. Dean wore facial hair only after this period, for instance in his solo movie roles in specific cases where the role demanded, as in his stubbled drunkard's look for *Rio Bravo* (1959). When Dean snatches a man's toupée in a public restroom in *Money from Home* he uses it as a fake beard and mustache, part of a disguise to avoid paying train fare. Jerry went clean, always: even super-clean, with an exception being a brief disguise (that is, a Jerry who was not really Jerry) as a French barber in *You're Never Too Young*, and later, in *The Family Jewels* (1965),[3] mustached as an effete airline pilot and using shoe polish to simulate facial stubble as a white-jacketed gangster.

Interestingly, when Orson Welles came to Hollywood in 1939, he was criticized for the fullness of his facial hair and his beard more than for anything else. Generally in the 1950s, a man with facial hair, especially in a recognizable style, was thought either artsy or intellectual or ethnically entitled, as with Prof. Émile Flostre (Michel Auclair) in Stanley Donen's *Funny Face* (1957) or the ersatz plantation owner Col. Harlan Sanders touting his (Depression-era) southern-fried chicken. Walter Pidgeon was the brilliant genius loner in *Forbidden Planet* (1956): with a goatee. Clifton Webb often wore a goatee of one kind or another on *The Man Who Never Was* (1956) and to get him to shave as per the normal regulations of the British Navy at the time hell had to be paid (see Pomerance "Who"). Burl Ives has a mustache and goatee (a southerner again) as Big Daddy in *Cat on a Hot Tin Roof* (1958). Vincent Price has a goatee that sticks out in 3-D in *House of Wax* (1953). But for men onscreen almost always, the mustache alone was as far as one went toward characterization, using it to connect fastidiousness, eccentricity, pushiness and dictatorial mien, or arch dignity. The biggest stars went shaven, and Dean & Jerry were, and intended to continue to be, the biggest of the biggest stars.

[4]

With its proximity to the face, hair is immediately readable as an identity adjunct, a key to articulating oneself to the world. Fictional and cinematic detectives called upon distinctive wigs to mask their identities and pass through the world relatively undetected. Not for nothing did the quick-change artist Leopoldo Fregoli rely on a stock of more than a thousand wigs. In choosing wigs, one would be choosing styles. Hairstyles of the 1940s and 1950s fell into a distinct and limited set, each meaningful and instantly identifiable, slicked down or spiked up with cultural connotations that would have been immediately legible to audiences and performers alike.

To attend to Dean's curlicues and Jerry's military cut is not to suggest or believe that they were influencing hundreds of thousands of others to dress

3 For shooting which, Lewis invented the video assist.

their hair this way; or to believe that they were using hair to try to influence their culture. What it does call us to accept and think through is the fact that when they performed with these hairstyles eminently in place, audiences the world over understood immediately and implicitly how to see, how to accept, how to "read" their characters in the context of that hair. In short, the hair itself was as believable a part of the performance as the crooning and the babbling.

THE TIP OF THE NOSE

Jerry Lewis shared a monologue with the live television audience tuned into the May 20, 1951, broadcast of *The Colgate Comedy Hour.* We give gestures and stage directions in square brackets below. Tonight's show is almost done. He emerges from backstage looking happy but notably weary, in his standard tuxedo with his untied black tie dangling in the way that became *de rigueur* for him later on, when he wanted to be "the real" backstage Jerry, fresh from the dressing room:

> [*Applause. He briefly touches the tip of his nose. Nods to the audience. Touches his hands together. Smiles broadly.*]
>
> Thank you. Uh, ladies and gentlemen, we'd like to say, uh, you know, this is a very fabulous business, you know, this is a very fabulous business, television, y'have to run and change, so, you carry on, you knock your brains out [wrapping hands together]. The compensation is very, very . . .

very wonderful [quickly touches nose, pulls out pocket handkerchief to wipe hands]. You're entertaining an awful lot of wonderful people. People come to see you in the theater [mops face]. Amazing how people know so little about it, y'know. And the people in television don't particularly care to tell people about it because they like it to be sort of a mystery. With me [raises hands in surrender and picks up a thick Brooklyn accent] *I don't go fer none o'this*! [Audience laughter] I don't want people should be disillusioned [looks down, medium close shot, touches handkerchief to lips].

Jerry's tone is frank and confessional, as well as chummy, the way a friend who's an especially hard worker might take a quick breather and confide the secrets of his trade.

Nothing could be easier, of course, than taking that whole *spiel* to be in "bad faith," mere makeup and manipulation, a charade about the charade, a wholesale bamboozle. Yet, Lewis's perspiration is readable as coming directly from the labor of doing the show, no put-on at all, and gives us to recognize that like any and all stage artists, Jerry gives his all when "on," and perspiration couldn't be more normal. (This is *live television:* there is no time for a glycerin spray from the makeup person behind the scenes.) In film, we are guided by the editing and in television guided by the commercials *never to see bodily truths like this:* the sweat, the blinks, the coughing, the fact of the body. Jerry gives the audience the very formal compliment of confessing how wonderful they are at doing what they are doing: he and Dean are "entertaining an awful lot of wonderful people." Pure shtick, perhaps, but also pure sincerity, purely the only thing we are given to see that Jerry has in him right now.

But note how for his punchline, the moral of his little sermon, he shifts to a thick Newyorkese, inflected a little with Yiddish-English as in, "I don't want people should be . . . ." And what is his central message, his *ganze geschichte*?

I don't want people should be disillusioned.

He is explaining, point blank, what the comedy of Martin & Lewis is all about, speaking at least from his personal point of view. He is wary of, not opposed to or feeling himself to be above, committing illusion. Illusion of any kind. Illusion that is so artfully done it does not appear as illusion. If a presentation *were illusory* and *did not appear as illusion*, the audience could cruise along *taking it as real, believing it to be uncontrived.* And then, afterward, waking in the cold light of morning, they would feel let down by an intensive disillusionment as they realized that they had been hoodwinked. And worse, they would see suddenly that the "dream world" they'd thought themselves to be inhabiting, and inhabiting with such joy, never actually existed. How horrible this let-down would be, claims this Jerry who is talking to us now. *I don't want people should be disillusioned.*

He is also saying he wants his audience to catch an illusion, hold that illusion, take pleasure in that illusion; and therefore he is admitting openly that the staged performance is indeed, and with deliberate intention, an illusion. The maker of an illusion is pointing to what he is doing, and with scrupulous honesty.

If we look at the whole span of work that Martin & Lewis accomplished, what we see is obvious illusion following obvious illusion following obvious illusion. Far more than the illusions, the *obviousness* of them. "I don't want you should take an illusion seriously as a thing, I want you should know that an illusion is an illusion." Very Platonic. And more: "I want it should be the illusion itself, the illusoriness of that illusion, that gives you pleasure."

I STAND UP, I FALL DOWN

To know, and even happily, that we meet unblessed; not in some garden of waxed fruit and painted trees, that lie of Eden, but after, after the Fall, after many, many deaths.

—ARTHUR MILLER

[1]

For affirmation, a colossal negation. Once we ascended from the amphibia, left the waters behind, stood up on our own two legs (so that we could see what was a long way off and free ourselves from smelling the world from down low), and walked, we were ready also to march, and then to strut, and then to pirouette—all the while relying on secure knowledge that our legs would be pillars of support to keep us on high. To suddenly lose that support is to spontaneously collapse: the body, the spirit, and the whole history of the human race. The taller we grow, the further the head is from the ground that is about to receive us when we fall. To stand is to be on the precipice of falling. To be a walker is to be a tumbler.

But in comedy, the tumbler is a *tummler*.[1] In comedy, the fall is the pratfall, where the iconic body drops face-forward into the dirt. Henri Bergson reflected on the person suddenly becoming a thing (26): the old banana peel gag is a classic example, since when the person slips he becomes nothing but a weight subject to gravity. Certainly in all cases The Fall is a blatant querying of erect posture and all its superiorities and benefits. And a momentary debilitation, loss of rhythm, and situational puncture. A powerful tool for someone like Jerry Lewis, faced with the cool aplomb of someone like Dean Martin. Dean's postures are invariably confident: I'm standin' here, I'm not fallin'.

In other comedy duos, the Chief Goof is partnered with an Assistant Goof, not a super-stable icon of noble beauty.

Jerry's characters lived—as Arthur Miller put it—*After the Fall*. The fall and the Fall into disgrace, the Fall out of Eden, the Fall into confusion, the Fall out of gravity, the gravity of the fall. Entering gravity. The legs that were failing Lewis as he fell were, in truth, only "failing," as far as audiences could tell, since every pratfall was deftly conceived and executed with finesse, this depending on very subtle muscular capacities in the legs. As with Ray Bolger's "faulty" dancing as the Scarecrow in *The Wizard of Oz* (1939), so Jerry's frequent pratfalls: don't be deluded into thinking that the moves are not summarily athletic and far beyond an untrained person's capability. The fall had a shocking effect in its particular dramatic circumstance precisely because the audience never anticipated it, not, at least, precisely. The posture had been stolidly erect as an iron statue's. The pacing had been intensively muscularized. The stance had been proud or cramped, showy or diminutive, but always in control and always with exactly the right leg power for the pose. Poised with the power of the legs and then suddenly . . . BOOM! Note: BOOM!, and not KA-BOOM! IN KA-BOOM, the KA is the half beat that is the preparation, the announcement, the "get ready" and with Jerry there was no KA.

1 For more on *tummlers*, see "In the Playroom," above. Lewis knew them well when we worked the Borscht Belt in the early 1940s.

Jerry, then, was a figure who could both leg it and lose his footing. Lose footing on cue, lose it "by accident," lose it chaotically. He "attacked" Dean perpetually by making Dean's social and interpersonal footing unstable, by shaking up Dean's suaveness. Yet that suaveness always reappeared instantly, as though it had not faltered, as though with Dean faltering was impossible.

[2]

The legs are the central human embodiment of modernity, the source of the bustle. All of locomotive inventions, the wheeled cart, the train, the automobile, the aircraft are extensions of our preponderance to walk from here to there.[2] When the legs gain a mind of their own, s/he who is legging may run amok.

An especially telling example of legging it, one that, albeit screened after the Martin & Lewis break-up nevertheless looks back astutely to what was happening in the duo performances, can be seen in *The Patsy* (1964). Indeed, when we see the scene in the KLUTZ-TV 44 studio, it is virtually impossible not to believe Dean is standing just off-camera, preparing to enter and deliver a reprimand. A teen pop music show is being broadcast (shades of Dick Clark's *American Bandstand* [1956], televised by ABC from the Prospect Studios in Los Feliz from 1964 onward). Stanley Belt (Jerry)—he can really belt it out!—comes in from the wings, introduced to the rabid teen audience as composer of the newest hit and . . . Here Now!, ready to *lip-synch* it. Part of the comedy of this moment is the blunt declaration that lip-synching is about to take place, since in most televised and lip-synched singing the mystery of lip-synching was carefully preserved (as it is with Lina Lamont at the end of *Singin' in the Rain* [1956]).[3] Stanley's "hit" "I Lost My Heart in a Drive-in Movie," now proceeds fully, in a stunning array of jabbering and face-twisting, as seems only right since the song is full of strange band

2 See Sol Worth and John Adair's study of the Navajo, for whom walking is being.

3 The irony, of course, is that Debbie Reynolds's speaking voice was actually dubbed in parts of the film by Jean Hagen, who plays Lina Lamont. Betty Noyes dubbed several of Reynolds's songs. Earl J. Hess and Pratibha A. Dabholkar, *Singin' in the Rain: The Making of an American Masterpiece* (Lawrence: University Press of Kansas, 2009), 145–47.

sounds and incomprehensible lyrics (Stanley cannot remember them, except for the chorus, so the mouth movements startlingly [and hilariously] do not match what is heard—the record act again). To get to the microphone, Stanley crawled out of the wings, peeped at the audience hoping for friendship, and stooped; then with a very deliberate—too deliberate—pace he lurched forward (Frankenstein's monster reborn), as though instructing his body to make every calculated move. Right foot, move! Left foot, move! Right foot, your turn! Left foot, now you! Move that right foot. Move that left foot. One and-a two and-a three and-a four. (I am a spirit inside the body of a robot designed to look like a human being.) He became so obsessed with his own action of producing action that his action was acted upon, and now with the singing this pattern seems repeated, as though it's the only pattern his body knows. The show's host was standing with his hand-held mic on a tiny platform raised possibly six inches or so off the floor, and eager Stanley crashed into it with his feet, tripping his way up. Jerry "tripping himself up."

[3]

If walking was the baseline of the transport revolution, then shoes were the absolutely essential underlying precondition for that baseline. On June 22, 2018, three pairs of Jerry's "stage boots," all made by Florsheim—two stamped with his name inside of them; two in patent leather; two of which were "tap boots"—came up for auction, with expected prices of around $500 a pair. The shoes turned out to be size 10, the average size for a man's shoe (*Solomon's size, in fact, and the idiot didn't bid!*). The heels looked high—as in the kind of "elevator" shoes a performer would wear to increase his "height." Perhaps this was because of "metal Capezio taps attached to bottom," as the auction catalog indicated (*Property from the Estate of Jerry Lewis* 42). As for Dean's shoes, while it often looks as though he is wearing "elevators" we know that higher heels were both a fashion for men and a strict necessity for tap dancers. Shawn Levy writes, "Jerry and Dean were the same height—a sliver over six feet each—but audiences around the world have always carried the . . . impression that . . . : Compared with Dean, Jerry was lilliputian" (62). It is perhaps interesting that after Dean's death, no multitude eager to bid for his shoes was imagined by those who managed his estate.

Of course, Martin & Lewis's gags benefited hugely from the dream-vision of "little" Jerry, as Lucille Ball called him. Audiences needed Dean to be taller than Jerry, needed Jerry to shrink somehow, so that Dean could become a giant. Sympathy was cast downward toward Jerry, a sweet, harmless, innocent David looking up at a menacing, if crooning, Goliath. *Don't hit me!!* That Jerry's antics could well be read as violent, aggressive, and antisocial in themselves—a diminishment in the audience's judgment—letting him "fall down" made for a balance. Jerry may come to seem like a tree growing against a chain-link fence, adjusting its shape to bend and curl around it: so many years of being next to Dean has forced his growth to be receptive to Dean's dignified posture, has made Jerry seem to twist like a vine around a trunk.

To walk in Jerry's "stage shoes" implies another level of grace, of being "light on one's feet":

> I have spread my dreams under your feet;
> Tread softly because you tread on my dreams.
> (Yeats, "And He Wishes for the Cloths of Heaven")

What on earth would it be like to literally walk in another man's shoes, when the other man is Jerry? Jerry didn't learn to walk the "Jerry walk" because of those boots, but would he have walked that walk or squawked that squawk without them? Surely the very fact that they were being put up for auction suggests that some audience was prepared to believe he wouldn't have.

What about dancing in another man's shoes? If you owned those Jerry boots, would you dance the Jerry dance—say jitterbug as in *Living It Up*? Where is the magic, in the body or in the shoes the body wears? The self or the appurtenances? (See, for a rhapsody on this, *The Red Shoes* [1948].) If the dancer is in the body, where in the body—the fingertips, the brain, the knees? The dancer and strutter must use the legs, surely; but is the dancing and strutting *in* the legs? And might some of it have rubbed off on things that were proximate to that specific body—Frazer's "contagious magic"? It was certainly the case that when audiences were wowed by a Martin & Lewis routine—not the script, the acting-out of the script—they were seeing magicians at work and wondering, as we all are wont to do, "How did they do that?"

How? The extent of an arm movement as it sweeps through the air . . . the amplitude of a squawking voice . . . the precise length of a jaw drop . . . the length of time measured in seconds where one partner stares blankly at another's goofiness . . . the swerving hips . . . It all looks as though it's just simply, naturally, and obviously *there,* BUT HOW COULD IT BE? All of what we see in a Martin & Lewis routine is achievement. How is the achievement accomplished?

We often talk (casually) about the influence of an artist's *hand.* Wanting to shake hands, wanting a piece of paper with an autograph, wanting to buy an antique original letter signed, wanting a dedication in a book bought in a long line-up at a bookstore. The whole long Western tradition of creativity flowing out of the hand (the Sistine Chapel). (For an extreme case, see Robert Wiene's *The Hands of Orlac* [1928] or Fritz Lang's insistence that his hand be seen onscreen in his films.) But with Dean & Jerry, over and over and over, we have creativity flowing out of the feet, the "dance of the hours."

Yet our sense with movies, here and always, but perhaps nowhere more acutely than with Martin & Lewis, is that the feet are continually dancing away. The movement of the feet screams, "Distannnnnce!" As much as they draw us in, movies keep us at a distance, separated by screens as well as by the inexorable flow of time, with artifacts like Jerry's boots offering us the only possibility of touching "the stuff that dreams are made of," as Sam Spade (Humphrey Bogart) says in *The Maltese Falcon* (John Huston, 1941) (see Sobchack "Chasing"). But, *wearing* the past, encasing oneself in it, is the lure of vintage clothing of all kinds, on the feet and upward, a lure amplified by production-worn apparel. To own Charles Foster Kane's "Rosebud" (as Steven Spielberg reportedly does) is one thing, but Dorothy's Ruby Red Slippers are another, because—provided your feet are smaller than Judy Garland's—you could actually wear them. If you clicked the heels three times and murmured "There's no place like home," where would those shoes take you?

[4]

It might seem ineffable today, but when Dean & Jerry were in their prime there was nothing odd about a performer who had a full range of skills: patter as well as yuk as well as song as well as dance—and exhausted himself physically. The whole marathon. Dean: he sings everywhere; he dances in a routine with the Step Brothers on television, in *That's My Boy,* in *Living It Up*, and always smoothly and convincingly. His patter is elegantly timed. Jerry: he sings in *My Friend Irma* and in *The Delicate Delinquent*; he plays piano in *The Nutty Professor*; he conducts in *The Bellboy*; he dances in *That's My Boy* and *Living It Up.* In *Damn Yankees* he played Applegate and sang "Those Were the Good Old Days" in some hundred and eighty performances starting February 28, 1995, on Broadway; and then in the West End. Dean, for his part, sang every venue you could imagine . . . yukking his way between the songs. Dean was not only famous as a singer, he was famous universally, his voice strikingly available even when his picture was not. It was a relaxed voice, an at-home voice, a lullaby.

[5]

For a wisp of a moment in *Pardners*, Jerry lays aside his squeamish squiggle, his uptight bodily rictus, his slipping and his sliding, his hunching down in the face of The Great Other, and . . . strides. He is being educated by a cowpoke (Jeff Morrow) on what can happen during a robbery, and is told that in the gang there is a spy. "A spy!" he bellows, then clenches his teeth with seriousness, puts his arms to his side, and clomps across the room. (A parody of the movie cowboy clomping into the saloon.) Less a stride than a caricature of a stride, of course, but as all of Jerry's moves are caricatures we can penetrate the sheath of form and see plain, everyday Jerry-style striding. This is not the only time he strides on film, but it is a standout example. Dean would never stride with quite such exaggeration and self-consciousness, not even in *Rio Bravo*; his constitutional restraint and habit of underplaying would never have permitted it, onscreen or offscreen. Let us say that Jerry's big strides and Dean's big strides were differently big, but awkwardly or in harmony they were making big strides together, almost as if they were both wearing mythical ten-league boots. Always moving forward. Always progressing. And ahead of their time.

Yet progressing through precise arrangement and calculation.

When Stanislaw Lem (1921–2006) writes in 1986 about a futuristic navigator locomoting across some planetary surface in a *strider* (in translation by Michael Kandel), he could be describing Jerry Lewis. The immense strider was made by engineers who "wanted to put a man in the place the heart would be if the giant were living" (22). Imagine that Lem is writing about the Jerry we see lurching, scrambling, stumbling, jerking, tripping, slipping on the screen:

> He made his first, tentative, small step. In the lining of his suit were thousands of electrodes, sewn in supple spirals. Pressed against the naked body, they gathered the impulses from the nerves and muscles and transmitted them to the Goliath. Just as to each of the skeletal joints of the man there corresponded, in the machine, a magnified, hermetically sealed joint of

> metal, so for each group of muscles that flexed or straightened a limb there were cannonlike cylinders in which pistons moved, pushed by pumped oil. But the operator did not need to think or even know about all this. He merely moved as if walking, as if treading the ground with his feet, or as if bending his torso to pick up, with outstretched hand, a desired object. (23)

What if "the hundred-ton legs, thrusting forward, were halted too abruptly" (26)? The accommodation of the intelligence to the body supplying it, the coming to terms, as one grows *up*, with the legs, the nerves, the muscles all operate only with thought, operate under command, until a point comes when thought is no longer required, or when it is elided, and one merely trudges along through the day. The intelligence inside the Jerry character seems profoundly like the naked being inside the suit inside the Goliath, the spirals in the suit conveying every impulse to the pistons which stressed the hermetically sealed joints. For this one, however, thought is never *not* required. Dean, by contrast, moves as though unconscious, as though his daily life is a dream.

(Regarding movement and halting, especially halting too quickly: Jerry's legendary joint afflictions were produced, at least partly, by his doing that. The years of Percodan didn't help much.)

[6]

Consistent with the anti-Cartesianism of his jiggling persona, Jerry rarely moves in straight lines or right angles; rarely simply goes for a walk; but instead makes an endless series of arcing curves and Brownian jags around the stage or set. One wants to trace these movements as in a Bil Keane *Family Circus* cartoon, to reverse engineer the path he tracked around the stage or the set. Spirals, curves, reversals, re-reversals, stops and starts. Jerky jerky stops, leaning over, leaning backward, jerking to the side, starting up again without warning. Nothing could be more "organic," but getting from point A to B for Jerry was never a matter of moving directly "in a straight line," but always traumatically circuitous, indirect, hesitant, and belabored, a journey defined by countless detours and expending at least five times the energy that any other individual would use in traversing the same space. With Dean, of course, we see what looks like movement in the absence of energy, the definition of laconic; moving minimally, exerting barely perceptible effort to make his way through space. Even his dancing appears strikingly devoid of exertion, a matter of shuffling and swinging, assisted by gravity and the tendency for a limb in motion to remain in motion—Newton's Second Law. Dean's mobile tranquility was especially visible against Jerry's flailing limbs, stumbling steps, turning and turning and turning back yet again—all with verve—appearing incredibly energetic and exhausting. Was Dean's poise similarly exhausting? One saw the volume of perspiration that inevitably accompanied the end of a *Colgate Comedy Hour* show or sketch, mopped from foreheads, absorbed by shirts, jackets, pants, and of course footwear.

Here consider Dean's conundrum. While Jerry is unpredictable and unmappable in this way, he must find a way to make their paths intersect strategically on cue, make an entrance at the right time, find a place to stand at just the right juncture and remain there for just the right duration, move congruously with his own performance, all without colliding accidentally. Colliding "accidentally" is of course permitted, and is worked out. But actually colliding? Impossible. (Actual collision can produce injury. Injury causes trouble.)

Think, too, how Jerry's utterly un-fluid movement is exceptionally generous in its way. The Law of the Conservation of Energy states that the sum total of energy in the universe is a constant. Thus, whatever Jerry expends is absorbed by the people and things around him; absorbed and potentially used for good. Dean exercises a different kind of effect on his partner. One can imagine Dean's poise and calmness also available for absorption. Both energize their environment by twitching and lolling through it. Both contribute energy to the scene. Indeed, Jerry energizes Dean, who might well seem too relaxed, too lazy, to sing until Jerry spins around him, and then the voice comes out straight and clear. The straightness and clarity of Dean's voice only spurs Jerry on further.

In our own scholarly moment of eco-criticism, we find something bizarrely sustainable—if not totally generative—about Jerry Lewis's and Dean Martin's strange ways of helping each other move and grow.

[7]

How widespread is the belief that the healthy, proper, vigorous body is an athletic one. Athlete as supreme model—with muscular coordination, lithe movement, competitive strength, and speed. Even more than the body, the body's fluid dance. Athlete as sprinter, as boxer, as runner backward and forward, as climber, as contortionist. And not only the body in motion but the body in graceful motion. A body showing itself off. The ultimate body.

In *That's My Boy*, a long and bizarrely sedate opening sequence, almost cringe-worthy, has the quintessentially adolescent "Junior" Jackson (Jerry) in repeated confrontation with his aggressive, panicking, nostalgic father, "Jarring Jack" (Eddie Mayehoff, winner of *The Hollywood Reporter*'s Look Achievement Award for this performance), who has an insatiable need for his hyper-nerdy son to transform into the athletic hero he himself was in high school. Junior has every conceivable weakness, from allergy to awkwardness—there is not an iota of hope that he will become as agile and gorgeous as "gorgeous hunk" Bill Baker (Dean), whom we see jitterbugging with the super-svelte Polly Bergen at the school prom. Jarring Jack is non-plussed to see that the man who sired this paragon of masculinity, this Uber-male, is the diminutive, balding, wheezing Henry (Francis Pierlot). Audiences cannot but notice how Jarring Jack finds it positively incomprehensible that a jock like him, heroic fighter on the gridiron and by implication one of those stalwarts who went to war and kept the American flag flying high, one of those clear Alpha male types, could have produced a weakling son like Junior who has trouble even standing up. Sperm as destiny. (That is, immaculate conception in patriarchy, in which women play no role.)

Jarring Jack offers an exceptionally crisp portrait of a broad social condition that in the early 1950s took the form of a particular panic (that has changed form, but not intensity, today):

> A key aspect of this public panic was the idea of "degeneration." Underpinned by the rising "science" of eugenics, and supported by revelations about the poor physique of army conscripts, there was a widespread belief that urbanization and demographic trends were leading to the sturdy elements of the Anglo-Saxon race being swamped by an increasingly debased underclass. Because this impending national disaster was understood as arising from a crisis of manliness, many resulting interventions—the Boys Brigade, the Church Lads, the Legion of Frontiersmen, and others—took urban male youth as their focus.... [Robert Stephenson Smyth] Baden-Powell [founder of the World Scout movement] shared with many contemporary publicists a view given apparent support by the success of the Japanese in their war against Russia (1905–1906) that manly character

> and self-discipline (rather than economic or technological advancement) provided the foundation for national greatness. (Knights 49)

In *That's My Boy,* it is "manly character" that is present to excess—repeatedly startling excess in Jarring Jack, and absent—painfully absent, as the plot has it, in Junior.

One of Lewis's many guises is the stereotypical skinny "Jew boy." As such, he was at least implicitly the butt of jokes that were tinged with antisemitism; indeed, one can wonder whether antisemitism played a much broader role in Lewis's public reception (and, by obversion, Martin's). Many cultural stereotypes of the postwar era (which originated much earlier) consistently took jabs, casual but sharp, at Jewish masculinity. As Daniel Boyarin explains, "There is something correct—although seriously misvalued—in the persistent European representation of the Jewish man as a sort of a woman. More than just an antisemitic stereotype, the Jewish ideal male as countertype to 'manliness' is an assertive historical product of Jewish culture" (Boyarin 3–4, quoted in Desser 281). Boyarin is writing in 1997, perhaps in an echo of Dean & Jerry.

Lewis did not make a public spectacle of his Jewish identity, nor did Martin make a spectacle of his Italian Catholic one. Perhaps the closest Lewis came to publicly wearing a yarmulke was in sporting the propeller-topped beanie on episodes of the *Comedy Hour* while playing juvenile characters. The beanie as a sartorial signifier of youth was itself already firmly ensconced in American popular culture through Bob Clampett's children's television program—one of many based on puppetry—*Time for Beany,* aired on Paramount Television Network (1949–1954).[4] The title character's name was derived from his headgear. Presumably, at least with the Lewis version, the spinning propeller atop the cap meant that in myth if not in reality the wearer could fly, could be, in effect a *vogel. Vogel,* of course (a German word pronounced with the first letter as "f"), slides readily into *feigel* (angel) and thence into the common Yiddish epithet for the homosexual, *feigele.* As a characterological construct the feigele, it need hardly be said, was the "manly" man's worst nightmare.

Not for nothing was an iconic portrait of Jewish masculinity-as-beauty (Boyarin's deep thesis) brought to screen at more or less this exact moment by one of Lewis's Gar-Ron Playhouse chums Tony Curtis (starring opposite

4 Some will recall a later animated show, *Beany and Cecil.*

his wife, Martin & Lewis co-star and fellow Gar-Ron player Janet Leigh), in the biopic *Houdini* (George Marshall, 1953).

[8]

If Jerry was a hypomasculine *feigele*, Dean, on his part, was a hypermasculine *Vogel,* extraordinarily cultivated, oiled for perfect operation, and with a thoroughly lubricated singing voice: *Volare!* When Jerry met Dean for the first time, he used the epithet Harry Horseshit to describe him: "That was what we used to call a guy who thought he was smooth with the ladies. Anybody who wore a camel's-hair overcoat, with a camel's-hair belt and fake diamond cuff links, was automatically Harry Horseshit" (*Dean* 9–10). Jokes about Jerry's weak body constitute one of the major motifs of the Martin & Lewis oeuvre, along with astonishment at and adulation of Dean's Olympic one. In their radio show, scripted by a stable of writers who seem content to recycle much-used riffs, jokes at the expense of Jerry's physique are nearly as frequent as jokes about his early pompadour hair. In the *Comedy Hour* there are gym skits in which Jerry plays the proverbial "98-pound weakling"—in legion Charles Atlas ads placed tactically inside popular comic books, the "98-pound weakling" is the one whose ribs or matchstick legs were "showing." This shtick can be turned on its head. In *Sailor Beware,* Jerry the nerd-weakling is improbably harassed by a few dozen shapely girls. Escaping them, he must cross a road: two steps forward, two steps back, back, forward, forward, back, waving his arms as his long gangly legs don't quite carry him where he wants. On the far sidewalk, after a crowd of followers boards a bus (and he is left with the doors closing),[5] he falls to the sidewalk and is soon picked up by two MPs, as though he is a straw man.

In all actions the athlete shows military superiority, a capacity to fight for land and life and honor. The perfect body will save us. The athlete who will fight for victory is already the soldier in prototype. And why, after all, must the soldier be a muscle-man type? Marvin Harris:

> Our received wisdom in this matter is that males are naturally more aggressive and ferocious because the male sex role is naturally an aggressive

5 A beautiful foretaste of Hitchcock's cameo moment in *North by Northwest* (1959).

> one. But the link between sex and aggression is . . . artificial. . . . Sex is a source of aggressive energy and brutal behavior only because male chauvinist social systems expropriate sexual rewards, allocate them to aggressive males, and deny them to passive, nonaggressive ones. . . . The myth of the instinctively passive, tender, motherly female is simply an echo set up by male chauvinist mythology concerning instinctively brutal males. (106)

Sexual rewards: In every film they made together, Dean "winds up with the girl" and Jerry is almost always still trying . . .

Dean had Roman good looks, muscles, glow, casualness, healthy lack of self-consciousness, all of which already for audiences summed to a certain enviable archetype. Because Jerry was already typecast as "klutzy and inept," unable to fit in anywhere, unable to complete any task to other people's satisfaction—*but usually unaware of being that way*—he was ostensibly less predictably effective at physical labor, including fighting. He would use his mouth, and what language he could muster, but not his hauteur, his superior attitude, his hands.

Goffman suggests that for audiences, "watching is doing" (381). This would imply that gazing at Dean & Jerry, viewers "inhabit" one or the other, or both, of these bodies, very possibly to the point of unpleasant discomfort or at least strangeness. Dean & Jerry know this, and the embodiments they present are intended to lure viewer consciousness and in this way show us ourselves.

People considered underdeveloped or incorrectly developed or developmentally "abnormal" have often been subjected to corporeal corrections. Generally, without specific models (produced for us by particular athletes, stars, celebrities, and cultural icons in particular activities), the idea of regularized postures, limb usages, positionings, balances, and so on is up for grabs. Generally, at the very least in movie culture, the body awkward in motion is corporeally "wrong," that is, wrong for the corporeal ideals we espouse. But a cultural espousal of a form has its basis in cost and benefit to a controlling propriety, not in the forests of nature.

Frank Krutnik, who referred (somewhat slightingly) to Dean & Jerry as "the handsome man and his monkey," noted between Dean and Jerry a "conflictual harmony" ("Sex" 113). For Chris Fujiwara, Martin's "smooth imperturbability in the presence of chaos made him a perfect foil" (35). But Dean goes far beyond acting as a foil. He displays a kind of mindless grace, as though his body automatically assumes poses of Attic beauty; and balances itself in all environments with exquisite ease. This is a carefully performed exaggeration. In *Artists and Models*, when he sings about his "Lucky Day," he moves up and down the stairs with seemingly effortless grace. To move through the world mounting and remounting physical obstacles with such coordination of feet, legs, and torso, all while singing mellifluously—well, "Lucky Day" indeed! We do not see Jerry Lewis singing with graceful ease during the period he is working with Dean Martin; it happens for the first time in the 45 rpm singles he recorded for Decca shortly after the break-up and in *The Delicate Delinquent* (1957), as he sweetly covers Arthur Schwartz and Howard Dietz's "By Myself." Working beside Dean, by striking contrast, he is strutting the golf course in *The Caddy*; twitching around his sickbed in a strikingly immodest, blazing robe in *Living It Up*; jerking his way across the street in *Sailor Beware*; timidly meandering around the living room in *That's My Boy*; rounding the staircase with lawn chair and umbrella in hand, only to drop all of it, in *Hollywood or Bust*. . . . When, *post-Dean*, he changes disguise and places himself at a piano or stands coolly in a doorway or lounges on a couch or sits at a dinner table or holds a golf club over his shoulder (*King of Comedy*) . . . he is transformed as though by magic into a super-normal male, possessor and displayer of the "proper" body. The wounding, marring, utterly maculating twistedness is magically gone. He has become what "he was always supposed to be." But in the case of Jerry, and that of Dean & Jerry together, this "supposed" perfection was openly played out as *supposed,* in short they both exhibited a certain grace or klutziness *and queried its nature.* Queried, for entertainment and not for pedagogical improvement. As a team, they were far from stupid about the body; but they were also—importantly, we think—far from superior in attitude.[6]

The weak male, the loser, in this case he who is un-manned by muscular deterioration is culturally repressed. Jerry played at being the un-manned weakling, but no more frequently, and really no differently, than he played at being brash, played at being socially maladept, played at being vocally uncontrolled, played at everything (including, in *Living It Up*, at dying). If, as we have suggested, the world was a playroom for Dean & Jerry, surely it was all the world, everything they could lay eyes upon. There is no doubt that Lewis

6 Some have seen Lewis's performances as a cruel parody of the disabled and have made uncurious, punitive connections to his lifelong work to raise money for the Muscular Dystrophy Association. This seems highly problematic to us.

could spring around a stage or set like a veritable gymnast. (Not for nothing does he perform as an acrobat in *3 Ring Circus*.)

[9]

Nothing is naturally effortless; no movements are naturally graceful. The casual airiness Dean exhibits, again and again, wasn't there at the beginning for him, but through trial and error he learned how to show it. We can see Jerry's "klutziness" as indication of a person trying hard to manage himself but not yet having reached that level of success. Before we learn to manage legs, even to bring their existence or non-existence into our awareness and consciousness, we must work at our legs as a problem: how to make the extensions or their absence part of the self? Consider the struggle of walking: irregular uneven strides made possible only by a cane that bears part of one's weight, head bowed in apparently rapt concentration.

In *At War with the Army*, Jerry takes "audible" steps, walks as though under some internal direction. Pfc. Alvin Korwin (Jerry) enters a cabin to meet 1st Sgt. Vic Puccinelli (Dean) . . . is waved off . . . moves into an inner office to meet Supply Sgt. Miller (Danny Dayton) . . . is waved off . . . stands still . . . is told to go back to the first sergeant . . . turns . . . is told no, go around . . . looks confused . . . is instructed to use "that door" . . . looks at the door . . . takes a few steps that way . . . suddenly remembers to salute, raises a salute . . . sees that the Supply Sgt. isn't catching it, busy as he is with some document on his desk . . . creeps over in front of the desk, keeping the salute . . . sees that the Supply Sgt. still isn't catching it . . . squats down, lower, lower, lower, until his head is at the level of the Supply Sgt.'s head, still keeping the salute. The Supply Sgt. looks up, gives an irritated perfunctory salute back . . . at which point, shifting his balance, the squatting Alvin collapses to the floor. PUNCH.

(But the joke's not over.)

He gets up . . . clumps to the door . . . goes out . . . reenters the outer office from the outside door . . . walks up to Sgt. Puccinelli . . . and is rebuffed again.

The whole little routine is like the operation of a machine (Chaplin in *Modern Times* [1936]), the parts being gestures and the arrangement being cyclical. One thing after another, no move out of place. But also: every move an aria. That Alvin's legs cannot support him in a crouch, yet when he uses them to walk they work. Yet when he walks there is a curious form to his walking, something in blunt contradistinction to the many other creatures we see walking, marching, shuffling, standing, singing, and generally living on their legs in this platoon. This "form" is his stepping—Jerry's stepping—*as though to an unheard count.* One can virtually hear that brain at work: *Step, Step, Step, Step.* STOP. *Step Step.* STOP. *Clump clump clump clump clump* STOP. A silent voice, a silent "audible" track guiding, supporting, enticing, directing this brave but hapless soul.

We may recollect the general dictum, that the Army is filled with foot soldiers, that the foot soldiers fight *on foot,* that they "leg it" from place to place by marching, that legging their way through terrain is the fundament of their action.[7] All of the many soldiers we see behind and around Alvin merely walk, merely march, merely stand; walk, march, stand. Alvin, a different kind of creature, talks to himself, as it were. "Go there." "Come here." "Stand still." "Take a step, take a step, take a step, take a step, take a step." He is the only soldier in this platoon—perhaps even the only soldier in the Army; perhaps the only soldier in the Universe—who takes steps to get things done. Or takes steps *around* getting things done.

[10]

But what about Dean?

He can seem to be above walking, and often appears to be veritably gliding from place to place. A telltale—and celebratory—moment in *Artists and Models:* "Boodle-le-oo, boodle-le-oo / Boy have I got news for you..." Dean sings at a sidewalk stand where comic books are sold, then *lopes* forward. (As though an invisible "wagon" is drawing him along.) He turns and heads across the little street, which is to say, *toward the camera, and offhandedly between moving vehicles.* He raises his arms in preparation for boldly stepping onto the sidewalk, but we see him just step up, from behind, *eliding* the leg action. Now he's shticking with the incomparable Kathleen Freeman, who has a grocery bag, while behind him a little kid is loading up his wagon with her food. Graciously Dean takes the bag and lowers it to the wagon—again, no leg work. Now, as a little girl in candy-apple pink strides past to lead the way, he and the little boy start rhythmically "stepping" along: "I'm going to

7 Was it Napoléon Bonaparte who commented that an army marches on its stomach, not its feet?—in this way, of course, pointing sharply to the feet. Much more generally, as to marching, soldiering, and feet consult Sombart.

march, march, march along the / Avenue . . ." Then he's going to fly, fly, fly like little birdies do and he hops onto the wagon and flaps his wings as the boy pulls him along (a grip to end all grips). This is positively, absolutely, definitively *not* Jerry-walking, Jerry-twitching, Jerry-stomping, Jerry-strutting, Jerry-creeping, Jerry-whatever it is of the feet and legs that makes Jerry Jerry. The grace of seeing the wagon and hopping on in a fluid gesture—very much like water flowing upward—is a full contradistinction to Jerry's perennially getting the environment wrong.

Is every tiny graceful move of Dean's an implicit criticism of his partner's emphatic klutziness? If Jerry is the dancing tribe, frenzied, unpredictable, Dean is the totem pole around which the tribe must dance. Jerry's spasmodic extension of self works principally because there is a stationary, stolid, unaffected force to balance them. Dean always has secure footing.

Or, as in this *Artists and Models* routine, Dean gives up moving, and here lets a child move him (adorably) instead. Once again, and coming from Tashlin but applied to Dean not Jerry, the structural principle of contrast: if Dean is to hop on a wagon and be pulled along *so that he needn't trouble himself to walk*, the servitude of the puller is a requirement, and the more the puller looks like an already-disenfranchised type (ideally, a child), the more casual does Dean look allowing the routine. Like professional singers everywhere, he gestures with his arms, the extended arms, palms visible, a signal to watchers that he is working to hit a supreme note or to finalize his song.

Posed, Dean as though calls out: "Look, but do not touch!" We can look at Jerry looking at Dean's sculptural form, as though in a late nineteenth-century stereoscope card that played with the desire to look past flat surfaces, two-dimensional representations (like Dean's reflected image in the mirror seen at another point in the film), so as to apprehend—if not make contact with—the fully three-dimensional form so inadequately expressed in two dimensions.

"The rhythm of our breathing and the beat of our hearts are part of the experience by which we measure a work of art," writes Kenneth Clark (27). There can be no doubt of Dean's essential, composed, grounded rectangularity of form, nor of Jerry's peripatetic, usually open-mouthed, jerky, undirected encirclement:

> The relation of head to body determines the standard by which we assess all other proportions in nature. The disposition of areas in the torso is

related to our most vivid experiences, so that, abstract shapes, the square and the circle, seem to us male and female; and the old endeavor of magical mathematics to square the circle is like the symbol of physical union. (27)

Certainly Dean and Jerry are two manifestly antinomic forms, two abstract othernesses in the deepest sense of what Clark points to, so that in their routines we find them trying to achieve a physical union that seems categorically impossible yet also interminably desirable. To square the circle, and at the same time to round the square.

By virtue of posture, Dean never seems pathetic; Jerry never doesn't. What Dean does, by offering this self-image as Perfection, is to turn Jerry's everyday humility into a caricature, and it is the caricature that makes possible our ultimate and deeper understanding.

Dean's position is remarkably fragile, however. His persona exudes the sense that he does not *really* belong, doesn't really get the social nuances, because he came from humble origins and has not an aristocratic bone in his body. Of course, were his origins discernibly patrician, his position inviolable, there would be no comedy. In film after film, he is aspirational, striving upwardly through dress and bearing, as in *The Caddy*, trying hard to fit in with the country club set, even though he clearly does not belong, even if—or because—it involves snubbing his buddy, who is relegated to a serving role.

Very frequently Dean signifies American upward mobility—the story of his life. Thus the frequent reversion to a Cary Grant impersonation on radio and television, Grant being another icon of ladder climbing.[8] Despite Grant's own relatively humble biographical origins in Bristol, in a working- and middle-class American context his acquired accent screams privilege and Old World entitlement, a certain "natural" suavity, as in *Bringing Up Baby* (1938), where he cozies up to East Coast privileged elites (Katharine Hepburn et al.). In the Grant guise, Martin can slip into a persona of privilege, someone who doesn't strive to perform productive labor.

As to climbing, Martin never gives the impression of *needing* the heights but makes as though he is already where he should hope to be. He was not like Jerry, inside whom there was something undeveloped that threatened to

8 Grant's learning the voice and bearing that so many came to identify with him is often elided. If we look at him in *None But the Lonely Heart* (1944) or *Sylvia Scarlett* (1935, where he is an acrobat) we find a "lower," more vaguely Cockney type. He changed his class for George Cukor among others, the way many British citizens change their social situation by modulating their vocalization.

remain undeveloped no matter how hard he tried to develop it. Not only a kid who hadn't grown up; a kid who wouldn't grow up; a Peter Pan, yet one who would splutter and fall (like Icarus) if he tried to fly. Dean was his Daedalus, safe and stalwart and sensible on the ground.

[II]

Class and class issues being off the record in America (land of equal opportunity), the constant striving of Dean and of Jerry—their stretchy sketches—appears natural, part of their idiosyncratic natures, because it may not appear to be class striving. Less perceptibly, it was a portrait of The American Personality, never at home, never truly relaxed. Watching Dean & Jerry one could feel oneself bubbling in the American cauldron, mirrored approvingly by these two strugglers who belonged only because they so obviously didn't belong. Dean didn't belong with this *schlemiel.* Jerry didn't belong with this Casanova. Or: Dean belonged in order to be charitable to the *schlemiel*; Jerry belonged in order to venerate the Casanova. Legging it up and dropping into the *boue.*

Were they using their legs to *walk upward,* or to *hold a position*? Not on the discernable surface. On the surface the leggings were all personality.

Jerry is plasma, Dean is sculpture. Sculpted because filled out, chiseled, not gawky or molded. Sculpted because idealized *already.* Italian Marble vs. Play-Doh.

"I LIKE BLOOD!"

[1]

The comic-book movie has come to dominate the cinema box office, yet when it opened in VistaVision, *Artists and Models* was, as it remains today, a far more thoughtful consideration of the comic-book world in relation to the everyday. What contemporary comic-book films ask of their viewers is to dream their way into the animated universe, to believe in the characters as real, and to treat the stories, fabulously ornamented as they are, more or less like other dramatic adventures. What *Artists and Models* asked was that the viewer might think about how it comes to be that comic books exist in the first place and about the obsessions they nurtured.

While *Artists and Models* addressed the multitude of comic-book fans—an enormous multitude at the time, ravenous for comic-book material—what is more important is this question: expert as he was about comics as a form (having been an accomplished professional cartoonist and animated film-maker previously) and being in a powerful enough creative position by 1955, if Frank Tashlin had wanted to make a comic-book movie of any kind at all, how was his focusing on Martin & Lewis the absolutely perfect way of doing so? How do Martin & Lewis jibe with comic books? What is comic-booky about them?

One possible answer begins with the gap between plasticity and rigidity. Jerry could assume a series of distinct guises that were as supple and ever-changing as the drawn image, morphing, morphed, and altogether morphable, subject to endlessly mutating modifications, extensions, erasures, and re-drawings. Think of Henri-Georges Clouzot's *The Picasso Mystery* (1956), released just six months after *Artists and Models*, in which we see the evolution of individual Picasso paintings from a privileged vantage point on the other side of the canvas as it were (Pablo Picasso is painting on a pane of glass)—paintings that changed seamlessly from one thing to another with additional brushstrokes and continual alterations.

This plasticity—or "plasmaticness," as Eisenstein called it ("On Disney") —reaches its physical apogee in the massage sequence of *Artists and Models* but is also constitutive of Jerry's performance style, which shifts as quickly as the frames in a comic book. Eugene (Jerry) is being given a professional massage by a burly, heavily muscled Scandinavian Viking full of well-meaning zest and energy. Not butchering or twisting him but certainly kneading him like so much dough. Body – massage table – muscular hands – pushing and pulling, a living machine. Because Jerry's limbs so frequently indicate an impossible flexibility and limberness, a fantasy of negotiating the physical world with preternatural bodily litheness, we have no trouble assuming in this massage that his legs are twisted around each other, malleable beyond malleable. If this were to be taken as a serious massage, it might well commence and end this way, only. Instead, however, before we can count to ten, Jerry's masseurs have been wrapped up into nothing less than a living and breathing pretzel. And he is able to stand and watch.

"Plasmaticness" is the quality of unbounded change and motion, stretch and pull, release and contract. In his solo work later, Lewis very often appears to do things that live-action cinema cannot do. He becomes an animated character (without being technically animated). In *The Big Mouth* (1967), he leans over a dock and his legs extend impossibly far. In *The Nutty Professor* he finds himself waking up with his arms so long his hands are beside his feet.

As the viewer tries to engage with this plastic body, the viewing body becomes plastic in response, like Jerry in the prologue of *Hollywood or Bust*, first an American movie fan, then a British movie fan, then an Asian movie fan, then a French movie fan, then a Russian movie fan. Shape-shifting all around, cross-cut with shots of Dean rotating a globe onstage before a curtain. But, in order that the receiver not lose the receptive self altogether in the act of watching, there is the constantly reassuring, if irritated, presence of Dean as stolid, dominating master of the frame.

[2]

The dramatic stakes in Martin & Lewis stories are not the stuff of Action Comics #1, the first published appearance of Superman (June 1938) or of the Marvel Universe, but instead the stuff of *Archie* (1942–present). Archie and Veronica and Betty and Jughead, all residents of small-town "Riverdale" (fictional geographic location unspecified). Unlike today's comic-book action movies, where the Fate of the Universe hangs in the balance yet paradoxically no one seems really to care, the Dean & Jerry stakes rarely rise above the level of the casual everyday. If a plot ever swells to invoke a Cold War crisis, Soviet spies, and a missile testing site as in *Artists and Models*, it turns out to be nothing more than a farce. Thus, the comic universe here works in a totally different gravity than envelops superhero stories. Everything being plastic, no real danger is ever encountered, no real threat, no promise of destruction, no bomb to catch before it blows, no realistic derring-do.

Martin & Lewis themselves became fictional comic book characters in *The Adventures of Dean Martin and Jerry Lewis*, in which Dean & Jerry are hardly super-heroes—much less heroes of any kind—but instead, just a couple of regular guys. Jughead and Archie.

[3]

During the mid-1950s, approximately one billion comic books were sold each year in the United States—pop. 170 million—a market that meant almost $100 million in annual revenue for the predominately New York–based comic-book publishing industry.[1] But comic books, regardless of the magni-

1 For an exciting fictionalized account, see Michael Chabon's *The Amazing Adventures of Kavalier and Clay* (2000).

tude of sales, did not please every citizen. Ever since World War II, civic and religious groups had pressured federal, state, and local governments as well as the industry itself to censor so-called obscene and violent elements in comics, and by the mid-1950s comic books had been unofficially declared a national problem. Although surveys indicated that as much as one-half of the adult population read comic books, reformers focused on the potential threat of so-called crime and horror comics to children, arguing that the visual immediacy of illustrated panels had significant adverse effects on impressionable juveniles (Feder 1–6).[2] The reform movement was partially appeased in 1955 with the formation of the Comics Code Authority and the appointment of a comic-book czar, Charles Murphy, who had the power to enforce strict guidelines of industry self-censorship analogous to the film industry's Production Code Administration (Weisinger).

Associated with the growing "problem of juvenile delinquency" during the 1950s was this issue of comic book influence—what the host of the television panel show in *Artists and Models* (Art Baker) sententiously tells the audience is "the monumental problem confronting your children today" (as though it were children, not their parents, confronted by the "problem"). Purportedly devoid of any educational value, sermonizes the host, comic books are responsible for a "five-year old kid that was caught stuffing his grandmother in the trunk compartment of a car"—"an extreme example of comic book influence." When asked by this man if comic books influenced him to that extent, Eugene responds, "No, I didn't learn to drive 'til I was eight," and claims, indeed, that reading comic books *has* served an educational purpose:

> I learned how to grow poison plants in a windowsill flowerpot, how to keep the tarnish off brass knuckles, also how to start a fire by rubbing two gasoline cans together . . . how to make a hangman's knot, and . . . how to prepare rat poison so that it spreads like peanut butter.

Such absurd examples of comic book influence were just the type of "crimes" that comic book censorship ordinances sought to forestall; for example, one 1955 legislative measure prohibited the sale of any comic book that depicted the very crimes that Eugene reels off:

2 How far we have come: January 2023, rather than the Bible (or the Koran), newly elected U.S. Representative Robert Garcia (D-California) chose to get sworn in on an issue of *Action Comics* #1 (among other personally meaningful printed matter).

It shall be unlawful and an offense for any person to sell, offer for sale, attempt to sell, exhibit, give away, keep in his possession with intent to sell or give away, or in any way furnish or attempt to furnish to any child under the age of eighteen (18) years any "comic" book, magazine or other publication which, read as a whole, is concerned with an account of crime and which depicts, by the use of drawings, the following crimes as defined in the several chapters and articles of the Penal Code

(a) administering poisonous and injurious potions
(b) aggravated assault
(c) arson and other willful burning.
(Qtd. in Feder 58)[3]

The "dangers" of comic book influence are further represented in the film by the character of Richard Stilton (George Winslow), a vicious little boy left by his mother, "chair of the second elementary school district," at the publisher's office for babysitting while she goes shopping. Richard bites Mr. Murdock's thumb, throws a letter opener like a dagger at Eugene, and bellows in a deep voice: "Who cares about the Bat Lady! She's too tame—she stinks—no blood! I like blood!"

3 It would seem to have been comic books, not poison, disturbing legislators. Frank Capra's *Arsenic and Old Lace* came out eleven years previously; and there were legion other motion pictures showing images of poison and poisoning.

EYES TIGHTLY SHUT

[1]

An interesting and vital directional issue is raised in joking, where the comedian's and listener's inability to see a gag's punchline coming (even at the penultimate instant) makes for the explosive moment. To fail to discern that punchline, even in gross shape, is roughly equivalent to being abstracted out of an eclipse through hypnosis, anesthesia, physical departure, or kidnapping, etc., *right at the key moment.* Abstracted, one would have to think before reacting, but in comedy one reacts before thinking. Jerry's characters very often do seem abstracted in this way, that is, not ideal audiences for comedy, because at the key moment they *fail to find themselves funny*, seem to vanish into thin air at the laugh moment. This vanishing is performed through Jerry's use of the eyes, his blank look.

We see it over and over in Eugene's face as he confronts his buddy Rick in the bathtub in *Artists and Models*—he is for the briefest of moments, but repetitively, out of his body: what he does and says is preposterous, but *he doesn't get that.* It seems necessary for him to see Rick failing to get him before he himself grasps that he is impossible to understand.

[2]

Dropping out of a moment is one technical option available for closing off a joke, and there is more than one way to drop out of a moment. Close the eyes so that one cannot see where one is; magnify one's presence so that it eclipses one's moment in social space. Both are exemplified early in Norman Taurog's *The Caddy*, as Harvey Miller Jr. notably *doesn't* use his eyes at a moment of comic payoff and pays off in billboard proportion. Note that swiftly letting one's attention jump "onto a billboard" while talking face to face with someone is yet another way of "closing the eyes" to where one is. Harvey and Joe are being interviewed in their dressing room by an elderly female reporter, Miss Lorelei (Mary Newton), who is doing a story for the "*American Weekly*":

> LORELEI (ingratiating): You boys seem to have more fun than the customers.
>
> HARVEY (escorting her): Sit right down here and we'll find out just how everything came about. Where were you born?
>
> LORELEI (taken aback): Scranton.
>
> HARVEY (excited, trademark high-pitched squeak): Scranton!! Well, that *is* a coincidence.
>
> LORELEI: Were you boys born in Scranton?
>
> HARVEY (with a pronounced lippy pucker): No. *Then an eruption of buck-toothed laughter, but with the eyes screwed shut.*

By the style and magnitude of that trademark equine laugh, Harvey is making more than one direct statement:

[c] I do realize I just delivered a punchline, thus, a laugh is in order. I acknowledge and approve the expressive form called "laugh."

[d] So *I* myself will deliver that laugh, since I am so fervently convinced it is in order.

[e] I am momentarily, Miss Lorelei, forgetting your existence completely, notwithstanding that our whole little conversation happened only because of you. But also:

[f] My way of doing the laugh is not only a huge expression, it is notably huge—beyond laughter a kind of billboard advertisement for laughter.

The conversation with Miss Lorelei is small-scale, human, simple, situated, momentary—even forgettable. But the explosive laugh is proportionately scaled for a billboard. *I laugh and simultaneously announce that I am laughing.* More: *I laugh to you, Miss Lorelei, but I simultaneously announce to the entire world that I am laughing, I entertain you with my laugh much more than I could entertain you about whether or not we are from Scranton.*

Our breaking this fleeting moment into such minute detail is a particular choice of film-analytical methods. To understand the social world as essentially arcane and organized by mysterious and potentially unknowable principles (which seem to be silently and unreflectively grasped and abided by, by everyone else in a given situation) requires spelling out every possible implication, all of the connotations hidden behind every single denotation. What did s/he mean by that? How should I respond? How should I respond now? And what was that gesture all about? Is this method tiring? Yes it is. Welcome to our world. Welcome to Jerry's world. We take this one explosive laugh apart, just a little; but all of Jerry's guffaws could be taken apart this way; and all of Dean's calm postures of observation.

Dean watches, after all. Dean surveils.

As to that particular GUFFAW: the eyes *tightly shut.* The shut eye is an abrupt termination of wakeful presence, a withdrawal from the scene simultaneous with an involvement. *I do not see myself being here and now in the way that you see me here and now.*

Now the boys must rush out of their dressing room to do their stage routine. We jump into the audience as Harvey Miller is introduced and dances out from screen-right, grabbing the MC's hand and doing a Charleston, his head thrown back, a huge grin on his mouth, *and his eyes still shut.* Transported in delight. Carried away by nostalgia. In his own world. He quickly proceeds to accept the audience's raving applause, to quiet the band, to fiddle with the mic stand and upend it so that he can pretend with the round base that he's driving a bus: *what else does one do with a thing like this?* With the crowd he yuks along, "uh!-uh!-uh!-uh!," again with the *eyes closed in bliss* or else in unmitigated confusion and loss.

Dean steps out from left, as Jerry raises the mic way above his head. They banter:

JOE: Don't you want me to sing?

HARVEY: (In exaggerated Brooklynese): Yeah, but I t'ought we could do a song togedder boat![1]

"Togedder *boat?*" subtly mimics Dean. (There is an early-twentieth-century Lower East Side Jewish inflection to the addition of "both = *boat*" as a tack-on. The placement of the adverb at sentence's end, derived, like much Yiddish, from German. Dean is a long way from Yiddish, from German, and from Brooklyn.)

On "Yeah!!!" Harvey screws his mouth up one-sided and *shuts his eyes* as he yukks (Yuk: *Yeah, I know you think I'm ridiculous, but* . . .). Again: when Harvey laughs he closes his eyes. This as though to block any ongoing sights from disrupting the humorous moment, as he feels it, because just as he cannot seem to focus and cannot seem to locate he is also unable *not* to feel things. Nor is the humorous moment, for him, a cause for mirth; it has a musical perfection, a harmonic correctness, and with eyes closed he is savoring that perfection. Anything "out there" could constitute an interruption. Once again, optical reduction to a linear chain of eventful happenings, cause-event-effect, with no global perception of circumstance, framing, situation, or emotional moment. Yuk-yuk, and I am closing myself to reserve this for my exclusivity, my exclusivity that can appreciate harmony. And ... *I invite you to join me.*

Orson Welles is said to have remarked that it was very rare indeed to find an actor who could make you believe he thinks: not here in the dramatic moment, by what he says but elsewhere, generally. Jerry always, in character, makes us believe that Jerry—actor and character—thinks: but probably not the way we do. Dean's show of self never admits that he might be thinking.

1 After his break-up with Dean, Jerry's solo singing career began in earnest with the 1956 record album *Jerry Lewis Just Sings.*

[3]

Consider optical acuity without directional focus. *The Caddy*'s Harvey is walking on a golf course with his girlfriend, Joe's sister Lisa, surrounded by a huge crowd of onlookers. He peers ahead anxiously to try to see Ben Hogan[2] off-camera, way up ahead. Joe, meanwhile, is squinting and chewing a bun, unable to fully taste while also fully opening himself to the sight of the world. Harvey tells Lisa not to worry about money because he has bet a whole two weeks' salary on Hogan, whereupon she becomes distraught: "Harvey, what are we gonna do?!" He looks at her in a two-shot, squints in thought (squints his thought through), then turns his head to look off-left with a gleam in his eyes and his mouth opening in a grin, the open-mouthed, eyes-askance diabolical gleam. "Come wit' me, Lisa!" and he leads her off, with his mouth open and one eye screwed shut. *He's going forward from here, but he only half sees where to.*

Is shut-eyed Jerry living in an exclusive dream world while he moves through the day? Is Dean permanently in charge of this shut-eye, is he the baby sitter? As their films together progress through the 1950s, is Dean more and more exasperated at Shut-Eye who won't wake up? Does Jerry possess an alternate reality, a happy memory of the past, a hope for the future, stored away in there, privately mapped, to which he returns at any instant by shutting his eyes? A private reality so easily accessed, in fact, that he needs shut only one eye? Since we are given to *witness* this eye-shutting, again and again at the apotheosis of a comedic moment, can we gather that his interior world has some maximal value for him, outshining reality? That as a punch line he escapes to that inner world . . . That for him, the punch line is always something very private. . . .

Alvin's eyes are languidly closed in Hal Walker's *At War with the Army* as, shoveling out food to an army platoon, he sings, "The Navy gets the gravy but the Army gets the beans"—especially in a phrase, "Mammie I love ya," a direct imitation of Al Jolson, or in another phrase where twisting his hips he sings, "You get a wacky dame" with eyes tightly screwed shut. Soon later he is alone with Vic (Dean), who berates him: "I've been coverin' up for ye!" while Jerry stands before him abashed, head dropped, eyes closed. Eyes closed in shame? Or eyes closed in retreat to a sanctum? Or eyes closed because it's all a puzzle too difficult to make out without a struggle in the interior.

2 William Ben Hogan (1912–1997) was the major golf star of the 1950s.

[4]

Given the general priority of a star's eyes in the construction of the star face and the fact that in his own star portraits we find Jerry with bright eyes open and accessible, can we conclude from the prevalence and continuity of eye closings, through his career, that the retreat inward they suggest is a move of special, paramount importance to him as he works? We watched on YouTube an on-set interview with him in England, 1969, where he politely and intelligently answered a chain of questions; but one of them came a little closer to the bone than others and while speaking, cigarette in hand, he looked upward and with his free hand rubbed an eye half-closed. Are the exaggerated postures and gestures we so often see with him in fact extensions of the eye closings, ways of using the rest of his body to close himself off to everyday life by pushing his moves through the limits typically imposed in social convention? Escape by self-billboarding. Indeed, when the eyes are tightly closed, are not other physical gestures—including particularly the open mouth—dramatically emphasized, amplified, thrown out of balance? More mechanically: does he use the physical stretch in order to "close his eyes"?

The combination of open mouth and tightly closed eyes is infantile, of course: the baby yearning for food. In early life, as the optical system hasn't yet been developed for depth vision and focus, the idea of opening the eyes for navigational purposes is a premature conceit, it being far more important to get the mouth open wide enough to receive nourishment even badly aimed. We sometimes wonder, looking at open-mouthed closed-eyed Jerry, whether he is feeding, not preparing to utter; whether the tight closure of the eyes is a way of feeling the hunger of the interior, the open mouth being a passive receptacle.

While Jerry's eyes are closed, Dean, although he sometimes opens both eyes wide for effect (often in response to Jerry's antics), seems to take in everything around him yet to care about none of it. Total affectless surveillance. For Dean, the private unstated world is the one he's looking at, its arrangement, its secret interstices—not something inside him. Of course, given these two dramatic models of looking, Dean's and Jerry's, any viewer's way of responding to Martin & Lewis would depend on which road she chose, and how closely she was watching.

[5]

Double-Cross. Crossed eyes suggest roads intersecting, as though in looking at danger one must scout many directions at once, and when one does that, the lines of sight cannot fail to intersect. In *Hollywood or Bust* Dean asks Jerry at the craps table, "Can you throw snake eyes?" (i.e., a pair of ones on the dice) and Jerry responds instantly by giving a spasmodic eye cross, "*Snake* eyes!" In a moment he tosses plenty of "snake eyes." He is urgently cross-eyed as Julius Kelp holding up barbells in *The Nutty Professor*, a man on point of exploding, and here we may think him envisioning an immediate future, what in fact happens as though the eye crossing activates it: the gym weights smashing down to the floor and carrying his arms with them. In *Rock-a-Bye Baby* Jerry's Clayton Poole watches a group of men playing poker in a fire station, and when Salvatore Baccaloni[3] says he will cut Clayton's throat if ever he sees him with his daughter, Jerry gulps with horror and goes cross-eyed. One can easily recognize that the eye cross—technically speaking, *esophoria,* a particularly notable functioning of the ocular muscles, and relatively rare in the population although by moving an object closer and closer to the face one can artificially produce it[4]—is a signal for a character's being *in extremis,* a kind of plea for rescue, albeit silent; just as one can know that the tranquil smile conveys satisfaction, peace, rest. Crossed eyes have their own reality, their own force, quite independently of a catalogue of short-form symbols. They convey multidirectionality. They convey debility and/or pain. When Jerry's eyes are crossed, things are not going the way he wants them to, the world is confounded, he cannot find a pathway that will lead safely (and swiftly) from the surround, inverted as it is, into the private world of the self. That it is not infrequent for him to cross his eyes suggests the world is generally a confusing place.

Most typically in crossing the eyes, as one makes the left eye turn to look rightward, the right eye automatically does the opposite. The cross-eyed expression is a momentary stasis, a station between points, indicating a direction of action that is held midway, not taken to its final point of rest. But if

3 Italian operatic basso (1900–1969). He sang at La Scala, where he was influenced by Arturo Toscanini, as well as at the Royal Opera House, Covent Garden (singing in *Turandot*), the Philadelphia Grand Opera, and other companies.

4 We are grateful to Ariel Pomerance for briefing on crossed eyes.

the esophoric action were taken to its resting point, the left eye would swivel all the way around to look at the right eye looking. The right eye would look at the left. Without a mirror, the subject would be looking at the self, but also looking at the self's actual *looking*. Both the persona and the action would be viewed in an instant, a double-cross: who one was would be taking over what one was doing; what one was doing taking over who one was.

[6]

Withdrawals and Evocations. As much as crossed eyes suggest duplicity, doubling, and doubt, they also call up thoughts of disorientation and helplessness, thus, finally, a surrender to circumstance. In sudden loss of control is sudden passivity, a sense of being lost, the muscular flaccidity of stasis. As evocation at such moments, Jerry produces little more than a highly amplified vowel sound, which is the pure voice of feeling unshaped by learned, mastered, articulating movements of the glottis and tongue. The cross-eyed monster is thus also the fool, the outsider, at least the outsider apparent. Caught entirely off his guard, frozen in shapeless panic, inarticulate except in the base sounding of emotive tone, he challenges all the prescriptions and finesses of elaborate culture, all the sophistications and statuses, tactics and territorialities. He becomes a thing at once nonindicative and inactive, caught in the web of circumstance.

Dean sometimes crosses his eyes when he is completely exasperated, as he does in *Artists and Models* when (still in the bathtub) he is trying to decipher the telephone message which Jerry is trying to relay from Mr. Murdock without speaking. Most frequently, however, Dean brings forth a listlessly easygoing presence and relaxed response—he sees straightforwardly and also, of course, straight.

[7]

While Jerry looks idiosyncratic, a twitching river of expressive gesture, facial mobilization, and orchestration of vocal tone, spasm, and collapse, Dean, sensitive as he may be to any acoustical information coming out of Jerry's mouth, seems in attitude and response not to really see this partner he cannot stop looking at. He shows a fully receptive, yet also fully blank, or perhaps unconcerned, gaze. He has willing eyes, but doesn't see the rhythms. His musical timing has taught him how to wait for Jerry's riffs to finish, but he doesn't *appreciate* them. As time goes by, from 1950 onward, Dean's obliviousness starts to grow, and Jerry's antics become louder and more obstreperous to gain his attention. And Dean's glass of appreciation seems more and more empty, if not entirely nonexistent.

Dean never finds that he has to screw his eyes shut. He stands by Jerry's side with a posture that doesn't become frantic, even though it is occasionally violent. The look of Jerry's franticness suggests madness. The look of Dean looking at Jerry's franticness suggests overriding sanity, the hyper-sanity of imprisonment. The scripts these two played out repeatedly emphasize the zany craziness of Jerry's character, even when the craziness is childishness; and emphasize the too sober maturity of Dean's by comparison. Dean effects his demonstration of "sanity" by gazing at a twitching creature and not seeing him, a boundless font of impatience and vexed incomprehension.

[8]

Jerry's crossed eyes could be deeply troubling, even terrifying. But his eye cross is a flash of presentation, a signal that never becomes a sign. As quickly as the effect comes on it disappears, to be replaced by an oral configuration or a speechful burst, a muscular twitch of posture or groping limbs. We have no sense that the crossed eyes point to a character trait per se. Thus, the optical spasm works as an exclamation point in a continuing flow of action which can now be interpreted as a statement; looking at it in retrospect, once the exclamation has been made, we discover a chain of significant eventualities racing up to the point of contraction.

Jerry's tender eyes have seen wounds—in interviews they often, and dramatically, turn away—and can themselves be wounded. It is by virtue of what these eyes can see that the character feels struck, impressed, assaulted. With Lewis in offscreen interviews, however, one notices his sharp noticing, the way he regards and decodes the facial expressions other people direct to him: are they being critical, are they being amicable? Speaking over coffee with Jerry Seinfeld near the end of his life, we see Jerry in a coffee shop, leaning forward, his eyes almost bulging out of his head with tender and eager curiosity.

Dean has sleepy eyes. Half-open, half-closed. As if there were someplace else he would rather be or would perhaps like to get to, soon: an assignation, a business deal, more stimulating company, perhaps. A girl. In particularly uninterested moments, he sometimes looks like he might simply drift off to sleep on his feet.

ANOTHER INTERLUDE

POMERANCE

It seems to me the riddle inside the riddle here, let's call it *our* riddle for the moment, is something like this: how is it that Martin & Lewis made sense in their time? I mean, any kind of sense at all. To their immediate audience. It was possible for people to watch them, grasp what they were watching, have the desire to watch again.

Because there is clearly a presentation at one instant of two quite contradictory truths, the frenzied, neurotic, zany, uncontrolled, uncontrollable energy source; and the laid-back, even tranquilized, swinger who has eased into his situation, who is totally relaxed, who never seems to need to "move ahead." How is it, do you think, that this doubling could have been, in any way, appealing?

SOLOMON

Just because oil and water don't mix, doesn't mean that it isn't absolutely fascinating to watch the blobs and patterns take shape when you pour some oil into a cup of water. For me, this is Martin & Lewis in action, not really "doubling," but rather another kind of co-presence or co-existence where one substance, one partner, fills the open space left by the other, but fills it in any number of ways, be it emotionally, verbally, performatively, or visually. Martin was Lewis's "negative space" and vice versa.

POMERANCE

Yes, yes. But as to oil and water, or, if you like, *oiliness* and *wateriness*, what we have is a fundamental—in this case even chemical—contradiction. And I'm wondering what it was about America at the time, mid-1940s through mid-1950s, that made it so ripe for contradiction, so happy to be entertained by contradiction, so open to recognizing contradiction as a basic part of life. Because without that, nobody would have been able to tolerate Dean & Jerry for two minutes.

SOLOMON

Each embodied a key aspect of the American postwar dilemma. On the one hand, a burgeoning consumer culture was fired by the desire for leisure and a sense of self-satisfaction in the wake of a world war that had recently been won, a world now "safe for democracy." A new "happiness" betokened recognition of a culture full of visual and tactile delights, new possibilities, exciting horizons. On the other hand, there was always looming a dark denial: total neurosis as a response to the elephantine weight that was now placed on the individual with the rise of the Organization Man. A ballooning middle class could exist only with a middle-class work ethic, which demanded not only commitment but also diffuse propriety. Follow the rules, climb the ladder one step before the other. Boundless repressions needed to occur, desires held frustratingly in check at every moment—the desire to scream, to blurt something out in "inappropriate" situations, to move one's body in some non-functional and non-directed way, the desire to just drop everything and run away!

POMERANCE

So the urge to run away, to run amok, went along with—was married to—the felt need to conform, to look nice, to keep one's mouth shut. . . . We certainly see this almost totally unfettered urge and need coupled with a casual, naturalized restraint, in every moment of Martin & Lewis.

SOLOMON

In a way, the one cannot exist without the other, right? Yet, there is absolutely never any possibility of synthesis, "never the twain shall meet."

POMERANCE

So, whenever Jerry has fun he gets into trouble, he courts danger. And while Dean "cools it," he keeps being infected by the desire to have fun. I keep hearing Dean screaming at Jerry, "Will . . . you . . . calm . . . DOWN!!!!"; and Jerry blabbing at Dean, "Will . . . you . . . wake . . . UP!!!!!"

SOLOMON

I think that's right, although I think Dean is just as frequently stifling his own laughter as he is reprimanding or reining Jerry in, at least in the early days. But you didn't really say what effect Dean might have had on Jerry.

POMERANCE

Reminding Jerry, rhythmically, of the problem with breaking through boundaries, just at the instant that Jerry was breaking through boundaries. It's as though the consumer utopia was both delirious and frightening at the same time, both a source of relaxed pleasure, laying back in the new hammock from Sears Roebuck under a blue sky, and worrying that storms could be coming, could be, in fact, not so far away. Perhaps within one's sanctimonious daydream. And for the energetic wanderer, perhaps an eternal sense that a brick wall was just ahead.

SOLOMON

It's about RHYTHM, it's truly musical in its essence, and I find it as soothing as a lullaby even though I'm several generations removed from Martin & Lewis. You?

POMERANCE

Well, it's jazz. In jazz you have to have a strong motor beat and over that you lay a strong melodic line. You know, Dean was a vocal phenomenon when it came to melodic lines. But, as Sammy Davis (the maestro) always seemed to know, and to smirk at, he didn't have a beat. He *followed* some beat but he didn't have a beat. Jerry lived a beat, so much so it was often hard to figure out if there was a melody.

SOLOMON

That's as good a place as any to land, we said we'd write for one hour today, just like the *Colgate Comedy Hour*.

POMERANCE

Do you think audiences had the feeling when that show wrapped up each week that it was really done? That an ending had been reached? I mean this quite beyond network programming's hope that of course these watchers would tune in again next week. I mean, at the end of one particular show, did one sense a finale?

SOLOMON

The S-T-R-E-T-C-H that came at the end of those broadcasts kind of makes you contemplate the very idea of an ending, what it means for one thing to be finished and for another to begin. But, I think we're always looking forward to the next episode, to the next Martin & Lewis film, what a letdown after *Hollywood or Bust*, BUST!

POMERANCE

There's a beautiful line in Steven Spielberg's *The Fabelmans* (2022). "It's gone on so long you can't say 'The End.'" But—speaking of ends—let's think about the individual routines and their finale moments: do you think that generally, in their routines, Dean & Jerry knew where the end was when they began? Do you think the routines were mapped out? I don't mean timed, because certainly for television they would be timed, pretty accurately. And in film, one is literally counting the exposed frames as expense. But do you think they knew at the starting gun where their finish line was going to be?

SOLOMON

They were clearly working from a script and had rehearsed these routines, but there was always the chance of something spontaneous, something magical happening that wasn't contained in the script, that hadn't been rehearsed—Jerry blurting something out or breaking the fourth wall, Dean laughing or going off script, because he had forgotten his lines or was pretending to have forgotten them. I think they were both exceedingly good—in their prime—at keeping one another on their toes, upping the ante or doing something unexpected to see how the other would react. My sense is that in the nightclub act, this could go on for hours.

POMERANCE

This spontaneous inter-reactivity is really interesting as part of performance, I think, because it's the way relationships proceed in everyday life, when they're not part of some terrifying bureaucratic routine. People just fly along, interrupting each other (politely or bluntly), changing tack, sailing by the wind of the moment. So in their act, Dean & Jerry were doing something at once *fabulous* (specially attractive) and *natural.*

SOLOMON

Bingo! But, there are certain situations or settings where that is more socially acceptable. What is marvelous about Dean & Jerry's world, is that a sense of responsive spontaneity can occur in virtually any situation or setting. The films cycle through any number of genres and settings, the *Comedy Hour* even more so, but in nearly every case theirs is a world that feels spontaneous and unpredictable. What a world that would be to live in, so alive, so in the moment, so connected, so responsive to others!

POMERANCE

You know what Bingo is, right?

SOLOMON

I only know it as a game in which money can be made and a children's song about a dog.

POMERANCE

It's a five-by-five grid game in America and a larger-grid game in England. The origin is in Italy, roughly 1530. But what strikes me about that is that the Commedia dell'arte begins in Italy not even twenty years later. There is in the Martin & Lewis spontaneity something of an unheard voice calling out, "Bingo!!!" moment after moment after moment, as though all of life is Bingo. And of course you can trace the antics of Dean & Jerry back to the Commedia. Especially the unpredictability (which drove so many uptight Madison Avenue types out of their minds).

SOLOMON

I like where you took this. We could even consider their routines, all of them, lined up, in this way, a series of juxtapositions that accumulated until there was nowhere else to go.

POMERANCE

And on that somber note, do you think, in terms of the break-up of the relationship, they knew before it came that it was coming; or was it, perhaps, one more spontaneous kick that simply left both parties with no moves to follow?

SOLOMON

I think the writing was on the wall, since they had developed different aspirations—"we've grown apart," the old breakup cliché. We can read that dynamic from certain moments in the *Comedy Hour* and then in their last film together, *Hollywood or Bust* (more later). But it's also possible something else was going on, namely: one of them wanted to know where this "thing" was all going, a kind of teleology; and the other wanted to let it play out, to "live in the moment." Two radically different ways of "living it up."

POMERANCE

There's a terrific and profound moment near the finale of *Living It Up* when in matching tuxedos Dean and Jerry are "on the street" crooning together about their love of New York. Dean's voice could not be more mellifluous, romantic, or feelingful, and he is of course bang on key. Jerry is trying to do a duet, but his voice is a helpless screech.

Thinking about that screech, its exact timbre and phrasing, thinking about it as a musical riff, I begin to realize it's all over the place in Dean & Jerry's work, in the same way that Dean's taciturn, reproving look is everywhere. And I see, too, that all of their shticks on television, in film, onstage—all of their shticks are basically the same. The same little lunges and parries over and over. The settings change. The character names change for the settings. But the characters are always the two we expect to find. They are not the only comedic pair to work this way; but they are the only comedic pair to work this way *the way they worked this way.* This adds an element to the self-reflexiveness of Dean & Jerry: that as I watch a "library skit," for example, I am not actually seeing a library and what can happen in a library; I am seeing Dean & Jerry "doing their thing" pretending they're in a library: doing their playroom. So in one vision I see the library action and the performing-out of library action.

SOLOMON

I hear what you're saying, it's the dynamic between the two that is at the core of what they did together onscreen, onstage, and on radio. They discovered—or should I say, concocted—that dynamic early on, refining it a bit along the way, but really never varied from its essence. Certainly, neither ever played "against type" in their collaborative efforts. There is something immensely comforting in that stability and that consistency for a viewer and listener. The big brother knows his place in the family just as the little brother knows his, they each play their roles accordingly. As an audience, we can rely on that and choose to come back for more (or not). But, it must have grown tiresome for both of them even if some viewers would have been fine for Martin & Lewis to have lasted for another forty years. When a beloved sitcom ends, loyal viewers are heartbroken, but the "show must go on" for each, or so they say.

POMERANCE

And then, too, there's a kind of explicit social critique. They say to us, in a sense, *No matter what the circumstance, the fundamental reality is basically always the same.* They can be in a red convertible with a Great Dane, on a golf course with Ben Hogan, in an army barracks, crewing a submarine, dancing at a prom, inhabiting an apartment near Shirley MacLaine and Dorothy Malone, singing "That's Amore" with mom and pop, it doesn't matter: there they always are, this indecipherable pair. There they always and always and always are. Fused. Ampersanded. Bonded. And a mystery.

SOLOMON

How do you think Dean & Jerry play today, in 2023? Do you imagine young people "just don't get" the context and/or the references?

POMERANCE

Maybe in the way that you and I don't get—really get—the context and references of the world of the 1940s . . . but we can try to learn; and I think we hope that readers today will try, too.

PART III

THE TRUE VOICE OF FEELING

[1]

No matter how thoroughly unintelligible Jerry's voice seems to Dean, time and time again, no matter how weird, ungrammatical, alien, it surprisingly doesn't *feel* alien to audiences, who teach themselves early on to read meaning into his "nonsense."

[2]

Dean Martin's voice is a perfect example of true classical harmony, mellow, fluid, always phrasing perfectly, always on key. Always always on key the way that Jerry was, for all intents and purposes, always always off key. The voice that comes out of Jerry Lewis, almost every time (there are a few very notable exceptions), is, musically speaking, pure modernism, sometimes even twelve-tone modernism. It is an education to close one's eyes on Dean & Jerry's work, and just listen to the voices themselves—easy enough to do with recordings of their many radio shows. As we see them, Jerry's bodily contortions, arranged in linear sequence as he modulates from instrumentality to instrumentality when "expressing" syllable after syllable, merely convey the physical stress on his body at each instant—shades of the imitated symptomatologies that would be on show later in *The Disorderly Orderly*—and convey also a gesturally animated characterization of the speaker: a corral of "vocal" beings, some human, some not. Without witnessing the stress we are open to hearing the voice.

Jerry had been "vocalizing" mimically this way as long as people had seen him, but pointing to his vocalizing much less than working it, very notably in his record act. Call Jerry an organ with many stops, but that in fact would be too limiting. He is like a magical synthesizer (ahead of its time). That his musical mimes vary, geared tightly into the tempo and rhythm, draws attention to not only their bopping continuity but also, and importantly, their orchestrational variance: the notably unlike sounds of idiosyncratic instruments: how many such *unlike* sounds are possible in a band. Jerry is a one-man band. How many *unlike* forms of expression are possible from him?

But Dean is the featured singer glowing in a spotlight in front of the band, or so he thinks.

[3]

Emissions.

Dean usually speaks, directly and plainly. Speaks, as in "I am speaking now." Not screams, not cries. Just says. As to Jerry, there are considerable instances in his film and television appearances where he makes sounds hard to describe in conventional linguistic or acoustic terms: agonized bleats, painful whines, labored groans, sepulchral intonations, machine gun splatters, pre-pubertal mewling. These come out, no two alike and none ever exactly repeated, tonal portraits of the performing body and its vicissitudes at the moment, given the dramatic circumstance: that is to say, the onscreen Jerry-character at each situated moment points to the body of the performer "being" him and the limitations and feelings of that performative body. Part of what makes for the musical comedy of Jerry Lewis is the disjunctive surprise produced with each sonic explosion, a surprise coming partly from the explosion's idiosyncrasy—it's like nothing we've ever heard (nothing *exactly*). Crucial, too, is this multiplied voice's "cubist" placement in the scene. A screen character (and the performer making that character) does not know, cannot know, will not know in advance of the sound, what kind of a sound it will be, at what amplitude, with what duration and vector. We often think of these sudden vocal manifestations as indices of what Herbert Read called "the true voice of feeling," a tracing of

> the discovery and evolution of "organic form" in English poetry. . . . I believe [organic form] to be the specific form of modern poetry, in so far as this poetry is specifically modern. But I would like to suggest that what is specifically modern about our poetry is not the form as such, but rather a realization that form is the natural effect of the poet's integrity. So what we are to be concerned with is not so much "the life of forms" . . . but rather the form of life. (9)

For Read, poetry was organic to the extent that it was sincere. In Lewis's characters, we have an uninterrupted flow of sincerity, a thoroughgoing organicism. The viewer's sense of this is cultivated by the vocal spontaneity, by the condition that no hiatus for reflection or calculation—however brief!—separates a causal event from the character's vocal address. There is a virtual animism at play here, the Jerry-body becoming an expressive thing that sounds on vibration and vibrates on touch. As the world touches him, he speaks. As time wears him, he grinds out syllables. As he sees, he says.

[4]

Sincerity in speech involves not only being true to one's feeling and condition but also being alive to, and present in, the flowing moment—regardless of how painful that might be. Consider as a fine example a tiny moment in

Tashlin's *The Disorderly Orderly*, a kind of retrospective pointer to all of Jerry's work beforehand. Jerome K. Jerome is speeding away in a maroon ambulance (!) but suddenly needs to stop. So he rams his foot down on the brake. As the foot goes down it pushes the brake pedal entirely through the floor of the vehicle so that the sole of his shoe is now scraping against the road. Smoke is rising from his foot. His cheeks fly back in agony and he cries, in helpless surrender, "Oh! Pain! Pain!" Here:

- integrity and organicism are absolutely intrinsic to the event, first through the body's affiliation with the vehicle and second through the heat and reverberation moving up through Jerome's leg.
- Jerome's leg is owned and acknowledged vocally by Jerome himself, in the claim, "I am here; I have a body; my body has legs; one of my legs has pushed through the floor; my foot is on the road; my foot is burning."
- Further, as Jerome's foot is being used in this event to brake the vehicle, in driving he has entirely surpassed the technology of the car itself, its design, its manufacture, and is replacing both the brake pedal and the brake system with his own "braking system," which is also, ironically, "breaking." Can we think, perhaps, that Jerome *is* the ambulance (a medical emergency)?
- But at the same time Jerome/Jerry (can it be coincidence that the two names are so similar?) is aware of his position in the sight of some knowing observer—call it an actor's consciousness of the camera's framing, or a character's desperately prayerful consciousness of a guiding spirit watching over him. When he screams, he is being instantaneously responsive and feelingful: but responsive not to the foot on the road but to a viewer's *noticing* the foot on the road. He is telling *somebody* that there is pain. As soon as *we see the smoke*, and thus accurately surmise that the friction between the foot and the road is working to slow and stop the car, we know; and *as soon as we know, he screams.*
- He screams, but is he really screaming to us, specifically? This is a demanding question, because aside from Mr. Tuffington (Everett Sloane), who is on a stretcher in the back, and now about to fly away, there is no one else to whom Jerome could possibly be speaking. And the absence of a listener, a diegetic listener, coupled with the intensity of his expression help indicate his poetic nature in the first place. Poetic nature: that what is paramount to him is expression of feeling, not

communication. The critic and poet Paul Goodman once said, "A young poet should write plenty of essays in order to get rid of all his ideas. Poetry has nothing to do with ideas." That Jerome must be effectively alone when he screams is central to the moment.

- Clearly, too, this scream nicely replicates and indicates a broad-based human experience, the calling out to no one when a sharp sudden pain hits. A hammerer hits his finger, "Pain! Pain!" This is not a request for help, it is a woeful dirge celebrating the knowledge that *no request for help will bring help*, that one is *beyond help*, beyond the social frame in which relationships might augur some possibility for mutual endeavor and thus some rationale for communication. This scream is not a communicative scream.
- One also picks up here an innocent and heartfelt willingness to share the self openly and fully, since "Pain! Pain!" will *seem* to be intelligible language—meaning in sound—whether or not it is (this is why Jerome uses *words*) and in this respect can be received and interpreted (by the audience of whom the character is surely, in some way, conscious) as indicating all of the following, and in no particular order: (1) a negative feeling, (2) an *immense* negative feeling, (3) a feeling that is entirely and purely—unalloyedly— negative, (4) here! . . . now!, (5) that is, *right* here, in the closest location to this crying mouth, which is this very body, (6) somewhere, *down there!*, (7) my body down there, my body, my body down there, (8) and therefore pain that is entirely and uncorruptedly *mine*, (9) *my* pain, the pain in *my* body, my body that you are seeing, (10) pain as creature and manifestation, even as you see only an index of pain, which is (11) the smoke that (12) I am smelling, and that is causing me to think (13) my foot is on fire and (14) I will die in flames. Pain! Pain!

He shares because the pain that is of him and in him is now converted into a transactable cry, a cry that has become, perforcedly, content. Content as consonant and vowel. "P" to bring the lips together. Lip closure requires jaw movement, jaw movement is distinctly visible (puppet-like). "Ain" to rhyme with "rain," "drain," "contain," "gain," "main," and "stain." This is pain in the main, pain that stains from the inside out, pain that drains him away even as it might drain away itself, pain he gains but does not wish to gain, or cannot think about wishing to gain since the gaining has invaded his castle.

"Oh! Pain! Pain!" The *Oh!* as surprise, since as the face contorts the eyes pop open. I pushed on the brake to stop this ambulance, but I did not think

I would find my foot burning on the road. Why would I have thought that? Why would I have *thought?*, I was in motion. The viewer sees the action of the brake pedal as animated comedy, going down, going down, breaking through the floor, the leg going with it. We *see* it happening from the outside, and the sight is comedic by way of the conjunctions it sharply without announcement presents (conjunctions that are entirely logical but that were not prefigured): foot + road + speed = friction. Jerome, however, notices, from within, that it has just happened: it happened before he notices that it happened. There was a split second of *Pure Visual Gag*: the event with the foot on the road, our seeing but not yet assembling the parts, no feeling at all. Then quickly we assemble the parts and he responds to our assemblage, "Oh! Pain! Pain!"

"Oh!" I react to your having seen something here.

That is: *YOU told me what was going on,* and now I respond with surprise (Oh!) and feeling (Pain! Pain!). You: my world? My protector? The one who sees to it that I am alive because you surveil?

We have to be the surveillers now. Dean is off having his own career.

On surveillance, life, and preservation it is imperative to think of the stone rolled from the tomb, the vigil, the idea of vigilance that is essential to cinema watching (and who knows this better than Jerry Lewis?). You are always keeping vigil, you saw, it was mine to know that you saw, therefore what you observed *can be happening.* Happening because of vigilance, because of observation. If you don't see it, it didn't happen.

[5]

Voices and cacophonies:

In the April 29, 1951, *Colgate Comedy Hour* broadcast, we find "two young men from the University of Vienna," dressed in tasseled fez-like caps and heavy coats with fur-trimmed collars and sleeves, "Professors Martin and Lewis," invited to address the Cure the Common Cold Committee. At first, an exceedingly rambling, long-winded introduction from their host—a perfect spoof of the academic's inability to hold any audience *briefly*—prevents them from speaking. It is only after Dean strikes the speaker and knocks him out that the two "men who have completely outwitted medical science" get to say anything at all. Professor Martin bangs the gavel and then Professor Lewis holds forth:

PROF. LEWIS (in a thick Germanic accent): Ve haf no more noise hier! Ven de cold stghikes a nohm'l human being, [pause for emphasis] ... enough to make zomeone zick ... Is it ghright, Fritz?

Although he can barely make his words understood it hardly matters, since what he says is entirely self-explanatory—academicism as a way of stating the obvious in a way that is utterly incomprehensible.

PROF. MARTIN (in a heavy Italian accent, with immediate confirmation): That's a-right, Ernst.

This collegial affirmation is reflexive and unquestioning, a confirmation of loyal membership in the cabal—a tic of academic behavior.

PROF. LEWIS: We sit in the laboratory night-and-day-night-and-day-night-and-day.

PROF. MARTIN (as Dean, responsive as a juke-box): *Launches into the Cole Porter standard, "Night and Day,"[1] which Jerry joins very briefly but is cut off.*

This vocal interruption is a welcome change from the self-important monologue, but alas it is all too brief. We are forcibly returned to a testimony of academic activity. Too busy to do anything beyond the confines of their small laboratory or miniscule academic specialization, but nevertheless eager to show off just how much they have done and just how *indescribably busy* they have been in doing it, even if the results are completely and totally invisible, Prof. Lewis asks Prof. Martin a question:

PROF. LEWIS: You got de virus in de test tube? You got de test tube so ve can show dem vat we accomplished in our verk dat took us years and years and years? (*Conrad Veidt[2]-style eyebrow flicking.*)

Professor Martin produces an oversized test tube, the contents of which are transparent.

1 Written for the musical *Gay Divorce* (1932).

2 (1893–1943); star of, among many other films, *Casablanca* (1942). A German émigré to Hollywood, Veidt donated his salaries toward the fight against Hitler.

LEWIS (continuing, with the phial held gingerly): In dis test tube ve have three-hundred-and-thoity-seven thousand Cold . . . Tcherms!

PROF. MARTIN (quickly): That's a lotta germs!

Professor Lewis now prepares to proudly share the results of all their hard work, however invisible it may actually be, with the committee:

PROF. LEWIS: Ven ve discovered de cure for de cherms. . . .

But as he taps the test tube against the table, it breaks. The gathered committee gasps (that is, *inhales*) and recoils, but the two lecturing professors are unfazed. They have the cure, after all! Each produces a flyswatter from beneath his heavy coat and starts swatting wildly at the several hundred thousand germs they released into the room. The fly swatters are the celebrated "discovery" they have brought from Vienna, although the very same implements can likely be found in any corner store.

[6]

How would this 1951 "Cure for the Common Cold" skit have played in college classrooms, university dorms, or faculty lounges that year, just hypothetically since in 1951 nobody was importing media to the university nor was anybody calling television media? If this had been shown, would it have inspired illuminating discussion? Or in 1955? In 1960? In 1965? In 1970? In 1980? In 1990? In 2020? How would it work on campus tomorrow afternoon? A more pointed indictment of the academic enterprise would be difficult to find, after all. For an academic to watch it with glee would require the ability to tickle oneself. Can one say of the academy that such an ability, self-tickling, is alive and well there? More crucially: if the tenured professor does not laugh at Professors Dean & Jerry, *why not?* Dean & Jerry move us to wonder whether they are indicting the academic enterprise. If they are, what a hot-button issue that might turn out to be, even for professorial types settled back in their armchairs for a pleasant evening and putting tomorrow's PSY 235 out of mind!

Two learned professors, armed with flyswatters, intoxicated by—even self-flagellating with—the circularity and utter pointlessness of their discourse. Mutually reinforcing, one politely (read, slavishly) affirming the other, agreement guaranteed and signaled. What an august group must these two have joined, what a "high society"! Clothed in ceremonial academic robes, they are protected from the touch of the world (mocked, too, like the self-important travelers in Georges Méliès' *A Trip to the Moon* [1902], who congratulate themselves with great pomp at the end of that film). Are they aiming to reach an objective, however specious? Or only to elaborate a mindless celebration of their happy mutual agreement and (feigned) mutual admiration?

We are the experts! (Pay heed!)

We are the ambassadors of intelligence!

We are the ones you should listen to!

Nod along like good pupils while jotting down a few notes, why don't you.

After all, what we say is authoritative, that is, official. Never mind that it sounds like nonsense!

Through this braying, Dean & Jerry are not mustering even one syllable of disrespect for wisdom, for kindness, for compassion, for sensitivity, for precision of focus—indeed, for knowledge. They are not suggesting these goods are absent from schools; from academies; from the university sancta where "professors" breathe and grow. But they are definitively pointing to stuffiness. They are reminding us that wisdom is fun and that typically speaking, professorial endeavor is not. School is not a panacea. Wisdom and fun can be anywhere and everywhere, and in order to expand in the sunlight they do not have to be included in course curricula.

Neither Dean nor Jerry was ever awarded a college degree—both dropped out of school in the tenth grade, neither of them sticking around high school long enough for a diploma; for years after 1930, getting some kind of job was far more important—yet their performances were chockablock with a certain kind of cultural wisdom that rewards discussion, that responds to something more sincerely and authentically than a rote application of existing educational paradigms that confine their subjects to existing schemata already examined by "officialdom" and approved for worship.[3] *Allow me to count your footnotes. . . . Have you a good reason for failing to include reference to Dr. Bulkescheimer? . . . What evidence do you have to support these assertions? . . . What is the analytical ground upon which you are standing? . . . What you just said: who do you think you are to open your mouth and say that? . . .*

How does The Professor become The Emperor in his new clothes, and why are we not supposed to remind the Emperor and his subjects that the

3 As a fulsome exercise in stating, developing, and penetrating this theme see *The Nutty Professor* with great care.

man is naked? As the Emperor poses and prances, the attending and fully cognizant crowd is silent. A strange kind of silence with Dean & Jerry, too: if they are speaking up to describe reality, their chortling watchers are acting as though they don't hear.

[7]

Hearing did not require seeing. Episodes of the Martin & Lewis radio broadcasts—*The Martin and Lewis Show*—began (in 1949) with a vibrant clash of vocal styles, a double challenge to the ear, or a pair of challenges for two ears, with Deano singing a few bars of a song in his standard mellifluous fashion, then Jerry singing a few bars of the same song hopelessly off key. Dean had sung before, since the late 1930s, and went on singing, through movies and television and stage appearances. Jerry had a serious musical career later on, and certainly could sing as much on key as Dean if he wanted to—as was made very evident when he cut records. We will never know whether the radio show audiences took to this because they honestly thought a singer was being boxed by a blatant non-singer, or whether they sensed the special delights of this kind of performance.

What was the radio cacophony but a flagrant *mismatch*, a marriage gone impossibly wrong, a brotherhood of negativities, since Dean could not more obviously be a conventional crooner, following all the "rules," and producing what the listener was to feel as "harmony" while Jerry was a devious sort who (surely must have) calculated to dismantle all this.

The program, which was both a situation comedy and a variety show of sorts, maintained the illusion that Dean & Jerry were inseparable bosom buddies, professional collaborators as well as roommates who shared a bedroom. (Would not-so-well-to-do young performers be able in 1949 to find an inexpensive two-bedroom in Manhattan? Recall that in *Rope* [1948] the number of bedrooms is not given, but in any event, Philip and Brandon are *not* not-so-well-to-do [see Badmington].) On that same first broadcast, the announcer (early radio always, always, always had an "announcer" who lived, as it were, in the wings) explained, "Today is one of those rare occasions when Jerry and Dean have separate plans for the evening." Given that the show was on after suppertime and in radio prime time—initially Sundays 6:30–7:00 p.m.—"the evening" had to reference late night. And in fact the episode ended with Jerry "waking Dean up at 3 o'clock in the morning" to ask him a few questions, including, "Will you please move your bed a little further away from mine?"

Six years later on film, as we indicated in our shot analysis above, Eugene Fullstack of *Artists and Models* crawls through the boys' bedroom in order to get to Dean in the bathtub, but in doing this he steps over sheets and blankets: is he clambering over one large bed, or two beds side by side?—we are given no clear image.[4] The audience for Dean & Jerry was being conceived as entertaining a speculation of their intimacies, when in the real life of image production they were two entirely separate performers living separate lives and going separate ways unless they were in front of one audience or another. Note that when Jerry was running the Gar-Ron Playhouse and inviting friends to join in his productions, Dean was not on his list.[5]

The radio program itself is a domestic space, and the stars both live and work there, in a relationship that is intimate, domestic, and regular—amatory or not. The listener gets the idea of eavesdropping on "the boys" (as they are frequently referred to) going about their "daily" business, eating breakfast (June 12, 1949), or conversing with their somewhat dim-witted secretary Florence (Flo McMichaels),[6] seemingly a frequent visitor to their imaginary "home." Radio sound being as enveloping as it is for listeners at home, the illusion was that in tuning in we were literally visiting the boys' domain, literally sharing their space: on radio, space is entirely acoustic.

For his record act that preceded his affiliation with Dean, discussed above, Jerry was silent, posturing and gesturing to a song being played offstage. The whole thing was an elaborated lip-synch. Indeed, his vocal silence was the key to the yuk. But radio gave him opportunities to refine his vocal impressions, whether of a tough-talking gangster (June 5, 1949), or using a western drawl (June 12, 1949; July 5, 1949), or falling into a stiff upper-lip British accent

4 The Motion Picture Production Code, which would definitely have specified the number of beds two people could have together in one room, did not lapse until 1966.

5 Most likely, we think, Dean was not at all antic enough for the hijinks Jerry had in mind: he hosted Janet Leigh and her new husband Tony Curtis, George Gershwin's son Jerry, Larry Storch, and others. "We all loved to play games," Leigh said (qtd. In Levy 136).

6 (1919–1999), actor in film and television. She played Winnie Kirkwood on *Mister Ed* (CBS, 1961–1966).

(July 5, 1949). Was the listener at home to believe there were actually different personae visiting the radio studio? Did any radio listener at the time actually believe that? Or was the listener at home assumed to have agreed already to accept this singular Jerry figure as multidimensional, multifaceted, in fact wholly fragmented in personality so that he was all of these people in one body?

Dean worked radio with a double voice: when he sang, he was Romantic Mr. Moonlight; when he jibed at Jerry, he was impatient and unsophisticated.

Jerry's vocal switches were somewhat like impersonations without actually being them, since they had no actual live models. In what we call "impersonation," a comic type picks a living (but absent) model, and pretends vocally and facially to be that person.[7] The impersonator never gives the effect of actually *being* his model—that would be more than horrific. But he also never gives the impression of being himself—that would be more than tedious. Jerry does not use actual models, however, thus our suggestion his work can be *somewhat* like impersonation. Like Robin Williams, who came after him as an acolyte, Jerry imitated types, not individuals. He called up a type, as it were out of the air but in fact out of the cultural stereotypes—many of them minute and mundane—that he shared with his audience. What Jerry does is to launch into a loose personification that is the physical and sonic embodiment of what is already an impersonation of sorts, a stereotype, a composite of multiple performative types, most often encountered by audiences onscreen. He becomes a person who impersonates the "persons" of mediated drama. He is an impersonator of impersonations.

Listening to recordings of the radio show makes one wonder how visual were these vocal performances and what special delights could be seen by the live studio audience while being unknown to listeners.[8] The laughter one hears is sometimes not attributable to jokes. For the lucky attendees at

7 It may be that the last widely popular impressionist was Rich Little (b. 1938), who "printed currency" with his scathing takeoff of Richard Milhous Nixon. Other impersonators, such as Jim Carrey, stood out in the history of show business, and there are impersonators at work today, but generally speaking the form has eroded. There is a fascinating and unexplored "biological" link between impersonators and Canadians.

8 By contrast with radio production today, 1940s and 1950s radio "shows" were almost always produced in a studio with a live audience, whose shrieks and guffaws could find a home in the sound array. So-called laugh tracks (see, for

the studio, the stars' "domicile" had "visible" glass walls, and the stars were there to be met. For the home listener all of the goings-on had to be imagined from sound cues. (For considerably more on the limits and horizons of radio, see Verma.)

[8]

Sour Notes.

A particular, and much repeated, Jerry voice brings on an instant and spine-chilling sense of cacophony. With the voicebox constricted and the tone pitched against the top of the mouth, the body produces a screeching, even shrill vocal whistle, a diminishing of the size of the voice and a compensation through increased amplitude. Loud, harsh, extremely treble, and strained.

Strained to the breaking point.

Strained more than anything. (Dean, remember, is constantly dialing him back, with Jerry straining against the continual restraints placed upon him and upon his vocalizing, if not upon his very being-in-the-world.) As though the character is trying very, very hard to speak with others, squeezing the sound out with both hesitation and desperation at once. This special voice indicates an infantilized Jerry, since it calls up tonal memories of children trying to break into conversation out of eagerness to be noticed or attended to. Even in instances where Jerry uses this voice for expressing his character's opinion rather than clamoring for notice, he manages to draw exceptional attention to himself doing so. The speech content is thus much less important than the quality of the speech. The high-pitched screech is guaranteed to break through normal conversation, to pierce it like a spear. Other characteristics of Jerry's persona tend to accompany the tone.

He also often uses syllabic fracturing, breaking up fluid speech into singular articulations that have the *sound* of syllables whether or not, grammatically speaking, they are syllables in fact. Grammatically, Jerry's high speech is both a statement and a question, because assertions are phrased as though the speaker is asking about them. To add to the confusion, there is a frequent use of artful "dyslexic" inversion or syllabic transposition, as though the speaker

---

example, Woody Allen's *Annie Hall* [1977]) came later. Charles "Charley" Douglass's "canned laughter" ("sweetening") came into use beginning in the late 1950s.

is not comfortable with, or acquainted in, the "NORMAL" use of English. Language broken, then, but expressed through a hauntingly plaintive, high-pitched, whiny vocality.[9] Or used as a hoist: Dean, for his part, is often oddly well behaved with language, upping his social status or trying hard to.

Many physical comedians work by showing artful clumsiness, a clear display that the body is out of control negotiating the spaces of, and handling the materials of, the conventional world. Jerry certainly does this, but what he is doing here is a vocal match for this technique, therefore a signal that the character he is playing has trouble not only with physical objects and space but with language, intention, meaning, and expression: the tool for pointing to those objects and that space. Jerry's character has pointing trouble.

The possibility of hearing trouble—a condition certainly enforced upon the audience in these moments—is inherently rooted in a logical, cerebral, grammatical, expositional world structure. Deafness is principally a trouble when it is important to hear what people are saying, and it is usually important to hear what people are saying in order to fathom their alignments. Jerry insistently plays a character who doesn't get, or conform to, other people's alignments, who doesn't know the right word for the situation, who needs to expel syllables but not with conventional intelligence, who speaks to others as though he were some alien who never learned their language yet needs urgently that they should "get" him. By reinvoking linguistic incompetence, thus paralysis, he confronts his audience with a fundamental absence of capability, an impoverishment.[10]

Articulated language intercedes in our experience, forming a barrier against the world and a dense medium through which the world is translated for, and conveyed to, us. All of this is demolished by Jerry in these vocal routines: just as it is emphasized and reiterated in Dean's always-precise harmony. Language as boundary, definition, delimitation, positioning, navigation, recording, official history. At first one's emotional tendrils stretch out to graze against the colors and inchoate forms of things, to follow motion,

9 In *The Errand Boy* he pronounces a man's name "Habben-appen," when the "correct" pronunciation (the man insists) is "Wabenlotny." But Lewis has been part of scripting this film. Who would name a character Wabenlotny? Or Habbenappen. Or Benvedninton. Or whatever.

10 Various forms of linguistic "incompetence" present a fascinating issue that we do not investigate further here. See, for example, Sacks, *Musicophilia* 274–75 and *River* 169.

to be soothed by touch. But then words fly in, and after words compositions and arrangements of words. And then proscriptions and tendencies. And classifications, affiliations. Soon, conflict and defense. Jerry's language calls up a condition of lively attentiveness, willing participation without attachment. Freud's genital phase. Norman O. Brown reminds us, "The net-effect of the establishment of the boundary between self and external world is inside-out and outside-in; confusion" (143).

[9]

Consider Dean and then Jerry as possible instrumentalities, using as model something like Igor Stravinsky's 1913 effort, *Le sacre du printemps.*[11] Is there a place for Dean's harmonics inside the rattling machine? Do the spaces not expand endlessly for Jerry's percussive voice? The Jerry Screech has caused audiences to tighten the spine and withdraw, to squint the ears closed, and much the same happened with *Le sacre,* as Modris Eksteins shows:

> Regardless of attire, the audience on that opening night played, as Cocteau noted, "the role that was written for it." And what was that role? To be scandalized, of course, but, equally, to scandalize. The brouhaha surrounding *Le Sacre* was to be as much in the reactions of members of the audience to their fellows as in the work itself. The dancers on stage must have wondered at times who was performing and who was the audience.
>
> Shortly after the wistful bassoon melody of the opening bars, the protests began, first with whistling. When the curtain went up and the dancers appeared, jumping up and down and toeing, against all convention, inward rather than outward, the howling and hissing started. (11–12)

Of course, with Dean & Jerry—although to be sure, Jerry appeared to have noticed this more . . . much more—a culture of repressed pseudo-politeness grew all around. The howling and hissing, intentional as they may have been, were held back under the rubric of politeness, or smugness. Nothing to be heard.

11 *The Rite of Spring,* composed for Sergei Diaghilev's *Ballets Russes de Monte Carlo* and premiered (to a very displeased audience) at the Théâtre des Champs-Elysées May 29, 1913.

WHEN THE MOON HITS YOUR EYE

[1]

If Jerry's voicings were often agonies, Dean, for his part, rarely if ever appeared to be experiencing physical pain, or emotional pain, for that matter. Only the heartache of the troubador.

This isn't bodily pain, the kind that comes with having a body: the smoking foot as it scrapes the road. Dino is a paragon of suaveness, an icon of what the whole, hale, sane, ideal person should be if he or she is to stay always in control. Politesse, in the sense that Dean knows the same rules Jerry knows and knows how to negotiate them without friction. Coolness, because he never expresses a note or a gesture more than is called for. Swankness, because the stylish clothing fits his body so perfectly it seems to be him, whereas when Jerry wears stylish clothing it seems to be stuck on, as with one of those cardboard dolls that can be subjected to various costume changes.[1] This Dino doesn't hurt, but he desires. No remorse, no lovesickness that looks like actual sickness. Instead, lovesickness that looks like a smile. Keep up your energy for the hunt.

He is the cartoon set-up guy, victim of a bomb that goes off and leaves him a cluster of blackened threads with fuming bulging eyes, yet after a quick dissolve there he is put back together again. Humpty Dumpty in an ideal world. The Road Runner's Coyote (*avant la lettre*).[2] Out of Dean—out of what part of him we will never be able to determine—comes the floating voice of the hipper than hip, a voice sliding around in a drunken trance but then always finding the right note, a voice, finally, of contentment. "Ooble-le-ooble-le-oo."

[2]

Dino sang—less often spoke—of "love" countless times in countless songs to countless women (and only women—a very commonplace hypermasculine attitude of the time, virtually invisible as such to contemporary audiences).[3] This happens very routinely onscreen—"Here's to Love" (*My Friend Irma*); "I'll Always Love You" (*My Friend Irma Goes West*); "You and Your Beautiful

1 See, for example, *Playhouse Dolls* (Sandusky, OH: Stephens Publishing, 1949).

2 It was this cartoon quality that made Frank Tashlin (1913–1972), formerly an animated filmmaker, the perfect Martin & Lewis director.

3 Note, however, that at the same time watchers took the heteronormative proscription for granted they had no real trouble happily watching Jerry treat Dean like a dearly beloved bosom buddy for whom no sacrifice was too great. As Jerry put it, "Any two guys could have done it. But even the best of them wouldn't have had what made us as big as we are . . . it's the love that we had—that we still have—for each other" (*Dean* 277).

Eyes" (*At War with the Army*); "I Know a Dream When I See One" (*Jumping Jacks*); "That's Amore" (*The Caddy*); "Today, Tomorrow, Forever" (*Sailor Beware*); "When Someone Wonderful Thinks You're Wonderful" (*Scared Stiff*); "How Do You Speak to an Angel?" (*Living It Up*); "Innamorata" (*Artists and Models*); "Me 'n You 'n the Moon" (*Pardners*); "It Looks Like Love" (*Hollywood or Bust*)—

> It looks like love,
> It feels like love,
> And I confess,
> It's got me rockin' on my heels like love.
> (Sammy Fain and Paul Francis Webster)

—while always acknowledging, in his delivery and body language, directed simultaneously to audiences and to some diegetic prospective sex partner, indeed to listeners *as* prospective sex partners, that whatever love he could offer was unlikely to last beyond *the act,* beyond the concluding applause. With his dates as with his songs, when it was over it was over. Dean's act was always a self-indicating performance, in that way. Yet, true to the vaudeville tradition—of which Martin & Lewis were signal postwar representatives—onstage Dean worked unscripted but clearly well rehearsed, if not from practice in the wings then from hundreds or thousands of prior performances, each for a different audience, no one of which was individually memorable, much less worthy of commemoration. His every sung moment was a one-night stand.

Dean & Jerry's every performed moment was a one-nighter, too.

[3]

From *Living It Up*:

> DEAN (seated, with guitar, and in blue jeans [Homer is at the side, the apt pupil]):
>
> > You don't have to give me
> > Clever conversation
> > I just want affection,
> > Not an education.
> > (Jule Styne and Bob Hilliard)

That Dino's appeals to his audience were always partly carnal was only confirmed in Billy Wilder's *Kiss Me, Stupid* (1964), in which Dino's "Dino" makes it clear that intimate relations are a nightly physical necessity that must be satisfied whatever the circumstances, and for which he is perfectly happy, if circumstances demand, to compensate his partner monetarily. Jerry Lewis, reflecting: "My partner had established the ground rules well before we met: A real man has a wife and kids—and whatever he can get on the side. And Dean could get plenty" (*Dean* 88).

[4]

"All the way to Urbana for a one-night stand," Billy Wilder and I. A. L. Diamond have Joe (Jerry's pal Tony Curtis) say in *Some Like It Hot* (1959). The phrase "one-night stand" is originally theatrical, denoting the practice of giving one's show in a town so small the theater could be filled with paying audiences for no more than a single evening—the rise of the railroads during the late nineteenth century had turned vaudeville into a form of mass entertainment that served small towns as well as urban areas. In order to maximize bookings, performers were often obliged to play tiny municipalities and venues, this necessitating places for the performers to stay overnight and specialized agents to orchestrate the bookings, travel arrangements, and links with musicians. An unbroken series of dates typically therefore involved relatively short stopovers at many different places along the way. Lodging troubles. Lodging was the subject of a February 4, 1951, skit on the *Comedy Hour*, indeed, with two struggling young entertainers spending a night in a shabby theatrical hotel. They don't have enough money to pay for a double room, so they end up sharing a bed after Jerry absurdly emerges from Dean's suitcase, in a bit worthy of Georges Méliès' *The Devilish Tenant* (1909).

Could Dean ever have emerged from Jerry's suitcase? The patent unthinkability of Jerry toting Dean around and the obvious believability of Dean toting Jerry suggest a wealth of implication about these two, their relationship, their mutual regard across the chasm.

As to the move from town to town, Dean & Jerry were always far too busy to stick around, they gathered no moss; also far too busy in their act, moving from breath to breath. The quality of each yuk, each sung phrase, each double take, each squeak and squelch, each desperation, each embrace, each disciplinary frown—here today, gone tomorrow.

[5]

In the diegeses of Martin & Lewis sequences and sketches, one found a transactional economy: you want Dean's love, you gotta give him something; you want Jerry's attention, you gotta yank for it.

Thus, Dean is continually, if unawaredly, setting up the circumstances in which Jerry must squirm; Jerry's squirming is continually, if unawaredly, drawing Dean's (critical) attention. This balance/imbalance was clear enough—for Jerry much too clear—as the team careened toward catastrophe. Shawn Levy reports a growing tension between the stars on *3 Ring Circus* (1954), with Dean "saying he was fed up to the ears playing a stooge" (183) and eventually expressing resentment "at Jerry's increasingly authoritarian approach to material for the team" (195). When Jerry later met his agent Lew Wasserman[4] expressing a desire to break up the team, Dean reacted to the press, writes Levy: "To me this isn't a love affair. This is big business. I think it's ridiculous for the boy to brush aside such beautiful contracts" (197). Contracts, money, those were things of beauty. The proper place of "the boy" was sitting hopefully but not expectantly at the master's side. In the train car or the airplane, bustling from one bonanza to the next.

[6]

Hollywood or Bust was the last film Martin & Lewis made together, wrapping just before the break-up—by that time the two were barely speaking, a state of affairs Shawn Levy implies was long-lived, since from the beginning "there was an edge of cruelty to Dean . . . while Jerry was more like a puppy dog that kept wagging its tail even when it was being kicked" (72)—and the personal strain between them can occasionally be glimpsed or heard in their performances. In more than one scene, Dean appears to be genuinely piqued with Jerry's antics, his facial expressions betraying more of a scowl than the many episodes of the *Comedy Hour* from the early 1950s where Dean looks to be on the verge of laughing at something Jerry has done. Some measure of the

4 (1913–2002), ultimately president of MCA and arguably the most influential and powerful agent in American entertainment since 1945.

simmering performance Dean gives in the film might be related to what was happening behind the scenes. Lewis recalled,

> on the shoot of *Hollywood or Bust* . . . I was officially off the rails . . . I paid almost no attention to what I was doing, I barely bothered to learn my lines. I came up with unfunny ad libs that threw off the rhythm and the schedule of the shoot. After every take, I'd pace around the set grumbling, "That scene is shit"—when I was the one who had messed it up. I constantly picked fights.[5] (*Dean* 273)

The film also contains one of the most candid expressions of the transactional ethos of love that was inseparable from Dean Martin's fully developed screen persona. Dean is Steve Wiley, a smooth-talking small-time grifter perpetually on the make but now perilously in debt to a bookie who wants to collect even if collecting means violence. Steve ends up road-tripping with movie fan and delicatessen counterman Malcolm Smith (Jerry), from New York all the way to Los Angeles in a brand-new cherry red 1956 convertible Chrysler New Yorker (of which both claim they are the rightful owners after an onstage movie-theater giveaway at which both are holding seemingly identical winning tickets).[6] Along the way, they pick up redheaded aspiring showgirl Terry Roberts (Pat Crowley), who is hoping (as so many people young and old were at the time) for a Hollywood screen test.[7]

They stop to camp for the evening. Steve suggests "Let's Be Friendly" to her:

> Let's be friendly,
> but let's be discreet
> Should we accidentally kiss

5 Lewis recalled that his behavior was so egregious that Tashlin kicked him off the set, telling him, "You're a discourteous, obnoxious prick—an embarrassment to me and a disgrace to the profession. . . . Get your ass out of here and don't come back." (qtd. in *Dean* 274)

6 Steve has obtained a complete duplicate set of raffle tickets from the printer, but Malcolm has seen enough movies to have accumulated a shoebox full of raffle tickets (given out to promote moviegoing). The Chrysler New Yorker, in production since 1940, benefitted from a new high-output engine in 1956. New in this year's model was a record-player beneath the dash, though this possible amenity was not depicted in the film.

7 The clash between the red hair and the red car—two quite different reds—is echoed, interestingly, in Nicholas Ray's *Party Girl* two years later.

I'd give up the fight
And we could be more than just
good friends tonight. *[Terry tosses a blanket over his head]*
(Sammy Fain and Paul Francis Webster)

Nearby, Jerry is dozing in a hammock, wearing bold striped pajamas visible from miles away and with Mr. Bascomb, a massive Great Dane, beneath him. A glossy of Anita Ekberg is clutched at his chest. After Dean warbles his last line with his head poised just above Terry's—"We could be more than just good friends . . . . tonight"—he leans even closer to try for a kiss, and they have the following exchange:

TERRY: Nice music (pushing his head away forcefully and sitting up). Wrong lyrics.

STEVE: You have someone waiting in Vegas?

TERRY: I have a job waiting in Vegas.

STEVE: You know as soon as I saw you I figured you for a gambler. (Grabbing her arm) Relax, honey, we won't play for keeps.

TERRY: Look, it's getting kind of late, don't you think?

She explains her plans for when she gets to Las Vegas and notes the "undecided future" that Steve claims to be interested in. He impatiently lights himself a cigarette. As she continues to elude his grasp, she continues:

TERRY: Mr. Wiley, we were brought together because I had forty dollars, and you needed same. Well, you got my forty dollars, but that's all you get.

STEVE: I don't wanna get, I wanna give.

TERRY: Sorry, no takers.

(Terry then turns the conversation to Steve.)

STEVE: All right, what would you like to know? Where I was born or how I vote?

TERRY: Or, how an attractive man manages to stay single?

STEVE: You get better odds at a racetrack.

TERRY: Better than 50-50?

She is giving the chance of a successful relationship the same odds as a coin toss.

He responds with a 45-second monologue that dismantles the American dream so dear to 1950s media with the cold logic of a handicapper playing the horses.

> STEVE: That's only 50-50 on the toteboard. You know the minute you leave the startin' gate the odds are 6-to-4 'cause you're furnishing a rundown apartment. Then the odds drop 7-to-3 'cause you need a larger place, an extra room for the little monster that your ever-lovin' comes up with. Now the little monster grows, becomes a big monster: school expenses. Now you gotta start takin' everything that the crummy boss hands out 'cause you can't afford to lose your crummy job. Little junior's gotta go to college: "Dear pop, need money, met a girl." The odds are now 9-to-1 and you haven't even hit the far turn yet. By the time you get to the finish line, you gotta hurry up and die so you have enough money for your own funeral expenses. That's a bad deal.

Let's decode Terry Roberts for a moment. When she wonders how a single male (Steve) can stay unmarried, what exactly can she be surmising? That he's a bigamist, already married? Or—a reading that wouldn't have been given openly by most viewers at the time—that he's gay? The subtle implication beneath her question is: since obviously, all over America, attractive males are being pursued by women seeking marriage, you couldn't be male and attractive and also *not married* unless something else were going on.

The something else we read onto Dean is the constant fact that he's a serial philanderer, *serial* being the key word. Every conquest a link in a chain. At the same time, Jerry is one of his pursuers.

[7]

What was a constant between Dean & Jerry was a discrepancy between their displayed modes of affect for each other. Jerry was unendingly trying to grapple with Dean—touch, pat, embrace, surround, and so on. Dean was pulling back from this, as though under threat, and his song bits were often spurred by him sliding away from a Jerry gesture of affection.

This asymmetry was writ large over their entire body (pun intended) of work. What exactly it meant to audiences of the 1940s or 1950s—or today, for that matter—to see one man reaching out for another and the second pulling away from the first is discussed to some degree in Corber: a general culturally bound homophobia. But Dean & Jerry softened the stance. Jerry was "allowed" to be Dean's adoring fan, "allowed" to moon over him, "allowed" to twiddle him in many bizarre ways, and Dean was always in some sense policing the interaction despite a general air of begrudging tolerance. Dean buffered Jerry. Jerry needed buffering.

[8]

Terry has been watching Malcolm and Steve's relationship, indeed:

> TERRY (to Steve): He's off his rocker about you. (*That is, he'll do whatever you tell him to.*)
>
> STEVE (retorting directly, and completely missing her meaning): Why can't *you* be more like Malcolm?

In hot pursuit of Terry, Steve is failing to grasp what the audience and Terry have grasped quickly, that is, what she *can see—and has been seeing all along:* Malcolm is in love with him. Is her phrasing just a polite circumlocution? And is Steve inadvertently giving confirmation, since it is pretty clear that what he would like from Terry is exactly, precisely, and definitively what Terry has been suspecting Malcolm would like from him? Meanwhile, as Malcolm sleeps, the dog is loyally guarding.

But for Steve, Malcolm might as well not exist (a delirious fact for fans who loved Dean and hated Jerry, a blockage of sorts for anyone sympathizing with Jerry's character of the moment), his mental radio having been tuned to another station and the love song he had been humming now replaced by something completely different. But like the dog Malcolm is infallibly loyal. Steve has asked for milk and, eager to cater to his every need, Malcolm heads off to a nearby field to milk a cow—that turns out to be a bull.

With Malcolm we wonder, is he perceptually impaired? How can somebody who is looking for a cow mistakenly try to milk a bull? Or: how broad and deep is Malcolm's gender confusion, his inability to make clear distinction between "the male" and "the female" of a species, and in fact his determination to get milk out of a male? The joke's aimed-for laughter of course occludes all such thought, wipes it away in mirth. Is the film suggesting—perhaps none too subtly—that Malcolm's infatuation goes hand in hand with some embedded cognitive problem—he can't discern Steve any more than he can discern the bull? Dean's Steve, having no such problem, aims directly at the female in the vicinity.

Dean is forever hyperconservatively hetero, Jerry is forever treading a fine line between wanting a girl and wanting his partner. The tone of every performing moment between these two resonates with this conundrum.

Or could Malcolm's milk hunt have come from something like motherly love? Certainly, Jerry was interested in a kind of love that was utterly/udderly other than what Dean could or would give. Womanizing Steve has been physically forcing himself on Terry at every opportunity, but now he belatedly turns to see what Malcolm has been up to and spies him out in the field with a milk pan—another signifier of feminine caretaking—stuck on his head. The nourishing maternal love of mama-cow Jerry instantaneously rejected by the big aggressive bull(-shitter) Dean. Jerry wrote later of the abiding love he believed—no, that he *knew*—had existed between the two men. This was only when Martin was no longer alive to correct, interrupt, or negate his unapologetically sentimental version of the story (as he did so often in their stage, screen, radio, and television acts) or to offer his own retrospective revisionist history of their decade-long personal and professional relationship. In his 2005 memoir *Dean & Me: A Love Story*, Lewis is clearly still stinging from their breakup forty-nine years before:

> I dream about Dean pretty often, maybe once a month since he died [December 25, 1995]. In my dreams, he's almost always young, tan, still unbelievably handsome—indestructible. Sometimes, though, in these ultra-vivid late-night movies, bad things are happening—to him, to me, to both of us—and I'm powerless to stop them. Sometimes, my wife[8] tells me, I cry out in my sleep. (257)

8 Sandra "SanDee" Pitnick, from 1983 onward was Jerry's wife after Patti Palmer (Esther Grace Calonico), who divorced him after a long marriage.

THIS IS CARDBOARD

[1]

Colgate Comedy Hour, October 15, 1950:

> Finishing a spirited if partly off-key duet of "Marie"
> (Irving Berlin, 1928),
> Marie, the dawn is breaking,
> Marie, you'll soon be waking,
> To find your heart is aching . . . ,

Dean and Jerry take a unison bow, their two mouths wide open. But as the studio audience applauds, Dean announces that he has noticed behind one of the cameras someone signaling them that *only three minutes remain* in the broadcast and they must start wrapping up.

He starts miming in wildly exaggerated fashion.

Jerry joins in, mimicking the offscreen hand signals.

The two of them approach the camera. That is, they pointedly point out to their viewing audience that viewing is happening by way of a camera, a camera near them to which they can take steps.

> JERRY (bluntly, miming again): These fellas on the side are going like this.— (He mimes someone pulling hands apart, as in stretching taffy.) They don't want you people out there to know. You can't conceal these things to this audience! They pay money to buy Colgate and I want—put the camera on this man when he goes like this—hurry up, over there, do as I say this minute. (Stamps feet.) Put the camera over there when he goes like this—over there!

> DEAN (gesturing for the camera to follow him): You all think I'm mad.

The two segue, absolutely randomly, into a brief minstrel routine then into an exchange in Cockney dialect, followed by further ad-libbing. As they bring the show to a close, they make a dramatic point of noting each passing minute while looking over to the cameras:

> DEAN & JERRY (together): One minute.

> JERRY (confident): We can kill that in an hour.

Now thirty seconds remain. Jerry points offstage and Dean goes offscreen, only to return with the sign that says "30 SEC," which he shows to the studio audience and the camera and uses to fan himself before giving the cut signal and trotting offstage with Jerry right behind him.

Seven months later, May 20, 1951:

> JERRY (to cameramen): I gotta get over here??? What is it with you guys??? Just 'cause you wear an earphone you can direct people around. Maybe I don't want to go over there! . . . You're not close enough, are you? . . . Can you see all of me? I want they should see.

I want they should see! He doesn't want to hide it from us.

Later in the show:

JERRY: Let me show you what I mean about disillusioning people.... This ain't even a real tree. This is cardboard.

[2]

"This is cardboard."

Jerry's audience, perfectly and fully capable of detecting that this is not actually a tree, has tacitly agreed to go along with his little shtick—the conventional dramatic shtick used universally—and mentally treat it as one. But now, suddenly, he is bluntly addressing them and saying, in effect, "I noticed you have tacitly agreed to go along with a ridiculous gag of mine, that this cardboard picture of a tree is a tree, and by telling you now that I know the gag was ridiculous, and that I know you agreed to go along, I am actually addressing this silent agreement that *you*, and audiences like you around the world, keep offering show people like Dean and me." That flat tree has provoked something in Jerry.

If that tree-structure had been built by the designers to look much more believably like an actual tree (see Assheton Gorton's trees—"trees"—in Ridley Scott's *Legend* [1985] if you want serious inducement to *believe in trees* that are not trees) the audience might have reasonably thought it was that, not mere cardboard, and in such a case Jerry would be offering them a polite and helpful correction. But Jerry knows that the audience never was taken in, couldn't possibly have been; the audience was only putting on a show of being taken in, perhaps for his and Dean's benefit. Of course, in politely pointing his audience to the fact that (he knows) *they* were never taken in, he is distancing them from the "he" who knows this: in fact, *taking them in.*

Without elaboration we can say, and apparently audiences at the time could say, too, that television production could never possibly afford to bring an actual tree—or for that matter pretty much anything actual—into the studio. Viewers watched their screen addictively, knowing it was all fake. Knowing and suspending the knowledge; knowing and disavowing what they knew.

This is a moment that calls into question familiar conventions of televisual *mise-en-scène* from this period (in which most things, including trees, look an awful lot like so much cardboard). Jerry challenges certain of these conventions by making fun of sponsors, that is, openly pointing to them; by approaching the camera too closely, that is, by pointing to the camera; or talking to the audience in "direct" speech (Caldwell 47–48). Dean goes along, apparently happily. Dean & Jerry are a perpetual monkey wrench in the workings of 1950s broadcasting, constantly misbehaving, transgressing established boundaries, and troubling the assumptions of producers and audiences alike. As wholly fake as 1950s TV was, producers went to extraordinary lengths to cover that fakery. Jerry will later, onscreen, become a diegetic "monkey wrench" in all the dramatic circumstances the Martin & Lewis movies offer.

[3]

The Sponsor was in those days, and remains today, a universal subject for mockery as well as a sacred icon. In radio and early television, there was typically only the vaguest, if any, demarcation between the point where the program left off and the commercial began. The generally accepted belief was: nobody in his right mind takes commercials seriously, or sincerely claims to love watching them in preference to the programs and movies they rudely interrupt. Erik Barnouw does point out that some audiences claimed they found commercials "fun," but does not go so far as to suggest these audiences preferred them to programming (80). But this issue of preference rests upon the idea of distinction: that program and commercial message can be identified as separate and in some ways unrelated "messages." What happens, then, if commercials appear to bleed directly from, and leak into, programming? In the days before explicit "product placement," this kind of boundary blurring was hardly unique to Dean & Jerry. But, in their especially farcical and mocking style they not only blurred the program-to-commercial boundary, they pointed out the fact that they were blurring it, and by pointing this out they showed audiences that the pointing-out was aimed at them; in short, that viewers were not in null space but were actively watching a dramatized presentation that was explicitly commercially sponsored. The "fake" commercial, or the blurred commercial, screamed, "Look at you sitting there watching us goof around with the sponsors who are paying us to be here treating them with more respect."

But Dean & Jerry were exercising a singular form of mockery unknown at the time and unimitated since. They were essentially hustlers, grabbing for laughs, and nothing prevented them from slipping the sponsor into the hustle the sponsor was paying for.

During the age of the man in the gray flannel suit (a corporate ethos that Nunnally Johnson represented in *The Man in the Gray Flannel Suit* [1956] and that, taking satirical aim at the unholy alliance between the network television and advertising industries, Frank Tashlin sent up in *Will Success Spoil Rock Hunter?* [1957]), Martin & Lewis were perfectly willing to nibble at, even bite the sponsorial hands that fed them. Lewis tells the story of Martin refusing to give up the American Tobacco Company's Lucky Strikes—omnipresent for him—even though their radio program was sponsored by competitor Liggett & Myers for their Chesterfield cigarettes. (According to Jerry, Dean simply put his preferred smokes in Chesterfield packs [Lewis interview].) Later, they hustled Colgate.

The hustle is clean business practice; they're working for Colgate Palmolive. At the same time they're slyly filling their pockets by side-hustling cigarettes.

To look without preconception at Dean & Jerry's work is to see an unbroken chain of hustles—hustles for glamor and adulation, hustles for hysterical guffaws. You take an opportunity when you see it, because nobody is going to come around making you offers of opportunity you didn't reach out for, first. And taking opportunity when you see it, having the quick grasp, is a working-class strategy. When you're hustling to feed yourself, you know the difference between a cardboard tree and a real tree. The real tree doesn't come for free and even a cardboard tree costs something.

HUSTLERS

[1]

Dean and Jerry were world-class hustlers.

They shilled shamelessly through their entire careers. On the *Colgate Comedy Hour* they occasionally did their own commercials,[1] plugging the sponsor's products—this, even though most of the show's commercials were polished and sometimes animated productions made to flog Ajax, the foaming cleanser; Fab laundry detergent; Halo shampoo; and other Colgate products. There is a fascinating irony to Dean & Jerry offering, displaying, promoting, or otherwise attempting to be convincing about Colgate products. When they speak, they are not in character for sketches, yet at the same time they are not exactly speaking for themselves personally or taking the posture of company spokesmen. Who is it that has been using the Colgate toothpaste Jerry holds up to the camera beside his toothy face?

1 Barnouw reflects how in the 1950s and onward it was a frequent occurrence to find very famous celebrities showing up doing commercials (80).

Class advantages bring up taste. "Taste is a new empire brought within the reach of lower- and middle-class groups by the spread of leisure," Max Lerner wrote in the mid-1950s (642–43). As taste consider, for a telling example, the hustle of sport. Baseball was the American working-class game. You strove for a hit, or you strove to curtail somebody else's. You worked. And the harder you worked, the better you were. (Working-class ethic.) More: because by design the pitcher's timing was unpredictable (it is even more so today), the batter's swing was unpredictable, too, and the ball's being put in play was a total mystery. One had to spring into action, here, now, over there, even all the way over there. . . . Baseball as "Jerry's game." Golf was "Dean's." A much more middle-class sport. Take your time, make yourself comfortable with the ball, focus on it. Use good form—form defines the success of the swing. Make sure you dress properly for the links. Make sure you rent a caddy's services—as Dean does in *The Caddy*. And get a decent ball to play with, get a dozen, get an unlimited number.

Thus, we see Dean & Jerry hustling Dunlop Sport (est. 1910). Dunlop started marketing its high-end MAXFLI golf ball in 1922 and production was in heavy swing by the early 1950s. Catch Dean & Jerry on the *Comedy Hour*, February 10, 1952:

- In front of the curtain, following a skit, Dean & Jerry smile together in their matching tuxedos. Jerry proceeds, inexplicably, to introduce a song from Dean: "I'm going to introduce your song. So Max, fly away."
- Seemingly confused (Is this part of one of our gags?), Dean gives a nod of the head and replies, "Max? So fly away? I don't get this . . ."
- And now Dean looks on patiently while Jerry provides an inevitably circumloquacious explanation: "Well, your name is really Dean but I called you Max and told you to fly away because Maxfli is the name of a golf ball and *the sponsor doesn't want us to make any plugs!*"

(Doesn't want plugs, that is, of anything other than Colgate-Palmolive products, since the Company is indisputably possessive about Dean & Jerry and the expensive program time they are purchasing from NBC).

- Jerry approaches the camera and gives it a massive conspiratorial wink.

- But now, suddenly, Dean seems to click that Jerry is slyly doing a commercial for their favorite golf ball even though they are not paid Dunlop sponsors but in fact are being paid to advertise Colgate at that very moment! Dean smiles and starts nodding approvingly, then swings his arm as if tossing an imaginary golf ball. "We need the golf balls!" Don't pass up a split second's opportunity to get something for nothing.
- Jerry chimes in seamlessly, completing Dean's sentences before Dean can do so himself, as per normal. "—because we both play golf, so send them to the house right away!" Crossing his eyes . . . winking . . . and leaning toward the camera to make his appeal not to the consumer (as in a typical advertisement) but (in a surprising and openly self-serving reversal) to a manufacturer who is not sponsoring the program on which he is appearing. As he says these words . . .
- Dean lowers his head and adds his own plug, "MAXFLI!!!!"—even though the product name is barely audible because of the volume of the studio audience's laughter by this point.

(With Dean's complicity, what Jerry has managed here is a working-class boy's triumph, echoed by Dean giving the final punchline to the golf ball.)

- However, never one to leave off with a joke after the apparent punchline has been delivered if still another joke can presumably follow, Jerry goes on, holding his hands to his head while grimacing. Because he cannot possibly pretend the execs from Colgate aren't in his audience, ready to kill him!

JERRY: Oh, I can just see the sponsor now, squeezing all the Colgate toothpaste out of the tube and he's screaming something awful.

A face of imitated torment (but betraying actual delight), and the audience is in on the whole thing.

- Dean has taken hold of Jerry's arm and his other shoulder, and must physically restrain his partner from clapping and continuing with his ribbing of the sponsor if he is ever to sing his song.

DEAN: All right now, before you do anything else, Jerry, introduce . . . (*becoming forceful*) . . . introduce my song, and make it lovely.

- To which Jerry replies with the puncturing retort, "It's Academy Award time and he gets so carried away."[2]

The scene is in many fascinating ways prototypical of Dean & Jerry's work, not only here on the *Comedy Hour* but later in their duo films and even later in their solo work. Go for the punch, whether the punch is financial or semi-financial, or bold laughter. Don't think about it, don't send a telegram, don't make battle plans . . . GO FOR IT. Much of Jerry's apparently endless striving for effect in a comedic moment (switching facial expressions, postures, etc.) can be understood this way, going and going and going and going for it, as can Dean's precipitous and always canny standing by, looking for the right opening, and his seizing the chance to feed straight lines exactly on what would be taken as "cue," but was in fact improvised. You can improvise brilliantly only if you're hungry. Only if every breath is a search for sustenance.[3]

[2]

Nothing could be more mistaken than presuming the consumer heyday of the 1950s drew upon some widely shared wealth. Only some people could buy the broadloomed living room, the new pale turquoise Impala, or, around 1955, the new Frigidaire "Sheer Look" line described by Karal Ann Marling as having been:

> introduced to the public by fashion models holding their hands at stiff, right angles to match the lines of the merchandise, and dressed in the same snooty shades: Mayfair pink, Sherwood green, Stratford yellow, and

2 A little more than a month later, Humphrey Bogart was awarded Best Actor for *The African Queen* (John Huston, 1951) in the Academy Awards telecast on March 20, 1952.

3 It was only a year before art imitated life in *The Caddy*. After winning the Santa Barbara invitational golf tournament, a delivery of complimentary merchandise—including a new suitcase, several outfits of clothing, and six dozen brand-new golf balls—shows up for Joe Anthony (Dean) at the hotel room he is sharing with his caddy Harvey Miller Jr. (Jerry), courtesy of the Santa Barbara Businessmen's Association. A little nod of the head here to healthy egalitarianism, too, if not classlessness, because in the real world of golf and golfing arrangements, players were in one stratum and their caddies in another.

> a charcoal gray derived from men's flannel suits. If the pink refrigerator-freezer was a pathetic status symbol, a warning sign of cultural decadence, a mark of deadening suburban sameness . . . it was also a token of personal achievement, of an adventurous willingness to try something new. (266)

Social class differences were everywhere, if not everywhere to be seen. Indeed, *not* everywhere to be seen. There were biases against seeing social-class difference in America, after all; this was one of the horrors it was comfortably believed the pilgrims had happily left behind in England.

If you were in the working class, certainly from the Great Depression onward (Jerry was born in 1926, Dean in 1917), you did not have the world offered to you on a gilded platter by servants in spangling livery. You did not snap your fingers and whine that the cake didn't have enough icing. The life of the everyday, just like the life of the dream, was catch as catch can, race for the prize, reach in and grab if the grabbing was good. More than improvisation: surprise. An attitude to life that operated on the assumption that things happen, things eventuate, and all carefully architected plans are for nil. As *Variety* put it in one of the earliest reviews of Dean & Jerry's act, when they were playing the Havana-Madrid club in New York, hoping to score big with audiences and create the buzz that would lead to more and better future bookings, "Duo goes through a bunch of zany routines, apparently following a set format but improvising most of the way along the line" (Stal., "Night Club Reviews," September 25, 1946, 56). One scrambles for one's successes, moment by moment. One hustles. Two hustled. Dean, the boy from the small steel town in Ohio who wanted to get out, who took the opening he could see and ran, had the same essential way of being as his partner. Dino, son of barber, saw the coins going into the cash register early, learned that if one hustled one should be hustling to make a buck. Even if it was illegal, "There wasn't much else to do except a little stealing," he later recalled (qtd. in Freedland 4). Jerome Levitch, son of stand-up comedian, learned that if one was going to be hustling one should be hustling to get a laugh.

[3]

But there could be peril if you hustled across the stage line. Sitting too close to the performance could be a material hazard for spectators, but not, as it might turn out, spectators alone.

A Mrs. Deja experienced peril at the Chicago Paramount Theater when Martin & Lewis were appearing there:

> On August 1, 1951 at 4:10 PM. Mrs. Deja was seated in the 3rd row on the main floor, when she was struck in the mouth when the tip of Dean Martin's cane flew off. She was sent to the office of Drs. Walker and Cooper for first-aid, and they report . . . a ragged laceration . . . one lower tooth is loose. . . . It will require approximately two weeks before the wounds are healed; the tooth . . . [may] have to be extracted and replaced. (Letter from William H. Holden to Joseph Ross, September 12, 1951, Theatre Historical Society).

Note the permeability of the fragile stage boundary, generally speaking but especially heightened for performers like Dean & Jerry who toyed with it all the time. Here, however, is something fascinating for those who would research Dean & Jerry or research anybody working a long time ago. The more consideration we gave this little account, the more opaque it became:

1— A flying prop injures an audience member: easy to presume this was an accident, even though one assumes that nothing happening onstage is *actually accidental.*

2— Is the injury serious?, or does the correspondence elevate it? A mountain out of a molehill? Or a molehill blocking view of a mountain?

3— There is no account of Dean & Jerry wishing the injured Mrs. Deja well or any other response from them, *at all.* Others confabulate over their silence, however:

4— William H. Holden, who worked for Balaban and Katz theaters (offices inside the same Chicago Theater Building), was presumably acting on behalf of the theater regarding Mrs. Deja's injuries when he communicated directly—not with Dean or Jerry but with N. Joseph Ross, their lawyer, affiliated at the time with Pacht, Tannenbaum, and Ross at 6535 Wilshire Blvd., Beverly Hills (among whose other clients were Frank Sinatra and Bugsy Siegel). How did the unfortunate event come to be known by Holden? He was very likely not sitting in that audience.

5— Did lawyers at Pacht, Tannenbaum, and Ross have immediate concern that the event could (swiftly) turn into a legal matter? Pacht, Tannenbaum, and Ross was nothing if not a significant entertainment-business law firm. We can assume that in their work they were assiduous, but Ross[4] had not—so far as we can determine—sent a general letter to Holden or to Balaban and Katz warning that any untoward matters should be brought immediately to his attention.

6— Jerry reacts: Around noon on August 2, he calls a number in Beverly Hills from his dressing room, and is almost at the same moment reported unwell.

7— Jerry was already, it seems, on the cusp of "exhaustion." After their one-week gig at the Chicago Theatre, a newspaper report appears: "Jerry Lewis of the comedy team of Martin & Lewis is suffering from nervous exhaustion and has been ordered to 'take a complete rest,' it was announced today." Jerry needs a break, but the problem was caused by Dean's prop. Jerry's collapse forced a cancellation that would cost them considerably.

8— Could taciturn Dean have been exhausted as well, without giving the appearance? Did the cane accident onstage occur at least in part because, weary but smiling, his attention lapsed?

One should not automatically surmise that in show business, then and probably now, there rests, beneath the performance, a carpet under the fringes of which a great deal is swept. What exactly happened in the theater after the cane tip went flying? Ushers racing? People screaming? We don't know. Is there anything remarkable about how swiftly and easily this was all "handled" by powers that be, and kept away from the performers; or is it absolutely par for the course? We don't know. And whatever happened to Mrs. Deja afterward? We don't know. Certainly, Dean & Jerry had a lot of help behind the scenes breaking out of the possible, and unpleasant, limitations of legal trouble.

4 We are unable to be certain, but it is conceivable that Ross also represented Dean and Jerry's frequent producer, Hal Wallis. A year following the Chicago event, when young Sammy Petrillo and his partner Duke Mitchell were jostling to establish a career mimicking Dean and Jerry (Petrillo was the astounding lookalike who had played the baby in the "babysitter" skit's conclusion), Wallis initiated a conversation about stifling them with Dean and Jerry's lawyer and, as Shawn Levy reports, it was Joe Ross who responded to him (146). We can note that Dean and Jerry's legal representative was involved in as tiny a matter as eighteen dollars for unpaid phone calls and as potentially scandalous a matter as the theater injury to Mrs. Deja.

[4]

The phrase "we don't know" occurs and reoccurs above. Given the legion past situations, now faded from the scene, and from which no information has survived, a brief consideration of the process of researching "historical" film and television is merited:

Take the ganglion of information and speculation confronting us regarding the August 1951 happening at the Chicago Paramount. It points to the kind of complicated headache—and/or exhilarating wild-goose chase—that can come of primary-source research. One ends up "getting into the weeds" of messy historical minutiae, trying to track down someone's phone number to figure out who was on the other end of a 7:35 PM telephone call placed by Jerry Lewis on the evening of July 31 or in mid-day August 2 (while he was "exhausted"); the name of someone's lawyer(s), or the names of that lawyer's other clients. When one has access to nothing more than fragments of communication, it is like hearing the echoes of voices, often unknown, saying disconnected phrases. The slide can easily lead toward gossip.

Since the insider Kenneth Anger's[5] *Hollywood Babylon* (1965), a volume almost universally treated by "serious" readers as worse than worthless, we have tended as scholars to strategically ignore, if not scornfully disavow, the importance of gossip for writing histories of Hollywood. The tabloid press (at least insofar as the relevant periodicals have been preserved, microfilmed, or digitized by the relevant research libraries and institutions—which have, all of them, limits on what they can hold) has much to offer the historian. So do the files of countless lawyers (show-business professionals if ever there were) though they may be far harder to obtain even than copies of whatever tabloid might have covered Jerry's nervous breakdown in Chicago. Freedom of Information Act requests have become an invaluable tool for researchers of the Hollywood blacklist, but the same procedure is not available for researching private attorneys, with the distressing effect that reported lawyer tales are essentially only hearsay—but hearsay from voices we cannot identify in their saying. Were legal files ever to become more widely available, Hollywood history would probably need to be rewritten many times over should anyone have the patience and the willingness to read through the kinds of memos that

5 Anger (b. 1927) appeared in Max Reinhardt's *A Midsummer Night's Dream* (1936).

many film historians have made a habit of ignoring. In our case here, Pacht, Tannenbaum, and Ross clearly played a hushed role of some significance.

But even more enlightening—often shockingly so—can be directly presented oral comments from people "who were there" and never had their opinions, recollections, or observations recorded in any fashion. Of this *one would find nothing in the files.* For one telling example, the conversations taking place on a film set during shooting, which are not encapsulated or even hinted at in the Daily Production Reports. The real-life agonies, say, on the set of *Hollywood or Bust.*

Consider a tale about Lew Wasserman finagling to get Dean and Jerry on his side after they had freed themselves from Abner 'Abby' Greshler (1910–1993), with whose agency they were unsatisfied. Were any documents written and retained, in order to bring about the state of affairs Wasserman desired? When they traveled to LA and he had hopes of netting them—as we can read—he arranged for Herman Citron, the no. 1 agent in his crew, to go to Union Station to pick them up and chauffeur them—high-class treatment. Did Wasserman write to Citron to arrange this, or telephone him? And what exactly did he say? Fan magazines and the film industry trade press (some of which are digitized in online digital repositories like the Lantern Media History Digital Library, which has provided us with a number of primary sources) have been a boon to several generations of researchers, but there may well be a lot more elsewhere, unless it has already made its way into paper-shredders and incinerators, which in all likelihood is where where potentially illuminating evidence about the Deja affair ended up after the respective firms ceased to exist.

Unlike such treasure hunts, productive or not, tracking secondary sources generally sends one in circles, responding to the work of others, treading paths that are often well worn, concocting hypotheses relative to the existing scholarship, then testing, complicating, modifying, or falsifying them—in all of this having, usually, no way to be certain of the veracity of anything originally stated. Where did that information come from in the first place? Each of us has encountered scholars who, asked where something came from, gave a genial shrug of the vocal cords and said, "Actually I have no idea."

Somewhere there breathes an earnest researcher who is struggling in an archive to find out, "How much did Hal Wallis influence Frank Tashlin?" We, however, want to know, "What color was Hal Wallis's telephone?" Not a search for the meaninglessly picayune detail but a search for a Real Thing of the past.

IN STEREO

[1]

Martin & Lewis, like almost all other comics of their time, like many comics today, and like many non-professional comedians altogether, operated with stereotypes. Jerry wrapped in a flannel baby outfit suddenly becoming a baby (the baby so many thought he was). Dean with fake makeup scars all over his face becoming the hyper-gangster. These and so many other "preposterous" characterizations, going into a territory beyond parody, offer the audience admittedly simplistic, considerably exaggerated cutouts for seducing their ongoing commitment as the comedy progresses. The Jerry baby for example: far too immense to be a baby; far too much a lookalike for Jerry Lewis (who is always playing in some kind of infantile way, but in an adult body); dressed as a baby would be dressed, except that on an adult body the costume is nothing but laughable: yet for all this, if one is to engage in the jokes of the routine, one must keep telling oneself "This is the baby," very much in the face of openly denying that "fact."

In television skit-performance, there is very limited time for development of character and so stereotypes are often used for instantaneous pick-up and recognition. In films, preposterous, paper-thin characterizations, fakes that we love to accept even though we know they are fakes, may show up in bit performances, which tend to be relatively brief (contained in one or only a few scenes). A lovely example of the wildly stereotyped character performance is shown with bent old Miss Bessie Polk (Ida Moore) in *Rock-a-Bye Baby*. Ultra-archetype of the ultra-avid consumer, she watches television *only for the commercials*, having no interest whatever in the programming. Whenever one of the "multiple alternating sponsors" tells viewers to do something—drink Chicory coffee, smoke Superbo cigarettes, or take Burporex tablets—Miss Bessie consumes the corresponding product immediately, but when the commercials are over she gets out of her rocking chair and walks away from the set.[1] She explains to her devoted boarder Clayton Poole (Jerry), "You know I believe in loyalty to the sponsor," and thanks him for "running to the market every time one of those TV fellas says, 'Go to the market and get some.'" Scott Bukatman pays serious attention to Miss Bessie's television watching, standing upon Marshall McLuhan's observation that "ads push the principle of noise all the way to the plateau of persuasion." As to the lady's "loyalty to the sponsor," Bukatman observes, "What once we rendered to God or Caesar now (tenuously) belonged to Madison Avenue.... The more pervasive advertising becomes, especially when abetted by the power of television, the more it generates its own set of conditions: the *best* must always be *NEW and IMPROVED*" ("Idiocy" 183–84). Most viewers know television commercials as obnoxious interruptions of something "more serious" that they would choose to believe in, and the predisposition is exactly what is being caricatured through Miss Bessie and her inversion. *Don't believe this!—believe THAT instead!* That the characterization is not to be believed straightforwardly was precisely the point, and if Miss Bessie's character had taken up much more of the narrative space, the point would have disappeared. The only way to find entertainment, finally, is to commit oneself to the performance and believe in it, she says, effectively; and this is precisely what we do with her. *I don't want the audience should be disillusioned....* Completely far-fetched, the characterization is enthusiastically bought.

1 There is a parody of this 1958 sequence in Luis Buñuel's *The Discreet Charm of the Bourgeoisie* (1972), in the dining table sequence.

[2]

For Dean & Jerry (stereo)types worked for better or for worse. They themselves embodied and represented a pair of recognizable stereotypes. But onstage and onscreen, they brought together ethnic, biological, and gender stereotypes in a pairing that was both familiar and unexpected. They trafficked in stereotypes. Their "stage world"—a private universe that they created on TV, in movies, on the radio, and elsewhere—was populated by an array of types and stereotypes. Supporting players like Eddie Mayehoff, Fred Clark, Kathleen Freeman, Dorothy Malone, George Winslow, and many others embodied types much more than they did actual people, if not exactly ethnic then surely cultural types: the stuffed-shirt organization man (Clark), the "bossy" woman (Freeman), the attractive minx (Malone), the mature-beyond-his-years child (Winslow), the sputtering impotent blusterer (Mayehoff). These and so many others were always less fully formed characters than they were immediately graspable types—if mostly two-dimensional. If we can agree that Sergei Eisenstein's *Ivan the Terrible* (1944–1958)[2] was a "monodrama," as Yuri Tsivian puts it—

> in which his fellow characters, [are] conceived as various refractions of his self. . . . In the final analysis, the world of the film is that of Ivan; other characters are but extensions of his image . . . which means that characters around Ivan are kinds of proxies, or avatars, which behave, mutate or exchange functions according to what is going on in the hero's mind. (*Ivan the Terrible*, 51, 68)

—then all of the Martin & Lewis performances are "duodramas" in which everyone else to be met is little more than a representative proxy. More than the mental states of Dean or Jerry, it is fragments of their action that are represented in the types.

2 Conceived in three parts, only two were completed, with the second released only posthumously.

[3]

It was hardly Dean as a person whom Jerry, or anyone in the audience, would have seen or heard. It was Dean as the stereotype of the Italian American Catholic. Dean would never eclipse—or even try to—his Catholic, Italian, midwestern roots and upbringing, but his presence magnified, emphasized, and highlighted it. "It's no small thing to be a Catholic father of four," Jerry reflected long afterward, noting that Dean's first wife Betty "represented all the pain of his young manhood" (*Dean* 121)—a comment, we should not forget, from the creator and performer of one of the great religio-ethnic conundra of the twentieth century, "the lounge lizard Buddy Love, arrogant, condescending, suave, and garish as no self-respecting Jew in a predominantly anti-Semitic culture, demeaned by power and subservient to the defining gaze of others, dares to be" (Pomerance, "Who Was" 207). In some ways there is no coming closer to an identity than by acting it, so it is reasonable to think that Jerry, for years seeing the backstage "inside" of Dean, and having embodied the quintessentially non-Jewish Buddy, could understand the peculiarities of the Catholic torment. Understand, or at least recognize.

A Jew comprehending a Catholic? Surely some mutual understanding had occurred, as must have been the case with multiple interfaith marriages of the time.

Representation by stereotype was anything but abnormal from 1946 to 1956. Far more than through experience and social proximity, it was through stereotype that in this period (and even later) identifications centrally based on, and emphatically pointing to, ethnicity, race, religion, age, gender, and intellect were put forward and grasped on the American scene. Stereotypes were embedded in the fabric of American culture, Jerry's "Jewishness" and Dean's "Italianness" no more than others; Jerry's nerdiness and Dean's sang-froid and cool; Jerry's anxious fidgeting (all parts of his body) and Dean's suave ease. There was no escaping stereotypes, especially in visual media hell-bent on delivering characters and situations swiftly, economically, and strongly.

[4]

The word "stereotype" originated in nineteenth-century printer's jargon. It was an impression of an entire page of type and illustrations, composited and framed as a single piece. The use of stereotypes allowed printers to print one page while setting type for subsequent pages, freeing up their necessarily limited supply of moveable type—the essential element of the Gutenberg revolution. This allowed greater efficiency of print production, since typesetting and printing could be done simultaneously if enough laborers were available—somewhat in the same way that in the studio system, a camera crew could film a scene on one soundstage while a carpentry crew built a set for another scene in the corner or in an adjacent stage. Provided the stereotypes were kept in store, they also allowed for later print runs without repeating the time-consuming manual labor of setting the type all over again (and consider in light of this, Technicolor Inc.'s retention of black-and-white camera negatives—stereotypes of another kind—in storage so that new color prints could be struck later).[3] But one had to be aware that unlike the lines of moveable type from which it was impressed, once it was formed the stereotype was inflexible and could not easily be altered. Much easier than alteration was wholesale replacement with a new stereotype.

From a labor-analytical point of view, stereotypes were short cuts. While being a time saver, though, they also ossified complexities into rigidities.[4] The stereotype collected a group of individual, fragmentary parts, each of which has its own history of development, and lock-binds them into a singular configuration: waving the hand gesturally + devouring spaghetti and meatballs + losing one's temper + having curly dark hair + adoring Mama + drinking too much (wine) + warbling ballads ("Arrivederci Roma") + being a wise guy on the street = "Italian" (Dino).

Cinema has a long relationship with "types" and "stereotypes," whether the ones Sergei Eisenstein and other Soviet filmmakers used in casting their

3 See Haines.

4 And despite the efficiencies that resulted from its use, the stereotype could result in mistakes being perpetuated because of the difficulties of correcting what had already been cast. It is worth noting that printers used celluloid, one of the earliest plastics, to make stereotypes beginning during the 1880s.

films or the types and situations that were especially significant for silent cinema, as described here by Erwin Panofsky:

> There arose, identifiable by standardised appearance, behaviour and attributes, the well-remembered types of the Vamp and the Straight Girl (perhaps the most convincing modern equivalents of the medieval personifications of the Vices and Virtues), the Family Man and the Villain, the latter marked by a black moustache and walking-stick. . . . A checkered table-cloth meant, once and for all, a 'poor but honest' milieu, a happy marriage, soon to be endangered by the shadows from the past, was symbolised by the young wife's pouring the breakfast coffee for her husband; the first kiss was invariably announced by the lady's gently playing with her partner's necktie and was invariably accompanied by her kicking out her left foot. (Qtd. in Wollen, *Signs* 146)

Although it is easy enough to think that stereotypes are nothing but pernicious, the rhetorical and communicative efficiency of the stereotype and the sheer force of stereotypic repetition have made them remarkably durable as a form (even if some of the specific types Panofsky listed have faded).

Martin & Lewis were both easygoing and fluent with stereotypes, exchanging and expressing them with relatively little self-consciousness—so much so that the two men were often caricatures of themselves, so exaggerated as to not suggest any resemblance with the real world. They knew their audience was easygoing and fluent, too. The world they inhabited onscreen was caricatured. When Dean takes Jerry on a "vacation to Italy" as part of the September 21, 1952, *Colgate Comedy Hour* broadcast, they travel to a manifestly imaginary land of visualized stereotypes in which women crush grapes in large tubs to make wine and everyone talks with wildly exaggerated hand gestures[5]—at one point, the hand of the telephone operator abruptly and hyperexpressively protrudes from the telephone itself as with a stereotypically "Italian" hand gesture she explains something to Jerry. The restaurant-nightclub in *Scared Stiff*, the country club in *The Caddy*, the apartment building in *Artists and Models*, the hotel suite in *Living It Up*—all stereotypical exaggerations of the

5 A routine picked up by Lucille Ball and Desi Arnaz for the *I Love Lucy* show number 150, and produced with Lucy and Vivian Vance in a massive grape vat. Shot March 8, 1956, and aired April 16, this was later declared by Ball to be her favorite episode.

everyday. Cary Grant at the Warwick penthouse in New York had a hotel suite vaguely similar to Jerry's in *Living It Up,* but not half so sparkly.

In the 1950s, ethnicity was a centralizing attribute. Dean & Jerry invoked stereotypes about how Italian Americans and Jews related to one another (no minor issue for members of either group), including the anecdotal frequency of marriages between Jews and Italians or at the very least their mutual sympathy as types. Luigi Barzini writes of the similarity between "the Italians" and "the Jews":

> The Jews have the same disenchanted and practical outlook; are among the few people who laugh at their own foibles; they entertain a wary diffidence for other people's noble intentions and always look for the concrete motives hiding behind them. (191)

Whether or not it was demographically verifiable on a national scale or not, interethnic coupling surely impinged on both of their personal lives. Jerry's first wife was Patti Palmer, née Esther Calonico. In 1944, when they wed, "inter-marriage," as it later came to be called, was anything but popular. Currents of distrust and disaffection ran under the marital bliss, as became generally evident when these two divorced. Levy reports:

> [Jerry's parents] Danny and Rae were thrilled by the fame and fortune their son had come into. Now, to top it off, he was free of the meddling shiksa who'd stolen him away. "His parents were elated," said Patti, "for now they would have their son all to themselves." . . . "Their attitude—our son is finally back!—should not have surprised me. I had never been the little Jewish mama with real Jewish roots. To them I was Patti the interloper, the Italian outsider." (84)

Moreover, inside the uncountable American families with European roots there could be longstanding tensions and strains. "Jerry's family, like those of so many of his Jewish peers in the entertainment business, was part of the mass migration of Eastern European Jews to the United States at the end of the nineteenth century" (Levy 3; see also Bernardi, Pomerance, and Tirosh-Samuelson "Introduction"). In the Jewish community (eager to assimilate into American ways), being polite to outsiders was a good tactic frequently put in play, but many Jewish Americans thought behind their backs that the "others" were irredeemable *goyim.* As to the Italians, one nodded gracefully to them in the street but thought of them in the shadows as "wops," "dagoes," and "Ginos" and pointed to connections, real or dreamed, with the underworld.

Ethnicity was the crayon with which the unreflective and spontaneous sketched cartoons of the social world. "Every traveler in the tropics comes away with an unforgettable sense of the pervasive jungle enclosing him," writes Max Lerner. "America's jungle is its ethnic environment of a myriad of peoples. In such a tropical luxuriance every ethnic type is present, everything grows fast and intertwines with everything else, anything is ethnically possible" (77). Ethnically possible, but, in Dean & Jerry's world, hypervisible.

[5]

In both cartooning and the comedy that derives from it, for effecting a type little is more helpful than a hat.

Guy Davenport suggests the head as fate. The head can also be the font of stereotype. Dean's florid curls, Jerry's flat-top accompany Dean's smoldering lover eyes, Jerry's bulging eyes of incomprehension. The long-lost performative art of "chapeaugraphy," which flourished briefly around the turn of the century at the very moment when cinema was invented, is a remarkable demonstration of the power of stereotypes—for better or for worse—to condense meaning into a few recognizable figures. Onstage, this lost art made use of a circular piece of felt that could be twisted to form approximations of different hats that performers combined with curt and telling impersonations of specific famous people as well as more general (and necessarily stereotypical) performances of identity and occupation.

One did not need to have been an actual chapeaugrapher to make use of the signifying properties of specialized headgear and related modes of facial stereotyping. More casual and pungent uses were possible. Consider the prologue to *Hollywood or Bust:* Immediately following the Paramount and VistaVision logos, we see Dean Martin in a medium shot standing with one hand on a large globe in front of a theatrical curtain. Martin then introduces a series of national stereotypes in the form of movie fans of different nations, each played by Lewis in costume, including the American movie fan (*wearing a cap*), the French movie fan (*wearing a beret*), the Russian movie fan (*wearing a fur ushanka*). And yet, with loony Jerry, the joke always was that no matter which hat he was wearing, he was the same frenetic self.

Dean had a tendency not to wear weird, emphatic, or "ridiculous" hats. We'll see him in a straw boater, in a fedora, and in *Pardners* (and also later, in *Rio Bravo*) in a Stetson, but all these are working against stereotype. Even when Jerry stands next to Dean on a stage, wearing a matching straw boater, he looks preposterous while Dean looks a fashion plate.

In *Rock-a-Bye Baby*, Clayton is caught in Papa's (Salvatore Baccaloni) house alone with Sandy (Connie Stevens) while he is there to repair the television. He takes the picture tube out but still can't fix the thing: (a situation that will be surprising only for those who believe that you learn something important by taking things apart).[6] Now Papa comes home from the firehouse, where he's been indulging in red wine. Clayton must hide! Unable to find anywhere useful in Carla's bedroom, he hides behind the empty television. What follows is a virtuoso quick-change performance in which Clayton imitates various television personae while framed in close-up within the empty television cabinet. His salesman character requires a cowboy hat: "Howdy out there, neighbors. I know y'can look in on television everyday and buy for yer home." Wearing a hat has come to mean "wearing a hat." Sandy quickly rotates the channel-changing knob and Clayton, hatless, with a wide smile, says, "Hi out there in television land, and welcome to movie matinee." After an improvised commercial for Superbo cigarettes that has Clayton coughing and wheezing after lighting up, another turn of the knob reveals Clayton, again hatless, as the host of a children's program. Another turn of the knob shows Clayton in a bowler hat earnestly delivering a paid political announcement. The quick-change ends after two more turns of the television knob with Clayton in a tight-fitting skullcap delivering the weather report as a caricatured "Japanese" meteorologist.

[6]

Extremely stereotyped Dean & Jerry toys, and other substitutes, were easy to sell and became very popular. Dean-and-Jerry regalia included a number of different items, ranging from salt-and-pepper shakers to hand puppets, all this merchandise manufactured by specific retail companies who purchased the relevant licensing rights for a period of time and within a certain geographical range. Clothing, golf clubs, Dean & Jerry puppets. *Dean and Jerry puppets!* A child could play with them: talk like Jerry, talk like Dean, sing like Dean, even sing like Jerry. If sing like Jerry, sing on key? Sing what, "Everybody Loves

6 A set-up neatly reprised by François Truffaut in his *Stolen Kisses* (1968).

Somebody Somehow" or "Mammy" or "I Lost My Heart in a Drive-in Movie" out of the mouth of a ten-year-old?

A stereotype could separate from its model and have a life of its own. Through "Dean" and "Jerry" puppets, "Dean" *could* sing, but he didn't have to. He *had* to do only what the playful child invented for him to do. Invented on the spot. Was it easier, or harder, for a child to imagine and invent what "Jerry" would do than to imagine or invent Dean? Jerry Lewis often used the puppet "Jerry" that he put up before the cameras to do whatever he wished to invent, on the spot. Dean & Jerry came full circle from virtual playrooms on screens and magazine pages to children's real-world playrooms where likely they were the objects of rough play and no small amount of breakage. This invented (suddenly found) "Dean & Jerry" figuration should mystify us most, not what "really" happened to Dean Martin [né Dino Crocetti] (1917–1995) and Jerry Lewis [né Joseph Levitch] (1926–2017), but rather the way these two figures fired the imagination of innumerable individuals young and old, and allowed them to play out—or work through—their own scenarios and precarities, their own hopes, dreams, desires, and—yes—aggressions.

By manufacturing and selling these commodity play-withs like so much soap or laundry detergent, the producers, the stars, the corporations, and the marketers were also ceding the power to control these likenesses and how they might be used. Want to make them fight, then kiss and make up, both with equal vigor? Go ahead. Want to put Dean and Jerry in dresses? Go ahead. Want to feed them both to the family dog? Go ahead. Want to throw them in the garbage? Go ahead—that's what happened to most of them in the end after all, as to so much of the consumer culture which Dean & Jerry and countless others shilled.

The most elegant and bizarre merchandising form was the living imitation, of course. Stand up at a party and do a "Jerry," or a "Dean," in this way becoming a puppet yourself.

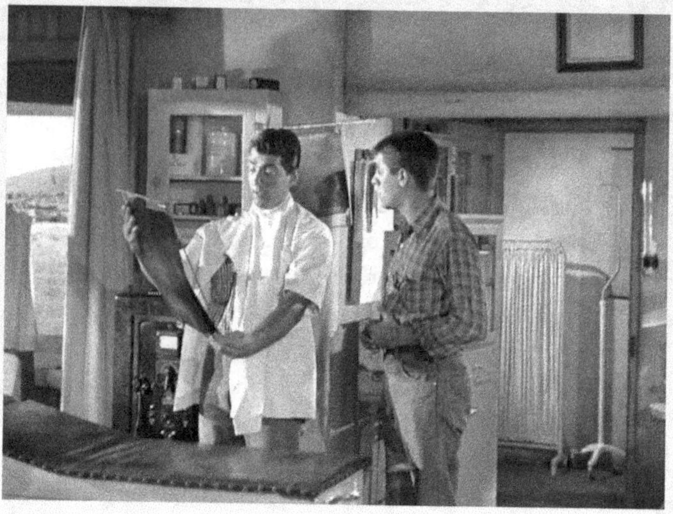

WITH THE DOCTOR

Dean & Jerry's movement from radio and television into motion pictures, after early July 1949, required some adjustments for them, because they had been the undisputed centerpiece of their entertainments, supported by fellow workers and technical hardware but never for a perceivable moment out of the limelight. Now they found themselves surrounded openly by a cast—sometimes a huge cast—of very talented supporting players who gave foundation to the movie business at least as much as to the star performers. (Indeed, they began in motion pictures as supporting players themselves, in *My Friend Irma* and *My Friend Irma Goes West.*) Generally, character actors had shown already, usually in numerous other pictures, what they could do onscreen—indeed, had shown that they could hold a scene very well on their own. You didn't have a movie story with only, or almost only, two characters, you built a world and that world would be populated with "(stereo)typical sorts."

In Martin & Lewis pictures supporting actors tended to seem typical of the diegetic personalities they were playing, not of "themselves"—which is the modeling Dean & Jerry were putting forward quite regularly. They were perfectly illuminated as newspaper publisher, hotel clerk, gas station attendant, nurse, doctor, masseuse, secretary, waiter, maître d', and so on. Yet at the same time as casting directors and actors' agents were working hard to populate these many roles (using precious files carefully organized, including head shots), the films themselves were sponsored and manufactured at studios, in Dean & Jerry's case substantially at Paramount, which meant performers had to be already well known to producers and directors there, and already well known, too, to the viewing public. Given that in Hollywood moviemaking of the 1940s, 50s, and 60s one could count on actors' capabilities uniformly—anybody could do virtually anything brilliantly—the real question was always who had the exact look that the character demanded, and who could work nicely with Dean & Jerry (cause minimal friction in a territory where friction was always possible anyway).[1]

There were a number of ways in which an actor might be cast in a supporting role, the major star roles ordinarily having been determined through deals in advance. They could be previously known by producers and directors; or touted by an agency (perhaps along with others of the agency's clients); or arrive by recommendation. From 1950 onward, filmmakers who wished to cast a performer who was not a citizen of the United States had to have the studio interface with the federal government requesting permission in accordance with the McCarran Internal Security Act (granted only when the government knew the full [real] name, passport number, birth date and place, role to be performed, length of stay in the USA, and the reason why an American actor could not do the work).

Here is some consideration of one tightly scripted and classical Martin & Lewis sequence that is signally dependent on supporting actors. We see

1 Star studies have produced fascinating accounts of major and minor stars, but most of the rest of the galaxy is completely and totally uncharted, as are actors who started out doing only character work and later became stars big or small. Many of the individual omissions are strategic, but we would argue that an entire class of "bit players" or "character actors" has been overlooked and it is precisely these individuals who gave texture to Hollywood's imaginary worlds.

not only the deftness and sureness of these players but the way Dean & Jerry modulate their screen presence so as to give accent to, yet make the story move forward against, each "bit" character.

In the "examining room" sequence of *Living It Up*, Homer's minder Steve lies unconscious on a hospital floor and Homer is cutting his hair shorter so he will be passable as "Homer" for some medical exams. Steve as Homer; Homer as Dr. Steve; Dean as Jerry; Jerry as Dean. Three medical specialists are coming from abroad to meet the patient.

[A] Dr. Emile Engelhofer (from Vienna): Sig Ruman, long-time Paramount character actor, with an enormous list of credits by this time, including *A Night at the Opera* (1935), *Ninotchka* (1939), *To Be or Not to Be* (1942), *House of Frankenstein* (1944), *Night and Day* (1946), *Give My Regards to Broadway* (1948), *Stalag 17* and *Houdini* (both 1953), and *The Glenn Miller Story* (1954). Bulbous eyes, pronounced goatee and mustache (in the style of Sigmund Freud as popularly imagined), and expert at bombastic spluttering speech. Thick Germanic accent. Homer pretends to be the French Dr. Nassau, an opportunity for Jerry to counter Ruman's Germanicisms with some of his trademarked "French." They've got Dean (the fake "Homer") laid out on a table under a fluoroscope and are fighting about using the device, since our Homer, "the boy who is very very ill," can't have this specialist see "nothing" inside the (perfectly healthy) patient. Ruman plays the scene spluttering, backing away, leaning forward with his face prodding Jerry's smooth escapes. (This is not the only Jerry Lewis film Ruman worked in.)

[B] Enter the real Dr. Nassau, forcing Jerry to push Engelhofer into Room A and switch (instantaneously) into a goateed and mustachioed stand-in for Engelhofer. Now we hear the Jerry "Germanic" accent against Eduard Franz's mellow-voiced, genteel French, which is of course not only authentic (in the true sophisticated Parisian style of the time) but accompanied by fluent English. Franz again with a long list of credits, including *Madame Bovary* (1949), *The Thing from Another World* and *The Great Caruso* (both 1951), as well as (Jerry Lewis's) "The Jazz Singer," a 1959 episode of the television show *Startime*, where he is the father. His trademark is the fluent, educated European doctor, professor, intellectual. When another entrance is made this genteel man is pushed over into Room B.

- As Dr. Lee, Richard Loo enters with numerous films under his belt including *Lost Horizon* (1937), *Island of Lost Men* (1939), *Across the Pacific* (1942), *The Keys of the Kingdom* (1944), *Back to Bataan* (1945), *The Steel Helmet* (1951), and *Hell and High Water* (1954). Homer converts to a fake "Dr. Nassau" again.
- But then Engelhofer comes out and Lee must be pushed into Room C while Homer sprouts painfully exaggerated buck teeth and becomes "Dr. Lee," mouth open most of the time. Before modern readers cringe too much about the blatant and patently offensive stereotyping here, it would be worthwhile to consider these images in historical context, not as a way of excusing them but as a way of explaining why actors as talented as Lee chose to fill these roles time after time after time. Hattie McDaniel famously said she would rather work on a film set playing a maid (as in *Gone with the Wind* [1939]) than work as a maid in another person's home.
- There is soon a catastrophe: Homer, "The gig is up!!!!": with all three specialists emerging and bumping into one another as klutzily as possible, while Homer and Steve flee.

DISSOLVE:

- Mr. Stone's office at the newspaper. He is seated with paperwork and the three consultants standing side by side next to his desk. Engelhofer does the talking. Bluntly: "There is nothing wrong with this person! And here is our bill!!!" Helpless spluttering from Stone, who looks as though he is suffering from the world's worst migraine. Fred Clark was the supreme expert at "headaches." His credits included *Flamingo Road* (1949), *Sunset Blvd.* (1950), *A Place in the Sun* (1951), and *The Caddy* and *How to Marry a Millionaire* (both 1953). Here, Homer/Jerry is "present" by strong implication and reference, and one can "read Stone's mind" as he pictures a healthy Homer pretending to be sick at his expense, steam rising from his bald head.

Many bit players, like Ruman, Franz, Loo, and Clark, were defined (thus, in screen work, somewhat contained) in large part by their physiognomy.[2]

2 As, today, are such performers as Steve Buscemi, Samuel L. Jackson, Christopher Walken, Uma Thurman, Maggie Smith, Tilda Swinton, and numerous others.

Each has a distinctive face, seemingly formed out of some plastic material and then used like a rubber stamp, the image of which is imprinted within multiple scenes across multiple films. In light of this, what is interesting about Dean & Jerry is the plasticity of their features, that by stretching they could stereotype a character but in "normal" posture they would look only like the star performers they were. Although the pseudo-science of physiognomy had been debunked by the time of the studio system (Gould *Mismeasure*), it still held strong residual purchase in the eyes of audiences and filmmakers alike whether or not it ever went by its proper name. Note Fred Clark's imposing forehead, purportedly a marker of intelligence but also of beleaguered exasperation. Clark was virtually always "exasperated" onscreen: one can easily imagine a casting director noting the need for an "exasperated" character and thinking, almost in reflex, Fred Clark.

In sequences like this one it is the head shot, as much as the actor's performing body, that is at stake. A close-up already captures the essential qualities of the person to the extent that they will be required in the film, a *carte de visite* in motion. This sequence is analogous to a game of three-card monte, with the card one expects to be turned forever replaced by another. And in this case all of the cards are face cards.

But playing cards work in some ways just like stereotypes. They are paper thin and insubstantial, visually designed to convey their identity as directly as possible with a single glance. The nature of card games also allows for them to be quickly and deftly manipulated, exchanged, and juxtaposed, as happens in this sequence (actors often were exchanged and juxtaposed in the process of casting a film). Although the Queen of Hearts signifies something quite different visually and symbolically from the Queen of Spades, in many cases the two were interchangeable as calculated equivalent values. Cinema has long had a fascination with these hand-held characterizations, so semiotically overdetermined, beginning perhaps with Méliès' *The Living Playing Cards* (1905) and continuing through *The Manchurian Candidate* (John Frankenheimer, 1962). Dean & Jerry used them to play their various hands in front of the cameras.

An added frill to the "doctor scene" joke: there is an implicit message here, that no matter the medical expertise you are searching for, what you will finally get is a face.

DEAN & JERRY FULL FRONTAL

There were two incommensurable cultural effects of the Martin & Lewis phenomenon. Beyond the entertainment they offered as pleasure, beyond the improbable zaniness and boundary fracturing, beyond the hairdos and the teeth, beyond the quirky voices and artful stumblings:

[A] *Balm.*

In an age riddled with tensions (the Cold War had started around 1947/48), they offered a vital valve. Europe was being carved up under Russian pressures, and America was finding an enemy in Russia. At the same time, the Korean peninsula was embattled, there were turmoils both inside and outside the scientific community over Edward Teller's development of a hydrogen bomb, and the marketplace was swept away in a delirium of consumer frenzy. That an atomic future seemed to be looming caused diffuse, widespread public panic as well as diffuse, widespread suspicion about science and scientists generally (note the "evil scientist" movie character type [see Hark]). How could culture be made safe for the Great Consumer Adventure, lent an aura of optimism, made fertile for capital growth? Everything we see in the Martin & Lewis routines is destructive cacophony *followed immediately by friendly harmony*. Bang!, Boom!, But!: *It's all for fun.*

Here is David Halberstam:

> Life in America, it appeared, was in all ways going to get better. A new car could replace an old one, and a larger, more modern refrigerator would take the place of one bought three years earlier, just as a new car had replaced an old one. Thus, the great fear of manufacturers, as they watched their markets reach saturation points, was that their sales would decline; this proved to be false. So did another of the retailers' fears—that people might save too much. Of the many things to be concerned about in postwar America, the idea of Americans saving too much was not one of them. The market was saturated, but people kept on buying—newer, improved products that were easier to handle, that produced cleaner laundry, washed more dishes and glasses, and housed more frozen steaks. What the leaders of the auto industry had done in autos with the annual model change, now, on a somewhat different scale, the manufacturers of home appliances and furniture were doing in their businesses. No wonder people bought more appliances. Suddenly, the old ones seemed inconvenient and outdated. (497)

[B] *Shock.*

For their addicted fans, the breakup of Martin & Lewis came as a complete and utter shock.[1] Their time was characterized by a pre-shock culture, com-

1 A similarly shocking, if more tepid surprise came as a result of Charles Van Doren's appearances on the television game show *Twenty-One*, which began only

pared to the world readers of this book are living in. No one embedded in popular culture in the 1950s expected to be shocked by that experience. The major shock of the John F. Kennedy assassination did not come until late 1963, the killings of Robert Kennedy and Martin Luther King years after that, and the Watergate hearings, a hugely shocking affair, a full decade later. Although there had been indications of trouble and tensions between Dean and Jerry, there had always been a fairly rapid reconciliation, with photo ops and television appearances in which Dean's arm was comfortably draped over Jerry's shoulders, sometimes segueing into a duet of "Side by Side" (as they did in the finale of the September 18, 1955, *Comedy Hour*). So, when the breakup did occur, ten years to the day from the beginning of their duo act, no one was really prepared.

Only in retrospect does the breakup seem inevitable. We may now be able to connect the dots to show the long lead-up to the split, to invoke its "inevitability," but this calculation is only legible with the benefit of hindsight. Perhaps that is entirely apropos, because retrospective teleology is one of the deep structures of the Martin & Lewis oeuvre, as our consideration of the opening of *Living It Up* suggested at the beginning of the book. Perhaps the specter of separation had always hung over them, but it was always just that, a specter, a figment of the imagination, a never-to-occur apocalypse, like nuclear annihilation. As a 1954 press release noted, "What our 'unofficial' press agents don't know is that they are right. We *are* going to split up as a team. We have even picked the date. It will be on July 25, 1996, which will be our golden anniversary as a team. We figure by that time we will have enough kids between us to keep us supplied in wheel chair grease and bifocals. We sincerely hope we have cleared up this ridiculous situation" (Dean Martin and Jerry Lewis, Press Release, March 18, 1954, qtd. in Hayde 273). Of all of the inconceivable and "ridiculous situation[s]" the duo had created as a team, Dean & Jerry not being partners was the most "ridiculous" and most inconceivable.

---

about two months after the breakup. Months afterward, a champion of champions on the show (isolation booth, headphones, seriously difficult questions), he confessed to . . . cheating.

SPLITSVILLE ON SCHEDULE

[1]

In broadcast radio, broadcast television, and motion picture production, there is a key sense in which timing is everything. Radio performers time their speech to the second, almost automatically after years of practice. The work of television performers must be timed to lead up to, and then be synchronized with, commercial spots and camera choreography—*Look here, count to three, then look there.* In film, every shot is timed and costed well in advance of shooting—costed to the penny. Most of Dean & Jerry's public performances were made and remunerated according to time constraints. Yet again and again they slipped off the clock, breaking out of time. Could we have loved them if they didn't?

Think of "comic timing" and its delicacies: the number of beats or half-beats between set-up and punch (speech pattern sets up the beats); the rate of movement forward between the set-up and the punch, especially the temporal interval between one joke moment and the next. Comedy is played through the ear, a form of music. Time and timing are all. But when you take the clock "in hand" and fiddle with it openly, when you break its springs (as Chaplin does in *The Pawnshop* [1916]), you step outside of comic convention: you do *meta-comedy.*

Performers working to a live crowd develop an acute sense of how much time remains in an allotted segment and, by gauging faces, how much patience remains in their audience. Waiting just offstage (at least metaphorically) in the wings of a live theater show was the threat of the "hook"—sometimes literalized—waiting to pull the performer offstage; or a stagehand poised to ring down the curtain if an act was running long. vaudeville (Jerry's father, Danny Lewis, earned his living there and Jerry admired it all his life) was America's first industrialized mode of entertainment, and as such it had to run like clockwork. In big-time vaudeville on the Keith-Albee-Orpheum circuit (the theater chain that later gave the vertically integrated RKO film studio its last two letters), managers monitored each act with a stopwatch in hand. Surviving in unpublished Managers' Report Books are careful notations of just how long each and every act ran, along with more or less detailed accounts and evaluations of the acts themselves. The more shows per day, the more money at the box office. If you had to do three shows a day, you were low on the totem pole. When you hit the top, you'd do one show a night and maybe make it to the Paramount on Broadway.[1]

Manager Samuel K. Hodgdon of B. F. Keith's Theatre in New York reported on a number of vaudeville acts during the week of January 18, 1904. For one:

> 3 KEATONS.—A man and a woman and 'Buster' Keaton. 'Buster,' of course, being the main feature of the act. He is undoubtedly one of the best juvenile performers in vaudeville. He seems to have a natural idea

1 A movie palace in Times Square seating more than 3,600 persons, 1926–1964. The crooning young Frank Sinatra was one of the major hits there. Dean & Jerry performed there in July 1951.

of comedy and does not overdo anything through his efforts. The act is really a big hit. *26 minutes.* (emphasis added)[2]

When short films were added to vaudeville programs starting at the turn of the century, they, too, were timed and had to "fit the bill." In early days just as later, the running time of a film dictated the number of screenings (sources of profit) the exhibitor could arrange in a day, thus the "take" for a week's rental of the property.

To run "over-time" in live performance was to take up somebody else's time spot, natural enough for self-anointed royalty yet at the same time hardly professional, unnoticeable, or "polite." But politesse was Dean & Jerry's target, not their policeman.

[2]

Whether audiences saw them in televised skits or in artificial but charming choreographed movie scenes, or heard them on the radio, one feature of Dean & Jerry's performance especially worth noting here—because it has gained almost no critical attention at all—is the strange quality of leisure they promised and offered. To be "off the clock," to stretch the moment, to languidly allow a patter or a routinized pattern to stay where it was, linger, swell, stretch, grow, and twitch, without external constraint, as seemed, and even without the repressive "respect" for the form that so many other performers had—this was nirvana. Nirvana even if Jerry's role was to produce almost unending anxiety and Dean's to unendingly quell it: push, pull. For their audiences, Dean & Jerry were an ultimate "break." To play with things; with words; with space; with rhythm; with forms; with norms; with temporality; even with the boundaries of production was not a decoration of their style, it *was* their style. The routine became a dream. The effect became unpredictable, unrepeatable, memorable only in the slippery way that dreams are memorable.

One has a continuing sense of Dean watching a clock and Jerry slopping around to miss his cues.

2 *Managers' Report Books,* vol. 1, p. 155, Keith/Albee Collection, University of Iowa Special Collections.

[3]

But, inevitably there did come a point, after stagehands held up cards with "1 minute" and "30 seconds" printed, when the show had to end: "Good night and God bless you all!" Roll credits. As Homer says, in what could be the throes of his last breaths, in *Living It Up*, "When the end does come, I want you to write about me, 'Exit, laughing.'"

Stop time meant breaking away from movement into stasis. And with stasis one was caught in the fascinating grip of the Martin & Lewis image: they were bugs trapped in amber and so were their viewers. A telling example is the producer and designer's choice of image for the standard *Living It Up* poster—Dean and Jerry caught in mid-air, legs spread energetically, faces contorted with feeling, a quality of vivacity and pulsation but: stilled. *Scared Stiff:* caught frozen in matching grimaces of horror. *Jumping Jacks:* floating down in twin parachutes (never to hit ground). *Pardners:* pointing matching six-guns or riding horses together, with the beasts' four feet almost all off the ground (thank you, Eadweard Muybridge). *You're Never Too Young:* Dean hoisting Jerry in drag. Caught, stuck, stymied, pinned, yet at the same time animated beyond animation, living it up. Living it up, but frozen.

Here is a telling case of temporal wandering:

In 1953, Martin & Lewis appeared on Milton Berle's *Texaco Star Theater* (NBC), to be aired live from Rockefeller Center—*live:* all action, camera-work, and commercials happening right here as we watch (not at all an atypical format for 1950s television). Nick Tosches recounts how they had gone to rehearsal and been sternly instructed by Berle that they would have *eight* minutes. "We have a timed show here, boys . . . Not ten. Not nine. I'm talking about eight minutes, on the nose." Both nodded comprehension and agreement. But

> they ignored the eight-minute warning. "Hold your horses, I'm not finished talking!" Dean hollered when Berle came out to introduce the next act. Jerry stuck his face into the camera: "Milton Berle! Big deal!" Berle hated it. The audience loved it. Berle loved it. (209–10)

[4]

After the split, July 25, 1956, as the two (officially) took separate paths through the forest of the entertainment business—and at a precise instant, quite as though by clockwork—one sensed each performer lurking invisibly in the "shadows" of the other's motion pictures. "Oh, *The Delicate Delinquent! It's Jerry without Dean.*"—"Oh, *Rio Bravo! It's Dean without Jerry.*"

Can one subtract something that was never conventionally added, however? (D + J) − D = J??? (D + J) − J = D??? But if we dare to think D & J minus D, or D & J minus J, what can we actually mean by *minus?*

This question, in its deepest and most abstract form, is what so many scholars and critics have failed to ask about Martin & Lewis. *How* is one imaginable without the other, in the end?

Dean & Jerry of course pioneered framing an answer to this exact conundrum. In a May 3, 1953, *Colgate Comedy Hour* skit, it was as though they were looking into the future:

> They are in the office of an insurance agent, taking out a million-dollar policy on their partnership, payable if "something should happen to either one of you." (*A circumlocution that can be funny for viewers who know that Jerry never circumlocutes, and also always circumlocutes.*) Initially pleased with the idea of having the policy, each suddenly realizes in a grimacing close-up shot punctuated by the familiar bars of the *Dragnet* theme music,[3] that he has created an enormous financial incentive for the partner to murder him. "People have murdered for less than that," the agent adds enthusiastically, to emphasize the magnitude of the sum. Just at the instant we see, in a two-shot of Dean & Jerry, the boys reaching the collective realization together and turning toward each other, nose to nose.

"You boys have nothing to worry about, you're more like brothers than partners." Onscreen, Dean & Jerry never ever played brothers. Indeed, Chris Fujiwara notes Dean's frequent appearances as "*surrogate* older brothers or fathers

3 Created and produced by its star Jack Webb, *Dragnet* was broadcast from 1951 to 1959 on NBC. Elements of the show, and especially the theme music (by Walter Schumann), were affectionately parodied on countless occasions.

whom the Lewis character desperately and ineptly tries to please, only to be met with a mask of disapproval or indifference" (37; emphasis added). But this *Comedy Hour* sketch pushes well past indifference. As Dean and Jerry leave the insurance office, neither feels safe turning his back on the other, however momentarily, and so they sidestep one another in an awkward *pas de deux* while passing through the doorway.

Shortly after Dean gets home to his wife (who has just had a visit from the plumber) things get sinister and ominous music is heard. He is a nervous wreck, peering behind doors and out the window. Fearful, he explains, "My partner's gonna kill me!" She chides him for behaving so suspiciously: "I'll bet you that Jerry's not behaving like you. No sir. Not Jerry. Why, he loves and he trusts you. And he'll come over here the way he always does—"

"—and kill me," Dean interjects.

But she goes on, "—full of faith, trust, and confidence."

The next shot of course shows Jerry crawling along the ground outside Dean's house, crickets chirping loudly around him (Dean has money, he's bought a suburban house with crickets in the vicinity: *When you wish upon a star* . . .). He is trembling, very afraid, and confides to a passing police officer, "My partner's gonna kill me." Gathering up his courage, he rings Dean's doorbell and makes his way inside.

Both of them are so afraid they barely notice one another, but abruptly they are face to face. SHOWDOWN.

Peaceably, however, they agree they are both being silly: "We're partners and pals," after all, says Jerry. When they hug, they both desperately pat each other down for concealed weapons. (Dragnet *again, a viewer's manual for police procedures.*)

Dean sociably offers to mix the drinks.

But Jerry, suspicious, turns to the camera and asks wide-eyed, "Gadzooks, should I go along with him?" (*Comic-book talk.*) We certainly don't want Jerry to be murdered, but even worse would be having to stop watching this skit. Sitting on the couch to wait, he notices a rifle hanging on the wall above the mantel. He lifts it down, not wanting a firearm to be so readily at hand for Dean. (*Nothing safer than a rifle in Jerry's hands!*) But now he picks up a ringing telephone, fearing the worst. It's the plumber, explaining how the homeowner can *do the job himself* and save a lot of money in the process. Jerry, ultra-paranoid, thinks the voice on the other end of the line belongs to a hit-man contracted to kill him.

Dean picks up in the adjacent room and thinks the same thing, believing the murder plot is meant for him.[4] The close shot of the two on separate extensions on two sides of a wall anticipates the split-screening of *Pillow Talk* (1959) by six years.[5] The episode was directed by Bud Yorkin.

Regarding this sequence, note:

- As with the opening of *Living It Up* (see "Can You Relax?" above), individually articulated single connections become retrospectively legible together, as a coherent transformation. A contract in an agent's office becomes a multiple murder arrangement. Of course, looking back, we can see how that happened; but in the office with the agent we are not at all anticipating it.
- The plumber on the phone does not and cannot know what we see going on in Dean's house, and the boys on the phone are catching only a fragment of a plumber's dialogue now taken out of context. Two worlds are colliding.

Structurally, this is classic Comedy, a story, as Northrop Frye taught, in which there are presented at one time doors to two houses and a space between. On both sides of the playing area, characters are ignorant of what is happening "over there." As he writes, "Comedy regularly illustrates a victory of arbitrary plot over consistency of character" (170). Some of the most arresting images show "the boys" on opposite sides of a wall, a cutaway view that allowed television viewers to see them reacting to, *but not seeing* one another in real time.

To hammer down on the detonator of our dynamite: looking back now, this 1953 playing-out seems rather obviously like a harbinger of the future, a kind of psychic looking forward. At the time, however, Dean & Jerry were going to go on like this forever.

4 This reprises an element of the scenario of Lucille Fletcher's radio play "Sorry, Wrong Number" and Anatole Litvak's eponymous film adaptation *Sorry, Wrong Number* (1948), in which a woman overhears voices plotting to kill her on the telephone but is powerless to do anything to stop them (Solomon 1995).

5 Lest we give excessive credit for innovations to producers of *The Colgate Comedy Hour*, it bears noting that Georges Méliès had often used cutaway sets some fifty years earlier in films like *The Inn Where No Man Rests* (1903) and *Tunneling the English Channel* (1907).

[5]

Not to imagine, however, that insurance policies are the stuff of fiction only.

Having bounced off one another onstage for six months in the mid-1940s, the two performers appeared as "Martin & Lewis" for the first time at Loew's State in New York, January 1947, with a contract that called for payment of $1,500/week (in 2023 dollars, roughly $17,500), and options for $1,750/week (in 2023, roughly $20,500). This was money not to be sniffed at. Their agent at the time, Abby Greshler, considered them so "valuable" (Tosches 145) he had them take out a $15,000 (in 2023 dollars, around $200,000) New York Life insurance policy, No. 20-796-917, with him as beneficiary. Needless to say, the boys' "value" increased, and was indeed considerably higher by the time the duo made Norman Lear and Ed Simmons's "insurance" skit. There was a business reality underneath their goofing; a grounding in real life. One might well suppose that the simulated trepidation in the comedy routine reflected a far more serious trepidation offstage; it surely could have done so, the comedy of a skit being, after all, instructive about life. To what extent would one of them benefit if the other disappeared?

"More like brothers than partners, perhaps"; but there are plenty of wide-flung tales about brothers and inheritance. Read *The Man in the Iron Mask.* Was this teaming constantly under pressure of collapsing from within?

[6]

Or was it love?

[7]

Very little can be said definitively about the "love and death" of the Martin & Lewis partnership. To the heart of darkness we cannot, and will not presume to try to, travel. Without doubt their shenanigans added up to an expensive demise, since more than a hundred and fifty million dollars worth of unexecutable signed contracts were in the vault, all of which had to be voided—and at cost. "Just like a divorce, the breakup with Jerry was expensive," Ricci

Martin writes. "They had to settle contracts for movies that wouldn't be made and nightclub appearances that would never happen" (32).

Worse, the separation turned a light on something that had never been quite so clear before: that perhaps the relationship had never been exactly reciprocal (in the way that audiences could so easily have assumed). From each side came a characteristic claim, repeated again and again like a mantra. Dean: it was never anything but money; it wasn't friendship. Jerry: "I fell in love with him immediately" (qtd. in Freedland 21). Dean concurred, "It was love at first sight. The kid looked up at me" (qtd. in Hayde 185). Money had nothing to do with that.

Possibly Dean's distancing from loving Jerry came in some way from his Catholicism, in which the word "love" has very particular meanings that, certainly at the time, were exclusively if not religiously heterosexual. In 1950s consumerist America, currents of male homosexuality or homoeroticism trickled, but perforce well below the surface of everyday commitments and relationships. Such currents were expressed in whispers or jokes, or were very substantially hidden, the subject of "put-downs," "teasing," and other banter ostensibly meant to deny a fact it probably confirmed. "The structures of secrecy and disclosure that organize gay male experience lead them to scrutinize constantly the behavior of other men for signs of homosexuality. For them, the slightly effeminate gesture or intonation of voice becomes fraught with meaning" (Corber 109). One can try to conceive the "meaning" that Dean could have taken when Jerry put on an "effeminate gesture or intonation of voice": perhaps he *wasn't putting it on.* The unsignaled kisses out of love or desperation or both; the gaze of adoration; the constant tickling; the sudden embraces. Regular pains of young manhood in the 1950s? Or irregular pains of a higher order? Or was Dean in the subterranean depths, hunting for a finale? Was he bone tired of being straight man for the "kid"?

[8]

A kind of tidy, but often highly unconventional, closure characterizes the typical finale of a Martin & Lewis film. One of the most dizzying cases is the moebius strip–like conclusion of *The Caddy*, the narrative of which is framed by an onstage performance by headliners Joe Anthony (Martin) and Harvey Miller Jr. (Lewis) taking place at a movie theater, outside of which a crowd of adoring fans has gathered. The viewer has been asked to believe that these two song-and-dance men's professional aspirations began not on the boards, but on the golf links. (In real life, both Martin and Lewis were avid amateur golfers, but professional entertainers.)

The plot of the film is a bit like a golf course in which the first hole and the eighteenth hole abut geographically—indeed, the film starts and ends backstage at the theater. Anthony and Miller shift down and up the California coast from San Francisco to Santa Barbara and then to Monterey, with Joe's egotistical acts of hubris (as he treats his ostensible best friend and lifelong pal Harvey increasingly like an underling) and Harvey's embarrassing shenanigans (which seem to erupt every time Joe is rubbing shoulders with high society) serving as metaphorical water hazards and sand traps along the way.

We end up back in paradise, New York's Paramount Theater, filled with an eager audience not so very dissimilar from the audience in which we are sitting to watch this eager audience.[6] The stage act, in fact, could well be a preface to a film screening coming up in just minutes; a film screening, like *this* film screening. But if we are not yet sufficiently befuddled, confused, and tickled, what comes next will do the trick:

Finishing their act, Joe and Harvey walk backstage where they meet, lo and behold!, a pair of up-and-comers hot to become The Biggest Thing in Show Business: Dean Martin and Jerry Lewis. (!!!!!!) Holding aside for a moment the technical means by which two Deans and two Jerries are made visible at once, consider the warping, jaw-dropping reality: Joe Anthony—that is, Dean Martin in the character of Joe—may "really" be the actor portraying him, namely Dean Martin, except that's impossible, because Dean Martin is the "Dean Martin" standing beside Joe, a second character played in "dual performance," we might say, by Dean Martin. Ditto Jerry Lewis with Harvey. Dean and Jerry are, then, at one moment:

- The actors underneath Joe and Harvey (all through this film);
- The novice characters whom Joe and Harvey are meeting backstage; and
- The actors underneath the novices.

6 Sitting to watch because it was not for several decades that movies could be seen other than in a theater.

Characters who are really actors who are characters who are really actors, who are . . .

Or wait.

Are we seeing the "real" Dean & Jerry performing at the Paramount—and heading backstage is it Joe & Harvey they meet, Joe & Harvey as up-and-comers?

WHO IS IT WANTING TO BE THE BIGGEST THING IN SHOW BUSINESS?

And who are we looking at?

Will the real Dean & Jerry please make yourselves known? Photographic and cinematic evidence leave even the well-informed viewer unable to tell the difference in this scene. Indeed, one can suppose that Martin and Lewis themselves cannot tell the difference, between their "on" characterizations as "Dean" and "Jerry" and what is backstage for them. A puzzle with no end, a twilight zone, an Escher, a mirror world as in *The Lady from Shanghai* (1947) or the *American in Paris* ballet (1951), a statement that is a question, an ending that is a beginning.

For all of us gazing in, the tissue is very, very thin.

[9]

The puzzle of doubling—the grand puzzle of the Dean & Jerry doubling—is nicely invoked in one particular finale. At the end of *Hollywood or Bust*, marching down a Hollywood movie premiere red carpet (shades of the beginning of *Singin' in the Rain* [1952]) are Jerry with Anita Ekberg and Dean with Pat Crowley. Leading them with dignity is the giant Great Dane, Mr. Bascomb. The boys are celebrating the Hollywood premiere of the-movie-within-the-movie, "The Lady and the Great Dane," at Grauman's Chinese Theater. This is the last motion picture shot of Martin & Lewis onscreen, here or anywhere. Since they walk right into the camera, mouths open (as in *The Big Swallow*), is this to be taken as a reality or as a dream? A tissue very, very thin.

[10]

> You see, there are only two classes of people, the magnanimous, and the rest; and I have reached an age when one has to take sides, to decide once and for all whom one is going to like and dislike, to stick to the people one likes, and, to make up for the time one has wasted with the others, never to leave them again as long as one lives. . . . I have elected to love none but magnanimous souls, and to live only in an atmosphere of magnanimity.
>
> —**MARCEL PROUST**, *SWANN IN LOVE*

Leslie Fiedler observed: "It was [Jerry] who truly loved, rather than Dean, who would only let himself be loved. And it was Dean who ended the marriage, of which Dean never seems to have been fully aware" (25). Jerry's memory of the tissue tearing—no surgical assistance in this case—puts it ten days after a cardiac arrhythmia that hospitalized him in early summer 1956. One day on the lot (inevitably Paramount):

JERRY: I've got to talk to you.

DEAN: Talk.

JERRY: You know, it's a hell of a thing. All I can think of is that what we do is not very important. Any two guys could have done it. But even the best of them wouldn't have had what made us as big as we are.

DEAN: Yeah? What's that?

JERRY: Well, I think it's the love that we had—that we still have—for each other. (*Dean* 277)

"He half-closed his eyes," writes Jerry, "gazing downward for what felt like a long time. Then he looked me square in the face."

CODA

The Fall is into Division, and the Resurrection is to Unity.
—NORMAN O. BROWN, *LOVE'S BODY*

In 1942, in Alfred Hitchcock's *Saboteur,* with the war raging, Norman Lloyd is dangling by his sleeve from Robert Cummings's hand on the torch of the Statue of Liberty. The seam of his jacket frays and comes apart, and Fry (Lloyd) plummets to his death.[1] Was Hitchcock hinting, perhaps, that America itself was coming apart at the seams? Fry, after all, represented a well-integrated Nazi cultural structure, and America, symbolized in the film by Liberty, was a well-integrated cultural structure, too; statuesque; solid;

1 Brilliantly homaged and revised in a flashback in the Coen brothers' *The Hudsucker Proxy* (1993) in which Paul Newman is saved from certain death dangling from the top of a skyscraper by his tailor's decision to double-stitch his pants despite being told that the single stitch was fine.

stable; unshifting. But was America well enough integrated? After the brutal social-class division of the Depression in the 1930s, the brutal interventionist-isolationist division during the war, and the brutality of the McCarthy hearings early in the 1950s, the idea of a single unified, harmonic social fabric, without any rents or blemishes, was more and more taking on the character of a myth, however idyllic things may have seemed on the surface. Division was, in truth, everywhere, and with the consumerist fever of the 1950s, more or less culminating during the time Dean & Jerry split up, division was heightened—even developed, since one had to go through life also suffering the anomic gap between the glorious rainbow future one dreamed of purchasing and the hard, cold reality of what one could afford to spend (if one could afford to spend anything at all).

Other significant cultural progressions of the early- to mid-1950s, outrageous as they may initially have seemed, worked to promote the myth of unity and coherence. In painting one saw Jackson Pollock's splatter canvases, but saw them at first as idiosyncratic and attention grabbing; except for art critics, viewers didn't compare and contrast them with what had come before, to see how Pollock was breaking away, or creating a gap. One heard Elvis on the radio, but did not in the beginning tag him as being either like anybody else or in opposition to other music because—again idiosyncratically—he swept cultural attention away. Onscreen one saw Montgomery Clift, Marlon Brando, Rory Calhoun, and James Dean as avatars of a new markedly non-military masculinity, but they did not visibly go into battle with the stars who had come before. If one looked to comedy, one found very conventional, even old-fashioned wit (executed superbly) with such as George Burns and Gracie Allen; or very conventional slapstick parody (executed superbly) with such as Sid Caesar and his crew (including Carl Reiner, Imogen Coca, and Howard Morris). Formal presentations were coherent, in some ways idealized, and reflected or promised some wild and wonderful bright new future born from some continuity that flowed from the present.

All except for: the presentations made by Dean & Jerry.

Here, flatly and bluntly in your face, was division, disparity, incompatibility, bizarreness, contradiction, incoherence, shock, impoliteness, tension, discord, discontinuity, unpredictability, utter unproductiveness, and "battle" all configured very intentionally as "natural," as belonging to the "everyday," in a multitude of "normal" social situations that, because of these two and their mutual incapacities, always, predictably, fell apart. Coming apart at the seams was everything in Dean & Jerry's routines. The social scene disintegrated, in plain words. And the falling apart was effortless, graceful, and happy, since the whole procedure evoked pleasure, surprise, a tickling, and an irrepressible joy. The swinger who couldn't stop posing, who couldn't wake up from his relaxation, and the ultra-jiving overeager man-boy whose body, social knowledge, language, and couth were all, fundamentally, untrustworthy: what a "pair," if one could even say the word. Dean neverendingly impatient with Jerry's interruptions and foibles; Jerry pushing and battering hard against Dean's too stolid, too unimpeachable, and far too comfortable form. Jerry never leaving Dean alone; Dean never fully approving of Jerry.

To appreciate this fracturing as entertainment, to laugh wholeheartedly at it, to clap one's hands in raves, to line up in the street for autographs, to assault the movie theater box offices—all this required an audience that understood, accepted, and indeed took for granted the idea of coming apart. Coming apart now, promising to come apart in just a moment, coming apart tomorrow and forever. Not—as would happen after July 25, 1956, to a great audience's great chagrin—*being apart;* but coming apart, the fabric tearing, the rip growing, the separation promised and still promised again at every breath—because between these "pardners" there never was what viewers all around, both on and offstage, would call unity. Unity? In America? From 1946 to 1956? Impossible. A nice dream.

To try to encapsulate the Dean & Jerry phenomenon visually is actually extremely easy if one is willing to restrict oneself to a two-shot. Choose literally any image that includes both and you will read that image—facial expressions, body language, etc.—as their essence. There are literally hundreds of thousands of two-shots of these men. But what is it that rested and jittered between them? That essence is infinitely mysterious, perhaps visually unrepresentable, if not invisible, and was the motive behind our jumping into this writing. To grab a moment from a routine certainly helps once a while to illustrate one particular point or another, but images of the routines would not, interestingly, help to discover what makes Dean & Jerry's work so vital and so unique. The shticks were not the relationship.

Nor did their shticks make Dean Martin & Jerry Lewis the biggest thing in show business. The shticks illustrated. They poked. They tickled. But what made Dean & Jerry so magnetic was only Dean & Jerry. The act that seemed unending, but that came to an end.

Endings are fascinating both currently and historically. Dean & Jerry would tell their audience how good they had been, and sign off smilingly, on television; onscreen they would giggle their way out of the story. There also existed a different, more open, sense of "closure" in which not every loose end needed to be tied off carefully as many screenwriting manuals of the time would insist. Indeed, the serialized structure of radio and television relied on such open-endedness, asking listeners and viewers to tune in for the next installment. "See you next week!" Nowadays, with Netflix and Co., the open ending is the only ending. Entertainment on the installment plan.

What one got in a Dean & Jerry show wasn't happy progress from any beginning to any ending; it was kaleidoscopic multiplicity, explosion, clashing, and clumsiness—all for fun. There was no single idea, no single conception or view, no single purpose, then, in a Dean & Jerry show or movie; what one got was multiplicity and fragmentation, but also shimmering scintillation.

Perhaps that has also been your experience reading this book. "You've been the most wonderful readers we could possibly have dreamed!"

IN THE LIBRARY

Altman, Rick. "Deep-Focus Sound: *Citizen Kane* and the Radio Aesthetic." *Quarterly Review of Film and Video* 15, no. 3 (1994): 1–33.

Andrews, Erin E., Anjali J. Forber-Pratt, Linda R. Mona, Emily M. Lund, Carrie R. Pilarski, and Rochelle Balter. "#SaytheWord: A Disability Culture Commentary on the Erasure of 'Disability.'" *Rehabilitation Psychology* 64, no. 2 (2019): 111–18.

Anger, Kenneth. *Hollywood Babylon.* San Francisco: Straight Arrow Books, 1975.

Badmington, Neil. *Perpetual Movement: Alfred Hitchcock's* Rope. Albany: State University of New York Press, 2021.

Baker, Nicholson. "The History of Punctuation." In *The Size of Thoughts*, 70–88. New York: Random House, 1996.

Bakhtin, Mikhail. *The Dialogic Imagination: Four Essays.* Trans. Caryl Emerson and Michael Holquist. Austin: University of Texas Press, 1981.

Balaban, David. *The Chicago Movie Palaces of Balaban and Katz.* Charleston, SC: Arcadia, 2006.

Barnouw, Erik. *The Sponsor: Notes on a Modern Potentate.* New York: Oxford University Press, 1978.

Barthes, Roland. *S/Z.* Trans. Richard Miller. New York: Hill and Wang, 1974.

Barzini, Luigi. *The Italians: A Full-Length Portrait Featuring Their Manners and Morals.* New York: Simon & Schuster, 1964.

Bateson, Gregory. *Steps to an Ecology of Mind: Collected Essays in Anthropology, Psychiatry, Evolution, and Epistemology.* Chicago: University of Chicago Press, 1972.

Bellour, Raymond. *The Analysis of Film.* Ed. Constance Penley. Bloomington: Indiana University Press, 2000.

Benjamin, Walter. *Charles Baudelaire: A Lyric Poet in the Age of High Capitalism.* Trans. Harry Zohn. London: Verso, 1997.

Bergson, Henri. *Laughter.* Frankfurt-am-Main: Outlook, 2019.

Bernardi, Daniel, Murray Pomerance, and Hava Tirosh-Samuelson, eds. "Introduction: The Hollywood Question." In *Hollywood's Chosen People: The Jewish Experience in American Cinema*, 1–18. Detroit: Wayne State University Press, 2012.

Boyarin, Daniel. *Unheroic Conduct: The Rise of Heterosexuality and the Invention of the Jewish Man.* Berkeley: University of California Press, 1997.

Brown, Norman O. *Love's Body.* New York: Vintage, 1966.

Bukatman, Scott. "Paralysis in Motion: Jerry Lewis's Life as a Man." In *Comedy/Cinema/Theory,* ed. Andrew Horton, 188–205. Berkeley: University of California Press, 1991.

———. "Terminal Idiocy (the comedian is the message)." In *Enfant Terrible! Jerry Lewis in American Film,* ed. Murray Pomerance, 181–91. New York: New York University Press, 2002.

Butterfield, Herbert. *The Whig Interpretation of History.* London: G. Bell, 1931.

Caillois, Roger. *Man, Play and Games.* Trans. Meyer Barash. Urbana: University of Illinois Press, 2001.

Caine, Michael. *Acting in Film: An Actor's Take on Movie Making.* Revised and expanded edition. New York: Applause, 1997.

Caldwell, John Thornton. *Televisuality: Style, Crisis, and Authority in American Television.* New Brunswick, NJ: Rutgers University Press, 1995.

Campbell, Edward Jr. *The Celluloid South: Hollywood and the Southern Myth.* Knoxville: University of Tennessee Press, 1981.

Cassidy, Frederic G., and Joan Houston Hall, eds. *Dictionary of American Regional English.* Vol. 2. Cambridge, MA: Harvard University Press, 2013.

Charney, Leo. *Empty Moments: Cinema, Modernity, and Drift.* Durham, NC: Duke University Press, 1998.

Chauncey, George. *Gay New York: Gender, Urban Culture, and the Making of the Gay Male World, 1890–1940.* New York: Basic Books, 2008.

Chion, Michel. *Audio-Vision: Sound on Screen.* Trans. and ed. Claudia Gorbman. New York: Columbia University Press, 1994.
Clark, Clifford Edward Jr. *The American Family Home, 1800–1960.* Chapel Hill: University of North Carolina Press, 1986.
Clark, Kenneth. *The Nude: A Study in Ideal Form.* Princeton, NJ: Princeton University Press, 1956.
Clayton, Alex. *Funny How? Sketch Comedy and the Art of Humor.* Albany: State University of New York Press, 2020.
Columbia University Bureau of Applied Social Research. *The People Look at Radio.* Chapel Hill: University of North Carolina Press, 1946.
Corber, Robert J. *Homosexuality in Cold War America: Resistance and the Crisis of Masculinity.* Durham, NC: Duke University Press, 1997.
Crane, David. "Projections and Intersections: Paranoid Textuality in *Sorry, Wrong Number.*" *Camera Obscura* 17, no. 3 (2002): 71–112.
Darwin, Charles. *The Expression of the Emotions in Man and Animals.* London: John Murray, 1872.
Davenport, Guy. "The Head as Fate." In *Objects on a Table: Harmonious Disarray in Art and Literature,* 25–51. Washington, DC: Counterpoint, 1998.
Davis, Mike. *City of Quartz: Excavating the Future in Los Angeles.* London: Verso, 1990.
Desser, David. "Jews in Space: The 'Ordeal' of Masculinity in Contemporary American Film and Television." In *Ladies and Gentlemen, Boys and Girls: Gender in Film at the End of the Twentieth Century,* ed. Murray Pomerance, 267–81. Albany: State University of New York Press, 2001.
Dick, Bernard F. *Hal Wallis: Producer to the Stars.* Lexington: University Press of Kentucky, 2004.
Dickstein, Morris. *Dancing in the Dark: A Cultural History of the Great Depression.* New York: W. W. Norton, 2009.
Didion, Joan. *Where I Was From.* New York: Vintage, 2003.
Eisenstein, Sergei M. "Eisenstein on Disney." Ed. Jay Leyda. In *The Eisenstein Collection,* ed. Richard Taylor, trans. Alan Y. Upchurch, 85–175. London: Seagull Books, 2005.
Eksteins, Modris. *Rites of Spring: The Great War and the Birth of the Modern Age.* Toronto: Vintage Canada, 1989.
Erickson, Kai T. "Notes on the Sociology of Deviance." *Social Problems* 9, no. 4 (Spring 1962): 307–14.
Feder, Edward. *Comic Book Regulation.* Berkeley: University of California Press, 1955.
Fiedler, Leslie A. *Freaks: Myths and Images of the Secret Self.* New York: Simon & Schuster, 1978.
———. "The Search for the Thirties." In *No! In Thunder,* 163–69. New York: Stein & Day, 1972.

———. "Whatever Happened to Jerry Lewis?: That's Amore . . . ." In *Enfant Terrible! Jerry Lewis in American Film*, ed. Murray Pomerance, 19–29. New York: New York University Press, 2002.

Foucaud, Edouard. *Paris inventeur. Physiologie de l'industrie française.* Paris: Prévot, 1844.

Frazer, Sir James George. *The Golden Bough: A Study in Magic and Religion.* London: Macmillan, 1906.

Freedland, Michael. *Dean Martin: King of the Road.* London: Robson Books, 2004.

Frye, Northrop. *Anatomy of Criticism: Four Essays.* Princeton, NJ: Princeton University Press, 2020.

Fuchs, Eduard. *Die Karikatur der europäischen Völker.* Vol. 1. Munich: Langen, 1921.

Fujiwara, Chris. *Jerry Lewis.* Urbana: University of Illinois Press, 2009.

Gabbard, Krin. "The Day the Clown Quit: Jerry Lewis Returns to *The Jazz Singer*'s Roots." In *Enfant Terrible: Jerry Lewis in American Film*, ed. Murray Pomerance, 91–106. New York: New York University Press, 2002.

Galili, Doron. *Seeing by Electricity: The Emergence of Television, 1878–1939.* Durham, NC: Duke University Press, 2020.

Genette, Gerard. *Paratexts: Thresholds of Interpretation.* Trans. Jane E. Lewin. Cambridge: Cambridge University Press, 1997.

Gish, Lillian. Letter to Alfred Hitchcock, March 28, 1975, regarding *Family Plot.* Alfred Hitchcock Collection, *Family Plot* file 200, Margaret Herrick Library, Academy of Motion Picture Arts and Sciences, Beverly Hills.

Glovinsky, Cindy. *Making Peace with Your Office Life: End the Battles, Shake the Blues, Get Organized, and Be Happier at Work.* New York: St. Martin's Griffin, 2010.

Goffman, Erving. *Frame Analysis: An Essay on the Organization of Experience.* Cambridge, MA: Harvard University Press, 1974.

———. *Relations in Public: Microstudies of the Public Order.* New York: Basic Books, 1971.

Goodman, Paul, with Percival Goodman. *Communitas: Means of Livelihood and Ways of Life.* New York: Vintage, 1960.

Gordon, Mel. *Lazzi: The Comic Routines of the Commedia dell'Arte.* New York: PAJ Books, 2001.

Gordon, Rae Beth. *Why the French Love Jerry Lewis: From Cabaret to Early Cinema.* Palo Alto, CA: Stanford University Press, 2002.

Gould, Stephen Jay. *The Mismeasure of Man.* New York: W. W. Norton, 1981.

———. *Time's Arrow, Time's Cycle: Myth and Metaphor in the Discovery of Geological Time.* Cambridge, MA: Harvard University Press, 1987.

Gunning, Tom. "The Cinema of Attractions: Early Film, Its Spectator and the

Avant-Garde." In *Early Cinema: Space Frame Narrative*, ed. Thomas Elsaesser, 56–62. London: BFI, 1990.
———. "Heard Over the Phone: *The Lonely Villa* and the de Lorde Tradition of the Terrors of Technology." In *Screen Histories: A* Screen *Reader*, ed. Annette Kuhn and Jackie Stacey, 216–27. Oxford: Oxford University Press, 1998.
Haines, Richard W. *Technicolor Movies: The History of Dye-Transfer Printing.* Jefferson, NC: McFarland, 1993.
Halberstam, David. *The Fifties.* New York: Fawcett, 1993.
Hall, Edward T. *The Silent Language.* New York: Anchor Books, 1990.
Hark, Ina Rae. "Crazy Like a Prof: Mad Science and the Transgressions of the Rational." In *BAD: Infamy, Darkness, Evil, and Slime on Screen,* ed. Murray Pomerance, 301–14. Albany: State University of New York Press, 2004.
Harris, Marvin. *Cows, Pigs, Wars, and Witches: The Riddles of Culture.* New York: Vintage, 1989.
Hayde, Michael A. *Side by Side: Dean Martin & Jerry Lewis on TV and Radio.* Albany, GA: Bear Manor Media, 2018.
Hayman, Richard. *Illuminated Manuscripts.* Oxford: Shire, 2017.
Hilsabeck, Burke. *The Slapstick Camera: Hollywood and the Comedy of Self-Reference.* Albany: State University of New York Press, 2020.
Hitchcock, Alfred. Note to Lillian Gish, April 9, 1975, regarding her letter. Alfred Hitchcock Collection, *Family Plot* file 200, Margaret Herrick Library, Academy of Motion Picture Arts and Sciences, Beverly Hills.
Hoekstra, Dave. "Comedy, Music and Romance." In Chicago Sun-Times, *20th Century Chicago: 100 Years, 100 Voices,* ed. Adrienne Drell, n.p. Chicago: Sports Publishing, 2000.
Huizinga, Johan. *Homo Ludens: A Study of the Play Element in Culture.* Boston: Beacon Press, 1944. Reprint, 1955.
Inman, David. *Television Variety Shows: Histories and Episode Guides to 57 Programs.* Jefferson, NC: McFarland, 2006.
Jerry Lewis House. Online at zillow.com/homedetails/1701-Waldman-Ave-Las-Vegas-NV-89102/7079852_zpid/?utm_campaign=iosappmessage&utm_medium=referral&utm_source=txtshare&fbclid=IwAR1sKVCngPlWLMow4XZwswQhHKfGkR6An1FeaKvOikwvp6UlVA9H8Zw1RdE&mmlb=g,48. Accessed September 15, 2020.
Kazin, Alfred. *Starting Out in the Thirties.* Boston: Little, Brown, 1962.
Knights, Ben. "Baden-Powell, Robert Stephenson Smyth (1857–1941)." In *Men and Masculinities: A Social, Cultural, and Historical Encyclopedia,* ed. Michael Kimmel and Amy Aronson, 48–50. Santa Barbara: ABC Clio, 2004.
Krutnik, Frank. "The Handsome Man and His Monkey: The Comic Bondage of Dean Martin and Jerry Lewis." *Journal of Popular Film and Television* 23 (1995): 16–25.

———. "Sex and Slapstick: The Martin and Lewis Phenomenon." In *Enfant Terrible! Jerry Lewis in American Film*, ed. Murray Pomerance, 109–21. New York: New York University Press, 2002.

Lazarsfeld, Paul. *The People's Choice: How the Voter Makes Up His Mind in a Presidential Campaign.* New York: Duell, Sloan and Pearce, 1944.

Lem, Stanislaw. *Fiasco.* Trans. Michael Kandel. New York: Harcourt Brace Jovanovich, 1987.

Lerner, Max. *America as a Civilization: Life and Thought in the United States Today.* New York: Simon and Schuster, 1957.

Levy, Shawn. *The King of Comedy: The Life and Art of Jerry Lewis.* New York: St. Martin's Press, 1997.

Lewis, Jerry. Interview by Sam Denoff, October 27, 2000. North Hollywood: Television Academy Foundation Online at https://interviews.televisionacademy.com/interviews/jerry-lewis. Accessed February 6, 2023.

———. *The Total Film-Maker.* New York: Random House, 1971.

Lewis, Jerry, and James Kaplan. *Dean & Me (A Love Story).* New York: Doubleday, 2005.

Lippit, Akira Mizuta. *Electric Animal: Toward a Rhetoric of Wildlife.* Minneapolis: University of Minnesota Press, 2000.

Longo, Vincent. "A Hard Act to Follow: Live Performance in the Age of the Hollywood Studio System (1920–1950)." Unpublished PhD dissertation, University of Michigan, 2022.

Managers' Report Books. Vol. 1 [1903–1904]. Keith/Albee Vaudeville Theater Collection. University of Iowa Libraries, Iowa City.

Marling, Karal Ann. *As Seen on TV: The Visual Culture of Everyday Life in the 1950s.* Cambridge, MA: Harvard University Press, 1994.

Martin, Ricci, with Christopher Smith. *That's Amore: A Son Remembers Dean Martin.* Lanham, MD: Taylor Trade Publishers, 2004.

McLean, Adrienne L. *All for Beauty: Makeup and Hairdressing in Hollywood's Studio Era.* New Brunswick, NJ: Rutgers University Press, 2022.

McLuhan, [H.] Marshall. *Understanding Media: The Extensions of Man.* New York: McGraw-Hill, 1964.

Melnick, Ross, and Andreas Fuchs. *Cinema Treasures: A New Look at Classic Movie Theaters.* St. Paul, MN: MBI Publishing, 2004.

Miller, Arthur. *After the Fall.* New York: Dramatists Play Service, Inc., 1964.

Miller, Jonathan. *The Body in Question.* London: Jonathan Cape, 1978.

Mills, C. Wright. *White Collar: The American Middle Classes.* New York: Oxford University Press, 1951.

Moriguchi, Chiaki. "The Evolution of Child Adoption in the United States 1950–2010: An Economic Analysis of Historical Trends." Discussion Paper Series A No. 572, Institute of Economic Research, Hitotsubashi University, Tokyo, 2012.

Perelman, Chaïm, and L. Olbrechts-Tyteca. *The New Rhetoric: A Treatise on Argumentation.* Notre Dame, IN: University of Notre Dame Press, 1969.

Pialat, Maurice, with Alain Bergala, Jean Narboni, and Serge Toubiana. "Le chaudron de la création: Entretien avec Maurice Pialat [The cauldron of creation: Interview with Maurice Pialat]." *Cahiers du cinéma* 354 (December 1983): 11–17, 58–66.

Podell-Raber, Mickey, with Charles Pignone. *The Copa: Jules Podell and the Hottest Club North of Havana.* New York: HarperCollins, 2007.

Polan, Dana. "Working Hard Hardly Working: Labor and Leisure in the Films of Jerry Lewis." In *Enfant Terrible! Jerry Lewis in American Film*, ed. Murray Pomerance, 211–24. New York: New York University Press, 2002.

Pomerance, Murray. "Bells Are Ringing: Notes on Rear Projection." *Film International* 15, no. 4 (February 2018): 37–55.

———, ed. *Enfant Terrible! Jerry Lewis in American Film.* New York: New York University Press, 2002.

———. "Who the Man Who Never Was, Was." In *Rule Britannia!: The Biopic and British National Identity*, ed. Homer Pettey and R. Barton Palmer, 243–65. Albany: State University of New York Press, 2018.

———. "Who Was Buddy Love? Screen Performance and Jewish Experience." In *Hollywood's Chosen People: The Jewish Experience in American Cinema*, ed. Daniel Bernardi, Murray Pomerance, and Hava Tirosh-Samuelson, 193–210. Detroit: Wayne State University Press, 2013.

Pomerance, Murray, and R. Barton Palmer, eds. *Autism in Film and Television: On the Island.* Austin: University of Texas Press, 2022.

Porter, Darwin. *Howard Hughes: Hell's Angel.* New York: Blood Moon Productions, 2005.

Property from the Estate of Jerry Lewis. Las Vegas: Julien's, 2018.

Read, Herbert. *The True Voice of Feeling: Studies in English Romantic Poetry.* London: Faber and Faber, 1953.

Riesman, David. *The Lonely Crowd: A Study of the Changing American Character.* Garden City, NY: Doubleday Anchor, 1953.

Sacks, Oliver. *Musicophilia: Tales of Music and the Brain*. New York: Alfred A. Knopf, 2007.

———. *The River of Consciousness.* New York: Vintage, 2018.

St. Paul, Pierre. *Music Hall Mimesis in British Film, 1895–1960: On the Halls on the Screen.* Teaneck, NJ: Fairleigh Dickinson University Press, 2009.

Schivelbusch, Wolfgang. *Tastes of Paradise: A Social History of Spices, Stimulants, and Intoxicants.* Trans. David Jacobson. New York: Vintage, 1993.

Simeone, Nigel, ed. *The Leonard Bernstein Letters.* New Haven, CT: Yale University Press, 2013.

Smith, Jacob. *Vocal Tracks: Performance and Sound Media*. Berkeley: University of California Press, 2008.

Sobchack, Vivian. *Carnal Thoughts: Embodiment and Moving Image Culture.* Berkeley: University of California Press, 2004.
———. "Chasing the Maltese Falcon: On the Fabrications of a Film Prop." *Journal of Visual Culture* 6, no. 2 (2007): 219–46.
———. "Thinking Through Jim Carrey." In *Closely Watched Brains,* ed. Murray Pomerance and John Sakeris, 199–213. Boston: Pearson Education, 2001.
Solomon, Matthew. "Adapting 'Radio's Perfect Script': 'Sorry, Wrong Number' and *Sorry, Wrong Number.*" *Quarterly Review of Film and Video* 16, no. 1 (1995): 23–40.
———. *The Gold Rush.* London: BFI, 2015.
———. "Sergei Eisenstein: Attractions/Montage/Animation." In *Thinking in the Dark: Cinema, Theory, Practice,* ed. R. Barton Palmer and Murray Pomerance. New Brunswick, NJ: Rutgers University Press, 2015, 77–88.
———. "'Twenty-Five Heads under One Hat': Quick-Change in the 1890s." In *Meta-Morphing: Visual Transformation and the Culture of Quick-Change,* ed. Vivian Sobchack, 3–20. Minneapolis: University of Minnesota Press, 2000.
Sombart, Werner. *Krieg und Kapitalismus.* Germany: Duncker & Humblot, 1913.
Spock, Benjamin, M.D. *The Pocket Book of Baby and Child Care.* New York: Pocket Books, 1946.
Tashlin, Frank. *The Bear That Wasn't.* 1946. Mineola, NY: Dover, 2007.
Tosches, Nick. *Dino: Living High in the Dirty Business of Dreams.* New York: Delta, 1992.
Tsivian, Yuri. *Early Cinema in Russia and Its Cultural Reception.* Trans. Alan Bodger. Chicago: University of Chicago Press, 1998.
———. *Ivan the Terrible.* London: BFI, 2002.
Turner, Victor W. *The Forest of Symbols: Aspects of Ndembu Ritual.* Ithaca, NY: Cornell University Press, 1967.
Verma, Neil. *Theater of the Mind: Imagination, Aesthetics, and American Radio Drama.* Chicago: University of Chicago Press, 2012.
Walsh, Tim. *Timeless Toys: Classic Toys and the Playmakers Who Created Them.* Kansas City: Andrews-McMeel Publishing, 2005.
Weisinger, Mort. "How They're Cleaning Up the Comic Books." *Better Homes and Gardens* (March 1955): 58–59, 254–55, 263.
Welles, Orson, and Peter Bogdanovich. "Orson Welles Interview." Folder 1, Box 1, Folders 2–10, Box 2, Wilson-Welles Papers. University of Michigan Special Collections Research Center, Ann Arbor.
Wojcik, Pamela Robertson. *The Apartment Plot: Urban Living in American Film and Popular Culture, 1945–1975.* Durham, NC: Duke University Press, 2010.
Wollen, Peter. *Raiding the Icebox: Reflections on Twentieth-Century Culture.* London: Verso, 2008.

———. *Signs and Meaning in the Cinema.* 5th ed. London: BFI, 2013.

Woodmansee, H. A. "Talking through Their Hats." *Motion Picture Classic* 27, no. 1 (March 1928): 63, 81.

Young, Paul. "Media on Display: A Telegraphic History of Early American Cinema." In *New Media, 1740–1915*, ed. Lisa Gitelman and Geoffrey B. Pingree, 229–64. Cambridge, MA: MIT Press, 2003.

CAN YOU LOOK UP?

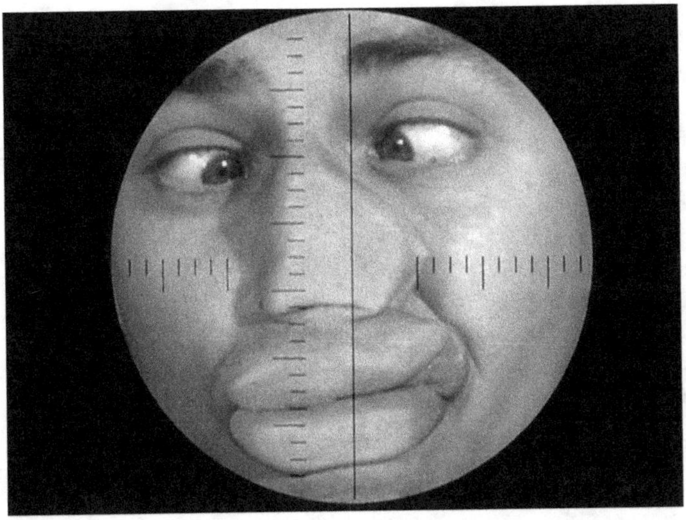

Note: Numbers in *italic* denote images.

the Store? (Frank Tashlin, 1963), 46, 89, 135n11, 151, 152;
Film locations and settings: Fontainebleau Hotel (Miami) in *The Bellboy,* 39, 39n14; *Ladies Man* dormitory, 38n13;
Jerry Lewis Theaters, The (1969), 87n6: brand of "good clean" fun, 87; commitment to G and PG films, 87; Staten Island theater secretly showing pornography, 87
Song Repertoire (solo): "By Myself" (Arthur Schwartz, Howard Dietz, 1937), 191; "Gay Continental, The" (Harry Warren, Jack Brooks, for *The Caddy*), 119; "I Lost My Heart in a Drive-in Movie" (David Raksin, Jack Brooks, for *The Patsy*), 180–181, 271; "Mammy" ("My Mammy") (Walter Donaldson, Joe Young, Sam M. Lewis, c. 1921), 76, 271; "Rock-a-Bye Your Baby with a Dixie Melody" (Jean Schwartz, Sam M. Lewis, Joe Young, 1918), 76; "Those Were the Gold Old Days (Jerry Ross, Richard Adler, 1955), 183–184 (*see also Damn Yankees*)
Liberace [Władziu Valentino] "Lee," 152, 152n9
Liggett & Myers, 252. *See also* Chesterfield
Li'l Abner (St. James Theater, New York, November 15, 1956), 77
Li'l Abner. see Lewis, Jerry, Films
Little, Rich, 234n7
Living Playing Cards, The [*Les cartes vivantes*] (Georges Méliès, 1905), 276
Lloyd, Harold, 82
Lloyd, Norman, 293
Lonely Are the Brave (David Miller, 1962), 64n6
Loo, Richard, 275
Los Angeles: Culver Theater (Culver City), 61; El Capitan Theater (Hollywood Blvd.), 33n4 (*see also* Martin & Lewis, *Colgate Comedy Hour*); Grauman's Chinese Theater (Hollywood Blvd.), 33n4, 290; Hollywood Blvd. (Los Angeles) (*see* Martin & Lewis, *Colgate Comedy Hour*); Melrose Ave. (*see* Hollywood studios)
Lost Horizon (Frank Capra, 1937), 275
Louis, Joe, 10–11
Lucky Strike cigarettes (American Tobacco Company), 95, 252
Lumière, Antoine, 94n16: Antoine Lumière et ses fils, 94n16; Cinématographe, 94n16
Lustre-Cream, 172
Lynn, Diana, 37

M

MacLaine, Shirley, 92, 133, 135, 142; sings "Innamorata," 240. *See also* Martin, Dean, Song repertoire
MacMurray, Fred, 146n2
Madame Bovary (Vincente Minnelli, 1949), 274
Magic Brain Remote TV Control, 35n7
Malone, Dorothy, 60, 111, *132,* 133, 141, 264
Maltese Falcon, The (John Huston, 1941), 183
Mamãe eu quero (Vincente Paiva, Jararaca, 1937), 105
Man in the Gray Flannel Suit, The (Nunnally Johnson, 1956), 252
Man in the Iron Mask, The. See *Vicomte of Bragelonne*
Man Who Never Was, The (1956), 173
Manchurian Candidate, The (John Frankenheimer, 1962), 276
Manhattan, *see* New York
Mansfield, Jayne, 95

Martin & Lewis, Films (*continued*)
Hollywood or Bust (Frank Tashlin, 1956), *1, 12,* 46, 67, 68n10, *72,* 85, 131, *144,* 156, 159, 191, 198, 208, 215, 217, 218, 242–243, 261, 269, 290; *Jumping Jacks* (Norman Taurog, 1952), 68n10, 159, 283; *Living It Up* (Norman Taurog, 1954), 17–22, *18, 19, 20,* 38, 43, 46, 75, 80, 85, *121,* 121–132, *158,* 159, *169,* 182, 183, 191, 217–218, 240, 267, 268, *272,* 273–276, 279, 283, 286; *Money from Home* (George Marshall, 1953), 46, 68n10, 172; *My Friend Irma* (George Marshall, 1949), 49n22, 68n10, 85, 183, 239, 272; *My Friend Irma Goes West* (Hal Walker, 1950), 49n22, 68n10, 112n4, 272; *Pardners* (Norman Taurog, 1956), *1,* 66–67, 97, 184, 269, 283; *Sailor Beware* (Hal Walker, 1952), 68n10, 189, 191, *307*; *Scared Stiff* (George Marshall, 1953), *52,* 68n10, 76, *81,* 95, 97, *100,* 101, 105, *110,* 110–114; 111n1, 267, 283; *Stooge, The* (Norman Taurog, 1951), *23,* 68n10; *That's My Boy* (Hal Walker, 1951), *31,* 44, 49n22, 68n10, 183, 187–188, 191, *202, 277*; *3 Ring Circus* (Joseph Pevney, 1954), 68n10, 135n11, 192, 242; *You're Never Too Young* (Norman Taurog, 1955), 37, 44, 74, 171, 173, *175,* 283
Film Locations and Settings: San Diego Hilton in *The Big Mouth,* 39; Sea World in *The Big Mouth,* 39
Martin and Lewis Show, The (NBC radio, 1949–1953), 73, 75–76, 155, 170, 232, 233–234, 272
Song Repertoire: "Ev'ry Street's a Boulevard in Old New York" (Jule Styne, Bob Hilliard, for *Living It Up*), 159, 217–218; "Here's to Love" (Jay Livingston, Ray Evans, for *My Friend Irma*), 239; "Hollywood or Bust" (Sammy Fain, Paul Francis Webster, for *Hollywood or Bust*), 159; "Marie" (Irving Berlin, 1928), 248; "When You Pretend" (Harry Warren and Jack Brooks, for *Artists and Models*), 42
Martin, Tony, 10–11
Marvel universe, 199
Mary Hartman, Mary Hartman (Syndicated, 1976–1977), 90n9
Mason [Charles]-[Jeremiah] Dixon Line (1863–1867), 76
Mathers, Jerry, 171n1. See also *Leave It to Beaver*
Maude (CBS, 1972–1978), 90n9
Mayehoff, Eddie, 133, 135, 264; winner of *Hollywood Reporter*'s Look Achievement Award, 187
Mayer, Louis B., 38
M[usic] C[orporation of] A[merica], 242n4
McCarran Internal Security Act. *See* Hollywood
McCarthy hearings (United States Senate Subcommittee on Investigations, 1954), 6
McDaniel, Hattie, 275
McLuhan, [Herbert] Marshall, 263
McMichaels, Flo, 233, 233n6
McQueen, [Thelma] Butterfly, 74
McVickers, Joe. *See* Play-Doh
Méliès, Georges, 130
Merton, Robert K[ingsley], 7
Metropolis (Fritz Lang, 1927), 5, 74n3
Midnight Lace (David Miller, 1960), 5
Midsummer Night's Dream, A (Max Reinhardt, 1936), 260n5
Miles, Vera, 146n1
Milland, Ray, 57n3
Miller, Arthur, 178, 179

ILLUSTRATIONS

FRONTISPIECE
Portrait of Martin & Lewis. Courtesy of PhotoFest, New York.

IN THESE PAGES
Dean watching Jerry on TV in *Artists and Models* (Frank Tashlin, Paramount, 1955). Digital frame enlargement.

AN AMERICAN UTOPIA
Dean and Jerry out west in *Pardners* (Norman Taurog, Paramount, 1956). Digital frame enlargement.

USER'S MANUAL

Dean, Jerry, and Mr. Bascomb in *Hollywood or Bust* (Frank Tashlin, Paramount, 1956). Digital frame enlargement.

CAN YOU RELAX?

The massage in *Artists and Models* (Frank Tashlin, Paramount, 1955). Digital frame enlargement; then, from *Living It Up*, Walter Baldwin (l.) with Jerry; Jerry hops a train; Jerry exhausted; Jerry on top of the train; Jerry in the radioactive car; Jerry astounded. All digital frame enlargements.

CAN YOU LISTEN?

Dean serenading in *The Stooge* (Norman Taurog, Paramount, 1953). Digital frame enlargement.

IN THE PLAYROOM

Jerry dances in *That's My Boy* (Hal Walker, Paramount, 1951). Digital frame enlargement.

SMASH AND CRASH

Spaghetti delivery in *Scared Stiff* (George Marshall, Paramount, 1953). Digital frame enlargement.

SONG OF THE SOUTH

Mr. Bascomb (uncredited) in *Hollywood or Bust* (Frank Tashlin, Paramount, 1956). Digital frame enlargement.

MOUTH TO MOUTH

Finger and mouth in *Scared Stiff* (George Marshall, Paramount, 1953). Digital frame enlargement.

KEEP GOOD RECORDS

Carmen Miranda imitation in *Scared Stiff* (George Marshall, Paramount, 1953). Digital frame enlargement.

UP THE ANTE

The bathtub scene in *Artists and Models* (Frank Tashlin, Paramount, 1955). Digital frame enlargement; Dean scared stiff in *Scared Stiff* (George Marshall, Paramount, 1953). Digital frame enlargement; Jerry guarding Dean's drink in *The Caddy* (Norman Taurog, Paramount, 1953). Digital frame enlargement; Jerry dictates a letter in *Living It Up* (Norman Taurog, Paramount, 1954). Digital frame enlargement; Jerry posing for Dorothy Malone (l.) in *Artists and Models* (Frank

Tashlin, Paramount, 1955). Digital frame enlargement; Dean gets clean in *Artists and Models* (Frank Tashlin, Paramount, 1955). Digital frame enlargement.

AN AMPERSANDED TRUTH
Dean schleps Jerry through the Bronson Gate at Paramount studios, Melrose Avenue, Los Angeles, in *Hollywood or Bust* (Frank Tashlin, Paramount, 1956). Digital frame enlargement.

INTERLUDE
Crooners in "New York" in *Living It Up* (Norman Taurog, Paramount, 1954). Digital frame enlargement.

GIVE ME A HEAD OF HAIR
Dean and Jerry in the doctor routine in *Living It Up* (Norman Taurog, Paramount, 1954). Digital frame enlargement.

THE TIP OF THE NOSE
Tommy Ivo (l.) with Jerry in *You're Never Too Young* (Norman Taurog, Paramount, 1955). Digital frame enlargement.

I STAND UP, I FALL DOWN
Jerry and Dean in the army in *At War with the Army* (Hal Walker, Paramount, 1950). Digital frame enlargement.

"I LIKE BLOOD!"
Jerry behind the billboard in *Artists and Models* (Frank Tashlin, Paramount, 1955). Digital frame enlargement.

EYES TIGHTLY SHUT
Dean the Adonis in *That's My Boy* (Hal Walker, Paramount, 1951). Digital frame enlargement.

ANOTHER INTERLUDE
Dean and Dean in *Artists and Models* (Frank Tashlin, Paramount, 1955). Digital frame enlargement; Jerry and Jerry in *That's My Boy* (Hal Walker, Paramount, 1951). Digital frame enlargement.

THE TRUE VOICE OF FEELING
Jerry in *The Caddy* (Norman Taurog, Paramount, 1953). Digital frame enlargement.

WHEN THE MOON HITS YOUR EYE
Donna Reed with Dean in *The Caddy* (Norman Taurog, Paramount, 1953). Digital frame enlargement.

THIS IS CARDBOARD
Dean and Jerry goofing with the clock on the *Colgate Comedy Hour.* Digital frame enlargement.

HUSTLERS
Dean painting the billboard in *Artists and Models* (Frank Tashlin, Paramount, 1955). Digital frame enlargement.

IN STEREO
Reading about themselves on the *Colgate Comedy Hour.* Digital frame enlargement.

WITH THE DOCTOR
Jerry visits the doctor in *Living It Up* (Norman Taurog, Paramount, 1954). Digital frame enlargement.

DEAN AND JERRY FULL FRONTAL
Jerry chauffeuring Dean and Polly Bergen in *That's My Boy* (Hal Walker, Paramount, 1951). Digital frame enlargement.

SPLITSVILLE ON SCHEDULE
Two paranoiacs, on the *Colgate Comedy Hour.* Digital frame enlargement.

CODA
Homage to Manet in *Hollywood or Bust* (Frank Tashlin, Paramount, 1956). Digital frame enlargement.

WORKS CITED AND CONSULTED
In the "library," *Colgate Comedy Hour.* Digital frame enlargement.

CONCORDANCE
Through the periscope in *Sailor Beware* (Hal Walker, Paramount, 1952). Digital frame enlargement.

ILLUSTRATIONS
Dean and Jerry meet themselves in *The Caddy* (Norman Taurog, Paramount, 1953). Digital frame enlargement.

www.ingramcontent.com/pod-product-compliance
Lightning Source LLC
Chambersburg PA
CBHW070750230426
43665CB00017B/2314
* 9 7 8 1 4 3 8 4 9 6 5 3 5 *